NEW CALEDONIA TRAVEL GUIDE 2024 EDITION

All rights reserved. No part of this publication may be reproduced, distributed, or transmitted in any form or by any means, including photocopying, recording or other electronic or mechanical methods, without the prior written permission of the publisher, except in the case of brief quotation embodied in critical reviews and certain other noncommercial uses permitted by copyright law

Copyright by Frank K. Knowles

Table of Content

Introduction

- Welcome to New Caledonia
- Overview of New Caledonia
- What's New in 2024

Chapter 1. Getting Started

- Travel Planning Tips
- Visa and Entry Requirements
- Currency and Banking

Chapter 2. Destinations

- Nouméa
  - City Highlights
  - Dining and Nightlife
  - Accommodation Options

- Isle of Pines
    - Natural Wonders and Cultural Attractions
    - Where to Stay
- Lifou
    - Beaches and Activities
    - Local Cuisine
    - Accommodation Recommendations
- Ouvéa
    - Relaxing in Paradise
    - Local Traditions
    - Best Places to Stay

Chapter 3. Activities

- Water Sports
- Hiking and Nature Trails
- Cultural Experiences
- Wildlife Encounters

Chapter 4. Cuisine

- *Traditional Kanak Dishes*

- *French-Influenced Cuisine*

- *Popular Restaurants and Cafés*

Chapter 5. Practical Information

- *Transportation within New Caledonia*

- *Health and Safety Tips*

- *Communication and Connectivity*

NOTE:

Embark upon an unparalleled journey as you immerse yourself in the very essence of this New Caledonia travel guide. Crafted not only to inform but to spark your imagination, nurture your creativity, and awaken the adventurer within you, this guide extends an invitation to step into a realm of exploration that is distinctly your own. Departing from the ordinary, you won't find accompanying images within these pages. Our firm belief rests in the idea that the true beauty of every discovery is most vividly experienced firsthand, untainted by visual interpretations or preconceived notions.

Picture every monument, each destination, and even the hidden corners of New Caledonia as exquisite surprises, patiently awaiting the moment to captivate and astonish you when you find yourself standing before them. We are steadfast in our commitment to preserving the thrill of that initial gaze, the sheer wonder that accompanies the revelation of something new. With this guide in hand, you stand on the precipice of an extraordinary voyage where curiosity is your sole mode of transportation, and this guide serves as your unwavering companion. Set aside any preconceived notions and allow yourself to be transported into an authentic New Caledonia of revelations—the enchantment of your adventure begins right here. However, keep in mind that the most enchanting images will be the ones etched by your own eyes and treasured within your heart.

In stark contrast to conventional guidebooks, this volume intentionally omits intricate maps. The reason, you may ask? We ardently believe that the most extraordinary discoveries unfurl when you let yourself lose track, allowing the very essence of each place to guide you while embracing the uncertainty of the path. Bid farewell to predetermined itineraries and meticulously laid out routes, for our aim is to empower you to navigate New Caledonia in your very own way, unburdened by boundaries. Allow yourself to be carried by the 'urrents of exploration, uncovering hidden gems that remain elusive on conventional maps. Summon the courage to embrace the unknown, trusting your instincts as you boldly venture forth, prepared to be pleasantly surprised—because the magic of your journey starts now, in a realm where maps are nonexistent, and the paths unfold with each step. The most extraordinary adventures await within the uncharted folds of the unfamiliar.

INTRODUCTION

Welcome to New Caledonia

Nestled in the heart of the Pacific Ocean, New Caledonia beckons with its unparalleled natural beauty, a fusion of indigenous Kanak traditions, and the sophisticated influence of French culture. This enchanting archipelago, situated northeast of Australia, is a haven for discerning travelers seeking a unique blend of tropical paradise and cultural richness.

The largest and most populous island, Grande Terre, is home to the vibrant capital city, Nouméa. As you step onto the shores of New Caledonia, the warm embrace of turquoise waters and the lush green landscapes will instantly captivate your senses. This is a land where coral reefs teem with marine life, dense forests hide cascading waterfalls, and pristine beaches invite moments of serenity.

In Nouméa, the cosmopolitan heart of New Caledonia, a harmonious coexistence of French elegance and Pacific island charm unfolds. Stroll along the waterfront promenade, where French Riviera-style cafes overlook the marina. Indulge your taste buds in a culinary journey that marries French gastronomy with Pacific flavors, creating a delectable fusion found nowhere else on earth.

The Isle of Pines, with its towering Araucaria pines and crystal-clear waters, is a testament to the untouched splendor of nature. As you explore its shores, you'll encounter the indigenous Kanak people, whose rich cultural heritage is interwoven with the land. The spirit of the Kanak people is alive in their customs, dances, and vibrant art, offering visitors a profound connection to the soul of New Caledonia.

Lifou, the largest of the Loyalty Islands, is a haven for beach lovers and adventure seekers alike. Picture-perfect bays invite languid days of sunbathing, while coral atolls beckon snorkelers and divers to explore the kaleidoscopic underwater world. Immerse yourself in the local way of life, savoring traditional dishes and participating in cultural ceremonies that provide a glimpse into the island's authentic spirit.

Ouvéa, known as "The Island of the Most Beautiful Lagoon in the World," lives up to its reputation with powdery white sands and vibrant coral reefs. This is a sanctuary for those seeking tranquility amid nature's wonders. Ouvéa's simple beauty is mirrored in its unhurried pace, offering a respite from the demands of the modern world.

For the adventurous souls, New Caledonia presents an array of activities that span from heart-pounding water sports to invigorating hikes through dense forests. Explore hidden coves by kayak, embark on a scenic horseback ride along the coast, or trek to the summit of Mont Panié for panoramic views that stretch to the horizon.

Culinary enthusiasts will find New Caledonia to be a gastronomic paradise, where French culinary techniques intertwine seamlessly with the freshest Pacific produce. From quaint local markets to Michelin-starred restaurants, the culinary landscape reflects the diverse influences that shape New Caledonia's delectable offerings.

Practical considerations seamlessly merge with the allure of the islands. Efficient transportation networks connect the main islands, allowing you to navigate with ease. Health and safety standards meet international norms, ensuring a worry-free journey. While French is the official language, a warm "Bonjour" and a friendly smile are universal, making communication a delightful part of the experience.

As you traverse the archipelago, delve into the tapestry of Kanak culture, where ancient traditions coexist with the vibrant pulse of modern life. Experience the joy of local festivals, witness traditional dances that echo stories of the past, and embrace the warm hospitality that welcomes visitors into the heart of New Caledonia.

Beyond the allure of pristine beaches and lush landscapes, New Caledonia is committed to sustainable tourism practices. The islands are a sanctuary for unique flora and fauna, and efforts are underway to preserve the delicate ecosystems that make this destination truly extraordinary. By treading lightly and embracing responsible travel, visitors become stewards of this natural paradise.

In conclusion, welcome to New Caledonia – a destination where azure waters meet emerald landscapes, where French sophistication harmonizes with Pacific island warmth, and where every moment is an invitation to discover the extraordinary. Whether you seek relaxation on sun-drenched shores, thrilling adventures in the great outdoors, or a cultural immersion that transcends time, New Caledonia invites you to embark on a journey that promises to be as unique as the islands themselves.

Overview of New Caledonia

New Caledonia, nestled in the heart of the South Pacific Ocean, is a captivating archipelago known for its diverse landscapes, vibrant cultures, and unique blend of French and Melanesian influences. This overseas territory of France is situated approximately 1,200 kilometers east of

Australia, comprising the main island, Grande Terre, and a collection of smaller islands, each offering a distinct allure to travelers.

New Caledonia's geography is a tapestry of contrasts. Grande Terre, the largest island, is marked by a mountainous spine, lush rainforests, and expansive plains. The coastal areas showcase pristine beaches with crystal-clear waters that vary from turquoise lagoons to deep cobalt-blue seas. The Isle of Pines, renowned for its stunning natural beauty, boasts white sandy beaches and towering Araucaria pines. Lifou and Ouvéa, the Loyalty Islands, offer a more relaxed pace, featuring coral atolls, limestone caves, and endless stretches of unspoiled beaches.

This tropical haven is a biodiversity hotspot, home to an array of unique flora and fauna. The coral reefs surrounding New Caledonia are part of the second-largest coral reef system globally, making it a paradise for divers and snorkelers. The terrestrial ecosystems house an extraordinary variety of plant species, with many found nowhere else on Earth. The island's rich biodiversity has led to its inclusion on the UNESCO World Heritage List, recognizing its exceptional natural value.

New Caledonia is a cultural melting pot, reflecting the convergence of indigenous Melanesian traditions and French influences. The Kanak people, comprising various ethnic groups, contribute significantly to the archipelago's cultural identity. Visitors have the opportunity to immerse themselves in the Kanak way of life through traditional ceremonies, dance performances, and visits to tribal villages. The European influence, particularly French, is evident in the language, cuisine, and architecture, creating a unique blend of Pacific and European charm.

Nouméa, the capital city, serves as the cosmopolitan heart of New Caledonia. This bustling urban center contrasts with the pristine natural surroundings, offering a taste of French sophistication amidst Pacific serenity. The city is characterized by its vibrant markets, chic boutiques, and an array of dining options that showcase both local and French culinary delights. The Tjibaou Cultural Centre, an architectural masterpiece, provides insight into the indigenous Kanak culture.

For outdoor enthusiasts, New Caledonia is a playground of possibilities. The diverse topography lends itself to a variety of activities, from trekking through the dense rainforests to water-based adventures like kayaking, windsurfing, and sailing. The Loyalty Islands, with their untouched landscapes, are ideal for those seeking a peaceful retreat, while the main island offers a mix of adrenaline-pumping and leisurely pursuits.

The gastronomic scene in New Caledonia is a delightful fusion of French and Melanesian flavors. Local markets are a treasure trove of tropical fruits, fresh seafood, and traditional Kanak ingredients. French-inspired patisseries and bistros coexist with beachside shacks serving coconut-infused delicacies. The culinary experience here is a journey through diverse tastes, reflecting the cultural diversity that defines the archipelago.

Traveling to and within New Caledonia is a seamless experience, thanks to well-developed infrastructure and modern amenities. The currency is the Pacific French Franc, and the official languages are French and Kanak languages. The archipelago's tropical climate means that visitors can enjoy warm temperatures throughout the year, although cyclones are a seasonal consideration.

In conclusion, New Caledonia is a destination that transcends the ordinary, offering a symphony of natural beauty, cultural richness, and a taste of the South Pacific with a French twist. Whether seeking adventure, relaxation, or a cultural immersion, this archipelago invites travelers to discover a world where the old and the new, the indigenous and the European, harmoniously coexist.

What's New in New Caledonia in 2024

As we step into the vibrant landscapes of New Caledonia in 2024, a plethora of exciting developments and experiences await the intrepid traveler. From cutting-edge infrastructure projects to emerging cultural trends, the archipelago is evolving, providing visitors with novel attractions and immersive encounters. In this exploration of what's new, we delve into the latest offerings, ensuring that your journey through New Caledonia is not only breathtaking but also filled with the freshness of contemporary experiences.

The architectural skyline of Nouméa, the capital city, is undergoing a transformative facelift. Urban revitalization projects are reshaping the cityscape, blending modern aesthetics with the rich cultural tapestry of the region. The emergence of innovative structures and public spaces promises a dynamic environment for both locals and visitors.

Travelers seeking a harmonious blend of luxury and sustainability will find solace in the new wave of eco-resorts dotting the pristine shores of the archipelago. These resorts are not just about opulence; they are committed to minimizing their ecological footprint, offering a guilt-free stay amid the breathtaking natural beauty of New Caledonia.

In the culinary realm, 2024 brings a fusion of traditional Kanak flavors with global gastronomic trends. Renowned chefs are experimenting with local ingredients to create innovative dishes that tantalize the taste buds. From open-air markets to haute cuisine restaurants, the culinary scene is a celebration of New Caledonia's diverse cultural influences.

For adventure enthusiasts, the year 2024 introduces a plethora of adrenaline-pumping activities. From zip-lining through dense forests to exploring underwater caves, the archipelago is positioning itself as a haven for thrill-seekers. Whether you are an avid hiker or a water sports enthusiast, there are new and exciting avenues to explore the natural wonders that make New Caledonia a unique destination.

Cultural festivals have long been a hallmark of life in New Caledonia, and 2024 promises a calendar brimming with vibrant celebrations. From traditional music and dance festivals that showcase the Kanak heritage to contemporary art exhibitions, the cultural scene is evolving, inviting travelers to immerse themselves in the rich tapestry of local life.

Connectivity is also undergoing a revolution, ensuring that even the most remote corners of the archipelago are easily accessible. Improved transportation networks and upgraded facilities enhance the overall travel experience, making it more convenient for visitors to explore the hidden gems scattered across the islands.

In the realm of conservation, 2024 marks the launch of ambitious projects aimed at preserving the unique biodiversity of New Caledonia. Conservation initiatives, both local and international, are working hand in hand to protect the delicate ecosystems that make the archipelago a UNESCO World Heritage site. Travelers are encouraged to participate in these efforts, fostering a sense of responsibility and appreciation for the natural wonders they encounter.

As the sun sets over the azure waters of New Caledonia, 2024 unfolds as a year of promise and discovery. Whether you are a nature enthusiast, a cultural connoisseur, or simply a seeker of new horizons, the archipelago beckons with open arms, inviting you to be a part of its ever-evolving narrative. New Caledonia in 2024 is not just a destination; it's an immersive journey into the heart of the Pacific, where every moment is an opportunity to embrace the beauty of the new and the undiscovered.

CHAPTER 1: GETTING STARTED

Travel Planning Tips for New Caledonia

New Caledonia, a stunning archipelago in the South Pacific, beckons travelers with its turquoise waters, diverse landscapes, and rich cultural experiences. Planning a trip to this Pacific paradise requires thoughtful consideration and preparation. Whether you're a first-time visitor or a seasoned traveler, these travel planning tips for New Caledonia will help ensure a smooth and enjoyable journey.

1. **Research and Understand the Destination**

   Before embarking on your journey, take the time to research and understand the destination. Learn about the different islands, their unique attractions, and the cultural nuances of the Kanak people. Familiarize yourself with the geography, climate, and local customs to enhance your overall travel experience.

2. **Choose the Right Time to Visit**

   New Caledonia enjoys a tropical climate, with distinct wet and dry seasons. The period between November and March is characterized by warmer temperatures and occasional rain, while the dry season from April to October offers milder weather. Consider your preferences for weather and outdoor activities when deciding the best time to visit.

3. **Budget Considerations**

   Establish a realistic budget for your trip, taking into account accommodation, transportation, meals, activities, and any unexpected expenses. New Caledonia, influenced by French culture, can be relatively more expensive than other Pacific destinations, so planning ahead financially is crucial.

4. Flight and Transportation

Research flight options and choose the most convenient and cost-effective route to New Caledonia. Flights usually land at La Tontouta International Airport, located near the capital, Nouméa. Once there, explore transportation options between islands and within Nouméa, such as rental cars, buses, or domestic flights.

5. Accommodation

New Caledonia offers a range of accommodation options, from luxury resorts to budget-friendly hotels and charming guesthouses. Book accommodations in advance, especially during peak seasons, to secure the best rates and ensure availability. Consider staying in different areas to experience the diverse landscapes and activities each region offers.

6. Language and Communication

While French is the official language, English is also widely spoken in tourist areas. Learn a few basic French phrases to enhance your interactions with the locals. Having a translation app on your phone can be helpful, especially if you plan to explore less touristy areas.

7. Health and Safety

Ensure that your vaccinations are up-to-date before traveling to New Caledonia. The archipelago generally has good health standards, but it's advisable to have travel insurance that covers medical emergencies. Practice common safety precautions, such as securing your belongings and being aware of your surroundings.

8. Currency and Banking

The official currency is the Pacific Franc (XPF). While major credit cards are widely accepted, it's advisable to carry some local currency for smaller establishments and markets. ATMs are available in urban areas, but they may be limited on some islands.

9. **Pack Accordingly**

Pack appropriate clothing for the climate and activities you plan to engage in. Lightweight, breathable clothing is ideal, and don't forget essentials like sunscreen, a hat, and comfortable footwear for exploring both sandy beaches and lush hiking trails.

10. **Respect Local Customs**

Embrace the local culture by respecting customs and traditions. Ask for permission before taking photographs of people, and be mindful of local sensitivities. Understanding and appreciating the Kanak way of life adds depth to your travel experience.

In conclusion, meticulous planning is key to a memorable trip to New Caledonia. By researching the destination, considering budgetary constraints, and embracing the local culture, you'll be well-prepared to explore the enchanting landscapes and vibrant culture of this Pacific jewel. Whether you seek adventure or relaxation, New Caledonia promises a travel experience like no other.

Visa and Entry Requirements for New Caledonia

New Caledonia, a stunning archipelago in the heart of the South Pacific, beckons travelers with its turquoise waters, lush landscapes, and unique blend of cultures. Before embarking on your journey to this paradise, it's essential to understand the visa and entry requirements governing your visit.

1. **Visa Types:**

New Caledonia offers various types of visas, each designed to accommodate different purposes of travel. The type of visa you need depends on factors such as the duration of your stay, the purpose of your visit, and your nationality.

2. **Tourist Visa:**

For short-term visits, tourists usually apply for a tourist visa. This type of visa allows visitors to explore the islands, engage in leisure activities, and enjoy the natural beauty of New Caledonia.

The duration of a tourist visa varies, and travelers must ensure that they leave the country before the visa expires.

3. **Business Visa:**

Travelers intending to conduct business activities, attend conferences, or participate in professional events may need a business visa. It's crucial to provide documentation outlining the purpose of the visit and the activities planned during the stay.

4. **Transit Visa:**

If New Caledonia is a layover destination en route to another country, a transit visa might be necessary. This visa permits travelers to pass through the country for a limited period without the intention of staying.

5. **Long-Stay Visa:**

Those planning an extended stay, whether for work, study, or other purposes, may need a long-stay visa. This type of visa often requires additional documentation, such as proof of accommodation, financial stability, and a clear outline of the intended activities.

6. **Visa-Free Nationals:**

Some nationalities enjoy visa-free entry to New Caledonia for short stays. The duration of the visa-free period varies, and travelers must adhere to the conditions specified by immigration authorities.

7. **Application Process:**

Regardless of the type of visa, travelers must follow a systematic application process. This typically involves submitting a completed application form, passport photos, a valid passport, proof of travel arrangements, and any additional documents specific to the visa type.

8. **Processing Time:**

The processing time for visa applications can vary. It's advisable to apply well in advance of your intended travel date to allow for any unforeseen delays. Some visas may be processed more quickly than others, so checking the estimated processing time is essential for proper trip planning.

9. **Entry Requirements:**

In addition to obtaining the appropriate visa, travelers must meet certain entry requirements upon arrival in New Caledonia. This often includes presenting a valid passport with at least six months of validity beyond the intended departure date, a return or onward ticket, and proof of sufficient funds to cover the stay.

10. **Customs and Immigration Procedures:**

Understanding customs and immigration procedures is crucial for a smooth entry into New Caledonia. Travelers should be prepared to undergo routine customs checks and, if necessary, declare any items subject to restrictions or duties.

In conclusion, thorough research and adherence to visa and entry requirements are essential steps in ensuring a seamless and enjoyable visit to New Caledonia. By understanding the specific visa type required for your purpose of travel and complying with entry regulations, you can focus on exploring the breathtaking landscapes and vibrant cultures that await in this Pacific paradise.

Currency and banking

Currency and banking play crucial roles in the economic infrastructure of any destination, and New Caledonia is no exception. As a French territory located in the South Pacific, it operates within the framework of the French economic system while also maintaining some autonomy. This duality is reflected in its currency, banking institutions, and financial practices.

The official currency of New Caledonia is the Pacific Franc, abbreviated as XPF (Currency Code). This currency is shared with other French Pacific territories like French Polynesia and Wallis and Futuna. The Pacific Franc is pegged to the Euro, meaning its value is directly tied to the Euro.

This linkage ensures stability in the currency, providing economic predictability for both locals and visitors.

When it comes to banking, New Caledonia boasts a well-established and reliable banking system. The major banks in the territory include Banque Calédonienne d'Investissement (BCI), Société Générale de Banque en Nouvelle-Calédonie (SGBNC), and Banque de Nouvelle-Calédonie (BNC). These institutions offer a range of services, including personal and business banking, loans, and investment opportunities.

Travelers to New Caledonia will find that banking services are readily available, particularly in urban centers such as Nouméa. ATMs are widespread, allowing convenient access to cash. It is advisable for visitors to notify their banks of their travel plans to avoid any potential issues with card transactions. Credit and debit cards are widely accepted, especially in larger establishments, but it's advisable to carry some cash for transactions in smaller shops or markets.

Currency exchange services are available at banks and currency exchange offices, providing the opportunity to convert major currencies into Pacific Francs. It's essential to be aware of the exchange rates to ensure fair transactions. Additionally, some hotels may offer currency exchange services for the convenience of their guests.

In terms of financial regulations, New Caledonia follows French banking standards and regulations. This adherence contributes to the stability of the financial sector, ensuring the safety of deposits and transactions. Visitors can have confidence in the reliability and security of the banking infrastructure during their stay.

For those seeking more specialized financial services, New Caledonia offers opportunities for investment and business activities. The territory has a thriving economy driven by industries such as nickel mining, tourism, and agriculture. Investors will find that the financial sector supports various forms of business activities, with the local government working to create a conducive environment for economic growth.

In conclusion, understanding the currency and banking system in New Caledonia is essential for a smooth and enjoyable stay. The Pacific Franc, with its connection to the Euro, provides a stable financial environment. The well-established banking institutions cater to the diverse financial needs of both residents and visitors. Whether you're a tourist exploring the vibrant landscapes or a business traveler engaging in economic activities, New Caledonia's currency and banking infrastructure are fundamental elements contributing to the territory's overall economic resilience and growth.

CHAPTER 2: DESTINATIONS

I. Exploring Nouméa: A City of Elegance and Culture

Nouméa, the vibrant capital of New Caledonia, is a city that seamlessly blends French sophistication with Pacific Island charm. Nestled on the southwest coast of Grande Terre, the main island, Nouméa is a gateway to the unique cultural fusion that defines New Caledonia. From pristine beaches to cultural landmarks and delicious cuisine, this city offers a diverse array of experiences for every type of traveler.

1. Baie des Citrons: The Heart of Nouméa's Social Scene

One cannot truly experience Nouméa without a visit to Baie des Citrons. This trendy bay area is the epicenter of social life, boasting a lively atmosphere day and night. During the day, the beach is a sunbather's paradise, and by night, it transforms into a hub of restaurants, bars, and clubs. Sample local seafood at one of the waterfront restaurants or dance the night away in a beachside nightclub. Baie des Citrons encapsulates the city's spirit of relaxation and revelry.

2. Place des Cocotiers: The Historic Heart

At the heart of Nouméa lies Place des Cocotiers, a historic square surrounded by colonial-style buildings and towering palm trees. This square is not just a picturesque spot but also a historical one, as it was the site of the city's first market in the 19th century. Today, it hosts events, markets, and is a favorite gathering place for locals. Take a leisurely stroll, enjoy a coffee at a sidewalk café, or simply absorb the atmosphere of this charming square.

3. Tjibaou Cultural Centre: A Tribute to Kanak Culture

Dedicated to the indigenous Kanak people, the Tjibaou Cultural Centre is a masterpiece of modern architecture set in a lush, tropical park. Designed by Renzo Piano, this cultural center showcases Kanak art, history, and traditions. Visitors can explore the museum, attend cultural performances, and gain insight into the rich cultural tapestry of New Caledonia. The serene surroundings and striking architecture make it a must-visit for both culture enthusiasts and architecture aficionados.

4. Nouméa Cathedral: A Symbol of Faith and History

The Nouméa Cathedral, also known as St. Joseph's Cathedral, stands as a symbol of the city's spiritual and historical heritage. This Roman Catholic cathedral, with its distinctive red and white façade, is a significant landmark. Step inside to admire the intricate stained glass windows and the peaceful ambiance. Whether you are a person of faith or an admirer of architecture, the Nouméa Cathedral is a place of tranquility and reflection.

5. Nouméa Aquarium: A Dive into New Caledonia's Marine Life

For a glimpse into the underwater wonders surrounding New Caledonia, a visit to the Nouméa Aquarium is a must. This educational and entertaining venue features a diverse range of marine life, including colorful coral reefs and an array of fish species endemic to the region. The touch tanks provide a hands-on experience for visitors of all ages. It's a fascinating journey through the aquatic ecosystems that make the waters around New Caledonia so unique.

6. Jean-Marie Tjibaou Promenade: Coastal Beauty and Art

For a scenic coastal walk that combines natural beauty with contemporary art, head to the Jean-Marie Tjibaou Promenade. This picturesque walkway hugs the coastline, offering stunning views of the turquoise waters and surrounding islands. Along the way, encounter art installations inspired by Kanak culture. The fusion of nature, art, and cultural elements makes this promenade a delightful and enriching experience.

7. Museum of New Caledonia: Unveiling the Islands' Past

Delve into the archipelago's history and ethnography at the Museum of New Caledonia. Located in a colonial-style building, this museum houses an extensive collection of artifacts, artworks, and exhibits that trace the region's past. From pre-European settlement to the impact of colonialism, the museum provides a comprehensive understanding of New Caledonia's complex history. It's an essential stop for those seeking a deeper connection with the islands.

8. **Coconut Square: Green Oasis in the City**

Escape the urban hustle and find serenity in Coconut Square (Place des Cocotiers). This green oasis in the heart of the city is an ideal spot for a leisurely picnic, a casual stroll, or simply unwinding in the shade of the towering coconut palms. The square often hosts cultural events,

adding an extra layer of vibrancy to this tranquil retreat. It's a place where locals and visitors alike come together to enjoy the simplicity of nature within the city.

Nouméa, with its blend of French elegance and Pacific Island warmth, is a city that captivates the senses. From the lively beaches to the historic squares and cultural landmarks, every corner tells a story of the unique identity of New Caledonia. Whether you're a history buff, a beach lover, or a culture enthusiast, Nouméa has something to offer. As you explore the city's highlights, you'll discover a captivating blend of tradition and modernity, making your journey an unforgettable experience in the heart of the Pacific.

Baie des Citrons: The Heart of Nouméa's Social Scene

Nouméa, the capital of New Caledonia, is a city that pulsates with life and culture. Among its many gems, Baie des Citrons stands out as the vibrant heart of the city's social scene. This trendy bay area, with its sun-kissed beaches, bustling promenades, and a kaleidoscope of restaurants and bars, encapsulates the spirit of Nouméa. As the sun sets, Baie des Citrons transforms into a lively hub of nightlife, making it an essential destination for locals and visitors alike.

The allure of Baie des Citrons begins with its stunning beaches. Soft white sands stretch along the bay, inviting sunbathers to lounge and soak up the Pacific rays. The crystal-clear waters are perfect for a refreshing swim or snorkeling adventure. Families build sandcastles, and friends engage in beach volleyball matches, creating an atmosphere of joy and camaraderie.

One cannot discuss Baie des Citrons without mentioning its diverse culinary scene. The waterfront is adorned with an array of restaurants, cafes, and eateries, each offering a unique gastronomic experience. From casual beachside cafes serving freshly caught seafood to upscale restaurants presenting a fusion of French and Pacific flavors, the options are as diverse as the crowd that frequents them.

What sets Baie des Citrons apart is its ability to seamlessly weave together the diverse cultural threads that make up New Caledonia. Here, French sophistication mingles with the laid-back Pacific Island charm. Visitors can hear the melodic sounds of French conversations, the rhythmic beats of local music, and the laughter of people from all walks of life coming together in celebration.

As the sun begins its descent, Baie des Citrons undergoes a magical transformation. The sky becomes a canvas of hues, painting a mesmerizing backdrop for the evening ahead. Locals and tourists alike gather to witness this daily spectacle. Some choose to enjoy the view from beachside loungers, while others take a leisurely stroll along the promenade, basking in the warm glow of the sunset.

When the stars emerge, Baie des Citrons awakens with a vibrant nightlife. The bay is dotted with bars and clubs that cater to every taste. Whether you prefer sipping cocktails under the stars, dancing to live music, or immersing yourself in the beats of a DJ, Baie des Citrons has it all. The nightlife here is dynamic, offering a mix of local charm and international flair.

One of the highlights of Baie des Citrons is its culinary fusion. The restaurants here do more than serve food; they tell a story of cultural intertwining. French chefs collaborate with local culinary artisans to create dishes that reflect the unique identity of New Caledonia. The aroma of grilled fish, the sizzle of garlic in a pan, and the tantalizing sweetness of tropical fruits converge to create a sensory symphony.

Beyond the culinary delights, Baie des Citrons hosts vibrant markets and showcases the work of local artisans. Stroll through the stalls to discover handmade crafts, traditional artwork, and unique souvenirs. Engaging with local artisans provides not only a shopping experience but also an opportunity to connect with the authentic culture of New Caledonia.

Baie des Citrons isn't just for night owls and party enthusiasts; it's also a haven for families. During the day, children build sandcastles, paddle in the shallow waters, and enjoy ice creams from seaside vendors. The bay's atmosphere is inclusive, making it a place where people of all ages can find enjoyment and relaxation.

For the adventurous souls, Baie des Citrons offers an array of water activities. Kayaking, paddleboarding, and jet skiing are popular choices for those seeking an adrenaline rush. The calm, clear waters provide an ideal environment for both beginners and experienced water sports enthusiasts.

Beyond its physical attributes, Baie des Citrons holds a special place in the hearts of the locals. It's a venue for community events, celebrations, and gatherings. From beachside concerts to cultural festivals, the bay becomes a canvas for expressing the vibrant spirit of Nouméa.

In essence, Baie des Citrons is more than a picturesque bay; it's a microcosm of Nouméa's identity. It's a place where the past and present converge, where diverse cultures harmonize, and where every sunset marks a celebration of life. Whether you're seeking relaxation on the beach, indulging in culinary delights, or dancing the night away, Baie des Citrons invites you to experience the heartbeat of Nouméa's social scene. It's a destination that captures the essence of New Caledonia—an intoxicating blend of natural beauty, cultural richness, and social vitality.

Place des Cocotiers: The Historic Heart

Place des Cocotiers, the historic heart of Nouméa, stands as a testament to the city's rich history and cultural significance. Nestled at the core of the capital city on the southwest coast of Grande Terre, New Caledonia's main island, this iconic square is a multifaceted space that has witnessed centuries of change and growth.

The origins of Place des Cocotiers trace back to the early days of European colonization. In the 19th century, as Nouméa began to take shape as a colonial outpost, the square emerged as a central hub for various activities. Initially known as La Place d'Armes, it served as a venue for military parades and public gatherings. Over time, as the city evolved, so did the square, transforming into the bustling civic space that it is today.

What makes Place des Cocotiers unique is not just its historical significance but also its architectural and cultural elements. Surrounded by colonial-style buildings and adorned with towering palm trees, the square exudes an old-world charm that harks back to an era when Nouméa was a burgeoning colonial settlement.

The architecture of the square is characterized by a harmonious blend of colonial and tropical influences. The buildings that line the square showcase intricate details reminiscent of French colonial design, with wrought iron balconies and facades that reflect the architectural trends of the 19th century. These structures, now housing shops, cafes, and administrative offices, contribute to the visual tapestry of the square.

At the center of Place des Cocotiers stands a majestic statue of La France Victorieuse (Victorious France). This statue, erected in the early 20th century, serves as a symbol of France's triumphs during World War I. Its prominent position in the square reinforces the historical ties between New Caledonia and France, a connection that has played a pivotal role in shaping the island's identity.

The square has evolved into a dynamic space that caters to the varied interests of locals and visitors alike. From leisurely strolls under the shade of the palm trees to vibrant markets and cultural events, Place des Cocotiers is a living canvas that reflects the pulse of Nouméa.

On any given day, the square becomes a lively marketplace, with vendors offering fresh produce, local crafts, and a variety of goods. The market atmosphere adds a layer of authenticity to the square, inviting people to engage in the everyday life of the city. It's a place where locals gather to shop, socialize, and immerse themselves in the vibrant energy of Nouméa.

Cultural events often find a home in Place des Cocotiers, further enriching its character. Music festivals, art exhibitions, and traditional performances contribute to the cultural vibrancy of the square. The open-air setting becomes a stage for expression, where artists and performers showcase the diversity of New Caledonia's cultural heritage.

For those seeking a moment of tranquility amidst the city's hustle, Place des Cocotiers offers ample opportunities. Benches and shaded areas provide a peaceful retreat for individuals and families looking to unwind. Whether enjoying a book, sipping on a cup of coffee at a sidewalk café, or simply taking in the surroundings, visitors can experience a sense of calm within this historical oasis.

The square's significance extends beyond its physical boundaries. It has been a witness to the social and political transformations that have shaped New Caledonia. From colonial times to the challenges and triumphs of self-determination, Place des Cocotiers has stood as a silent spectator to the evolving narrative of the island.

As a gathering place for both locals and tourists, the square fosters a sense of community. It's a space where diverse voices come together, creating a mosaic of experiences and perspectives. The cultural exchange that occurs within the square reflects the inclusive spirit of Nouméa, a city that celebrates its diversity.

In conclusion, Place des Cocotiers is more than a historic square; it is the beating heart of Nouméa. Its cobblestone pathways, shaded alleys, and architectural marvels encapsulate the essence of a city that has embraced its past while embracing the future. Through its rich history, cultural events, and everyday activities, the square remains a symbol of continuity and resilience. As visitors explore its nooks and crannies, they embark on a journey through time, discovering the layers of stories that have shaped this iconic space at the heart of New Caledonia's capital.

Tjibaou Cultural Centre: A Tribute to Kanak Culture

Nestled within the lush greenery of Nouméa, the capital city of New Caledonia, the Tjibaou Cultural Centre stands as a testament to the rich cultural heritage of the Kanak people. This architectural masterpiece, designed by renowned architect Renzo Piano, is more than just a building; it is a living tribute to the Kanak culture, offering visitors a profound and immersive experience.

The Tjibaou Cultural Centre is situated on Tina Peninsula, surrounded by tropical gardens and overlooking the serene waters of the lagoon. Its design is a harmonious blend of modern architecture and traditional Kanak influences, creating a space that is not only visually stunning but also deeply rooted in the cultural history of the indigenous people.

Upon approaching the cultural center, visitors are greeted by the striking sight of ten Kanak huts, known as "cases," arranged in a semi-circle. These cases, constructed with traditional materials such as wood and thatch, pay homage to the traditional Kanak way of life. Each case represents a different Kanak community, showcasing the diversity and unity within the culture.

The exterior of the main building is equally captivating. The curvilinear design mimics the shape of the traditional Kanak huts, creating a seamless integration of modernity and tradition. The use of natural materials, such as wood and metal, not only adds to the aesthetic appeal but also reflects the sustainability principles deeply ingrained in Kanak culture.

As visitors step inside the Tjibaou Cultural Centre, they are welcomed into a world of Kanak art, history, and spirituality. The museum within the center houses a vast collection of artifacts, ranging from intricately carved wooden sculptures to traditional masks and textiles. Each piece tells a story, weaving together the narratives of Kanak ancestors and their deep connection to the land.

The exhibition spaces are carefully curated to provide a chronological journey through Kanak history. From the pre-colonial era to the impact of European contact and the complexities of modern Kanak identity, the museum offers a comprehensive exploration of the cultural evolution of the Kanak people.

One of the standout features of the Tjibaou Cultural Centre is its commitment to interactive and immersive experiences. Visitors are not passive observers but active participants in the cultural narrative. Traditional Kanak music fills the air as skilled artisans demonstrate age-old techniques of carving and weaving. The scent of native plants and herbs used in traditional medicines adds a sensory dimension to the exploration.

The outdoor spaces of the cultural center are equally significant. The surrounding gardens, carefully landscaped with endemic plants, create a tranquil environment that encourages reflection. Visitors can wander through the pathways, pausing at various points to admire sculptures and installations that celebrate the spiritual connection between the Kanak people and nature.

The Jean-Marie Tjibaou Promenade, an outdoor extension of the cultural center, provides breathtaking views of the surrounding landscape. This coastal walkway, adorned with contemporary art installations inspired by Kanak culture, serves as a bridge between the traditional and the modern. It is a physical manifestation of the ongoing dialogue between the past and the present, a theme that echoes throughout the Tjibaou Cultural Centre.

Cultural performances, held regularly within the center, add a dynamic and vibrant layer to the visitor experience. Traditional dances, accompanied by rhythmic drumming, convey the energy and spirit of Kanak celebrations. These performances are not mere spectacles; they are expressions of a living culture that continues to evolve while preserving its roots.

The Tjibaou Cultural Centre also plays a crucial role in fostering dialogue and understanding between the Kanak people and the wider world. It serves as a platform for cultural exchange, hosting events that bring together artists, scholars, and visitors from diverse backgrounds. This spirit of openness aligns with the Kanak philosophy of "vivre ensemble" or living together in harmony.

The legacy of Jean-Marie Tjibaou, a prominent Kanak leader and advocate for cultural preservation, is intricately woven into the fabric of the Tjibaou Cultural Centre. The center, named in his honor, is a continuation of his vision to celebrate and safeguard Kanak heritage. It stands as a beacon of cultural resilience, a reminder that despite the challenges of history, the Kanak people persist in their commitment to preserving and sharing their unique identity.

In conclusion, the Tjibaou Cultural Centre is not just a museum; it is a living, breathing embodiment of Kanak culture. From its awe-inspiring architecture to its meticulously curated exhibits and vibrant performances, every aspect of the center resonates with the spirit of the Kanak people. It is a space where the past is honored, the present is celebrated, and the future is envisioned—a true tribute to the enduring legacy of the Kanak culture in the heart of New Caledonia.

Nouméa Cathedral: A Symbol of Faith and History

Nouméa Cathedral, also known as St. Joseph's Cathedral, stands proudly in the heart of Nouméa, the capital city of New Caledonia. This Roman Catholic cathedral is not merely a place of worship; it is a symbol deeply embedded in the spiritual and historical fabric of the city. With its distinctive red and white façade and commanding presence, Nouméa Cathedral is a testament to the enduring faith of its community and a silent witness to the historical transformations that have shaped New Caledonia.

The architectural grandeur of Nouméa Cathedral is immediately striking. The façade, adorned with intricate details and statues, reflects a blend of European and Pacific influences. The red roof tiles and white walls create a visually stunning contrast against the backdrop of blue skies, hinting at the cathedral's colonial heritage. As you approach the entrance, the towering spire and the overall sense of solemnity evoke a feeling of reverence and awe.

Step inside, and you are greeted by a sanctuary that exudes both simplicity and grace. The interior of Nouméa Cathedral is a sanctuary of peace, with its high arched ceilings, elegant columns, and soft lighting. The stained glass windows, crafted with meticulous artistry, filter sunlight into a spectrum of colors that dance across the pews. It's a place where the play of light and shadow enhances the spiritual ambiance, inviting visitors to reflect and find solace.

The cathedral's history is intertwined with the broader narrative of New Caledonia. Construction of Nouméa Cathedral began in 1887 during the era of French colonization. Its completion in 1897 marked not only a significant milestone for the Catholic community but also a tangible expression of the enduring French influence on the island. Over the years, the cathedral has weathered the passage of time, witnessing the various chapters of New Caledonia's history unfold.

Nouméa Cathedral holds a central place in the religious life of the community. Regular masses and religious ceremonies are conducted within its sacred walls, providing a spiritual anchor for locals and visitors alike. The cathedral's role goes beyond religious services; it serves as a gathering place for major events such as weddings, baptisms, and funerals, binding the community together in moments of joy and sorrow.

The cathedral's connection with the local Kanak culture is also evident. While its architecture reflects European influences, the Catholic rituals and ceremonies conducted within Nouméa Cathedral often incorporate elements of Kanak traditions. This blending of cultures is a reflection of the broader cultural diversity that defines New Caledonia.

Throughout its existence, Nouméa Cathedral has undergone renovations and restoration efforts to preserve its architectural integrity. These endeavors are not just about maintaining a historic building; they are acts of preservation aimed at safeguarding a cultural and spiritual landmark for future generations.

Surrounding the cathedral is a quiet yet impactful cemetery, where the final resting places of many prominent figures in New Caledonian history can be found. The cemetery, with its weathered tombstones and statues, is a poignant reminder of the individuals who have played pivotal roles in shaping the island's destiny.

Beyond its religious and historical significance, Nouméa Cathedral is also a beacon for architectural enthusiasts. The fusion of Gothic and Romanesque elements in its design, coupled with the tropical setting, makes it a unique and captivating structure. Visitors with an eye for architectural detail will find themselves marveling at the craftsmanship that went into creating this enduring masterpiece.

In conclusion, Nouméa Cathedral is more than a religious edifice; it is a living testament to the intertwining of faith and history in the heart of New Caledonia. As the faithful gather for worship, as tourists admire its architectural beauty, and as historians unravel the layers of its past, Nouméa Cathedral continues to stand as a symbol of resilience, continuity, and the enduring spirit of a community shaped by both faith and the passage of time.

Nouméa Aquarium: A Dive into New Caledonia's Marine Life

Nouméa, the capital city of New Caledonia, is a destination that boasts not only cultural richness but also a stunning array of marine life. Among the city's gems is the Nouméa Aquarium, a fascinating institution that provides visitors with a unique opportunity to dive into the underwater wonders of the surrounding Pacific waters.

The Nouméa Aquarium is strategically located to offer an immersive experience in the diverse marine ecosystems that characterize New Caledonia. The aquarium serves as a window to the underwater world, showcasing the incredible biodiversity and the importance of preserving these delicate environments.

As visitors step into the aquarium, they are greeted by the mesmerizing sight of vibrant coral reefs, bustling with life. The carefully designed exhibits simulate the natural habitats of the region, allowing guests to witness firsthand the beauty and complexity of the marine life that thrives in New Caledonia's waters.

One of the key features of the Nouméa Aquarium is its focus on showcasing the unique fish species endemic to the region. These include the dazzling parrotfish, the intricate seahorses, and the graceful lionfish. The aquarium takes pride in being a home to several species that are exclusive to the waters surrounding New Caledonia, offering a rare opportunity for visitors to appreciate the richness of this marine ecosystem.

The immersive experience is enhanced by interactive exhibits, including touch tanks that allow visitors to get up close and personal with some of the marine life. This hands-on approach not only provides an educational experience but also fosters a deeper connection with the marine environment, encouraging a sense of responsibility towards its conservation.

As visitors move through the aquarium, they encounter exhibits that highlight the delicate balance of the marine ecosystem and the various threats it faces. Educational displays on coral bleaching, overfishing, and plastic pollution convey the urgent need for conservation efforts. The Nouméa Aquarium plays a crucial role in raising awareness about the challenges that marine life in New Caledonia and around the world is confronting.

One of the standout features of the Nouméa Aquarium is its commitment to research and conservation. The facility actively participates in marine biology research projects, collaborating with scientists and institutions to better understand and protect the marine life of the region. Visitors have the opportunity to learn about these research initiatives and the positive impact they have on the preservation of New Caledonia's unique marine ecosystems.

The aquarium also serves as a platform for marine education programs. School groups and educational institutions regularly visit, benefitting from guided tours and interactive sessions that promote a deeper understanding of marine biology and conservation. The goal is to inspire the next generation of environmental stewards who will play a vital role in preserving the oceans for years to come.

Beyond its educational and conservation missions, the Nouméa Aquarium is a place of wonder and awe. The large viewing windows provide panoramic views of the aquarium's main tanks, where schools of tropical fish gracefully swim amid vibrant coral formations. The ambiance is serene, allowing visitors to lose themselves in the beauty of this underwater world.

For those seeking a more immersive experience, the aquarium offers unique opportunities such as guided snorkeling and diving sessions. These experiences allow adventurers to venture into specially designed tanks, surrounded by the marine life they've come to admire. It's a chance to witness the underwater ballet of fish, the delicate movements of corals, and the overall harmony of life beneath the surface.

The Nouméa Aquarium goes beyond being a tourist attraction; it is a hub of scientific knowledge, a catalyst for conservation efforts, and a source of inspiration for those who have the privilege of exploring its exhibits. It is a testament to the commitment of New Caledonia to protect its marine heritage and share it with the world.

In conclusion, the Nouméa Aquarium stands as a beacon of marine conservation and education in the heart of the Pacific. It invites visitors to embark on a journey of discovery, where the mysteries of the deep are unveiled, and the importance of preserving our oceans becomes evident. As a vital institution in the capital city, the Nouméa Aquarium ensures that the wonders of New Caledonia's marine life are not just seen but also understood and cherished by generations to come.

Museum of New Caledonia: Unveiling the Islands' Past

The Museum of New Caledonia stands as a cultural bastion, its colonial-style façade an embodiment of the rich tapestry that is New Caledonia's history. Nestled within this

architectural gem lies an expansive collection that weaves together the threads of the islands' past, offering visitors a profound journey through time.

Upon entering the museum, one is immediately struck by the diversity of artifacts that adorn the halls. The exhibits, carefully curated and displayed, unveil the nuanced story of New Caledonia, from its pre-European roots to the complex interplay of cultures in the present day.

The pre-European section transports visitors to a time when the islands were home to indigenous communities. Ancient tools, pottery, and ceremonial objects provide a tangible connection to the daily lives and spiritual practices of these early inhabitants. The artifacts speak of a harmonious coexistence with nature, as evidenced by intricately crafted items designed for hunting, fishing, and agriculture.

As the narrative unfolds, the impact of European exploration and colonization becomes a focal point. Models of colonial-era ships and depictions of the first encounters between Europeans and the indigenous Kanak people serve as poignant reminders of the profound changes that swept across the islands. The arrival of missionaries, the establishment of settlements, and the influence of European powers are all explored in meticulous detail.

The colonial period, marked by a complex interplay of cultures, is a key chapter in New Caledonia's history. The museum's exhibits shed light on the challenges and triumphs of this era, illustrating how traditions evolved in the face of external influences. Religious artifacts, colonial-era furniture, and portraits of key figures evoke the ambiance of a bygone era, inviting visitors to contemplate the fusion of European and indigenous elements.

The Impact of colonialism extends beyond material culture; it is etched into the islands' very identity. Displays documenting the resistance to colonization, including the Kanak uprisings, provide a sobering reflection on the resilience of indigenous communities in the face of significant adversity. The museum doesn't shy away from the complexities of this period, presenting a nuanced portrayal of the social, economic, and political transformations that shaped New Caledonia.

The 20th century ushered In a new era, marked by significant social and political changes. The quest for identity and autonomy comes to the fore in exhibits that explore the struggles for independence and the challenges faced by the Kanak people. Photographs, documents, and personal accounts weave a narrative of determination, solidarity, and the ongoing pursuit of self-determination.

Art plays a prominent role in the museum's narrative, providing a visceral and emotional dimension to the historical accounts. Paintings, sculptures, and contemporary installations offer diverse perspectives on the islands' past and present. The intersection of traditional Kanak art with modern expressions reflects the ongoing dialogue between heritage and contemporary identity.

The museum is not merely a repository of artifacts; it is a living institution that actively engages with the community. Educational programs, workshops, and cultural events contribute to a dynamic and evolving understanding of New Caledonia's heritage. The museum's commitment to inclusivity is evident in its efforts to amplify indigenous voices and foster cross-cultural dialogue.

A visit to the Museum of New Caledonia is not just a passive experience; it is an immersive journey that prompts reflection on the intricate layers of history. The artifacts, carefully preserved and presented, invite contemplation on the enduring legacy of the past and its relevance to the present. The museum stands as a testament to the resilience of the Kanak people and the evolving identity of New Caledonia—a narrative that continues to unfold, inviting visitors to be part of the ongoing conversation.

Coconut Square in Nouméa: A Verdant Retreat in the Heart of the City

Nouméa, the sun-kissed capital of New Caledonia, is not just a city of bustling markets, azure beaches, and colonial architecture; it also harbors a serene haven known as Coconut Square. Nestled in the heart of the city, this lush oasis offers a welcome reprieve from the urban hustle and bustle. As one strolls through its leafy expanse, shaded by towering coconut palms, a sense of tranquility envelops the visitor, creating a harmonious blend of nature and city life.

In the midst of this verdant retreat, the square acts as both a physical and metaphorical centerpiece—a place where locals and visitors alike converge to escape, reflect, and connect. Coconut Square, also known as Place des Cocotiers, stands not merely as a botanical enclave but as a living testament to the symbiotic relationship between nature and urbanity, a testament to the city's commitment to green spaces and community engagement.

The prominence of Coconut Square extends beyond Its botanical allure; it serves as a historical and cultural landmark, adding layers of significance to its already enchanting ambiance. This essay aims to unravel the myriad facets of Coconut Square, exploring its botanical wonders, historical roots, cultural resonance, and the vital role it plays as a communal space in the heart of Nouméa.

The defining feature of Coconut Square is, of course, the majestic coconut palms that give the square its name. These towering emblems of tropical splendor punctuate the landscape, casting dappled shadows on the cobblestone paths below. The rhythmic rustle of palm fronds in the gentle breeze provides a soothing soundtrack, a natural symphony that accompanies visitors as they traverse the square.

Beyond the coconut palms, the square hosts a diverse array of flora, creating a mini-ecosystem within the city. Lush tropical plants and vibrant flowers add bursts of color, transforming the square into a kaleidoscopic garden. As visitors wander through the meandering pathways, they encounter a botanical tapestry that reflects the biodiversity of New Caledonia itself. It is a living showcase of the islands' endemic plant species, a testament to the region's unique ecology.

Coconut Square's history is deeply intertwined with the evolution of Nouméa itself. In the 19th century, the square served as the bustling marketplace of the city, a vibrant hub where traders, locals, and sailors converged to exchange goods and stories. The echoes of this historical vibrancy still resonate in the architecture that surrounds the square—a harmonious blend of colonial structures and modern amenities.

The transition from a bustling market square to a green oasis reflects Nouméa's commitment to preserving its historical heritage while embracing the need for urban green spaces. The cobblestone paths, historic fountains, and shaded benches pay homage to the square's market past, providing a picturesque backdrop for those seeking respite in its leafy embrace.

Beyond its botanical and historical dimensions, Coconut Square is a dynamic cultural space. Throughout the year, it serves as a canvas for a myriad of events and festivals that celebrate the diverse cultural tapestry of New Caledonia. From vibrant art exhibitions to traditional music performances, the square transforms into a lively venue where creativity converges with nature.

The annual Coconut Festival is a highlight, drawing locals and tourists alike. This event showcases traditional crafts, culinary delights, and performances that pay homage to the coconut, a symbol deeply embedded in the cultural identity of the islands. The square, animated by the festivities, becomes a cultural agora—a space where traditions are shared, and community bonds are strengthened.

In the day-to-day life of Nouméa, Coconut Square assumes the role of a communal living room. It is a space where locals gather for a leisurely afternoon chat, families picnic beneath the shade of the palms, and children play freely on the grass. The square fosters a sense of community, creating a shared space that transcends social boundaries.

Local vendors and food stalls often set up shop around the square, offering an array of culinary delights that tantalize the taste buds. The aroma of freshly brewed coffee mingles with the scent of blooming flowers, creating an olfactory symphony that enhances the sensory experience of the square.

In essence, Coconut Square encapsulates the soul of Nouméa. It is not merely a botanical haven or a relic of history; it is a living, breathing space that mirrors the city's identity. As the sun sets

over the Pacific and bathes the square in a warm glow, one cannot help but appreciate the delicate balance between nature and civilization that Coconut Square embodies.

For those who wander through its shaded avenues, Coconut Square offers a refuge—a place to pause, reflect, and appreciate the simple joys of life. It is a sanctuary where the pace of the city slows, and the natural rhythm of the islands takes over. In the heart of Nouméa, Coconut Square stands as a testament to the enduring connection between urban life and the untamed beauty of the Pacific, inviting all who enter to partake in its timeless serenity.

II.   *Exploring the Dining and Nightlife Scene in Nouméa: A Culinary Odyssey*

Nouméa, the vibrant capital city of New Caledonia, is not only a paradise for beach lovers and nature enthusiasts but also a haven for those seeking a diverse and delectable culinary experience. The city's dining and nightlife scene reflects its rich cultural tapestry, blending influences from the indigenous Kanak people, the French settlers, and the diverse communities that call Nouméa home. From exquisite French cuisine to traditional Kanak dishes and international flavors, Nouméa offers a gastronomic journey that caters to every palate.

Culinary Marvels

1. **French Fusion Delights**

Nouméa's French heritage is unmistakable in its culinary landscape. Le Roof, a seaside restaurant, boasts breathtaking views and serves up a fusion of French and Pacific flavors. Imagine indulging in escargot while overlooking the turquoise waters of the Pacific—an experience that captures the essence of Nouméa's unique charm.

For a more intimate French affair, La Chaumière offers a rustic atmosphere and an extensive menu featuring classic French dishes. From coq au vin to bouillabaisse, the chefs at La Chaumière masterfully blend traditional French recipes with local ingredients.

2. **Kanak Gastronomy**

To truly immerse yourself in the local culture, exploring Kanak cuisine is a must. Tiet, a traditional Melanesian feast, is an experience that goes beyond food—it's a celebration of community and tradition. Local guides often organize Tiet experiences, where visitors can enjoy a communal meal of yams, fish, and coconut-based delicacies while learning about the customs and stories of the Kanak people.

For those seeking a contemporary twist on Kanak cuisine, Chez Toto is a popular spot. The restaurant infuses modern culinary techniques with traditional flavors, offering a unique and flavorful dining experience.

Nightlife Extravaganza

1. **Waterfront Elegance**

As the sun sets over the lagoon, Nouméa transforms into a city that knows how to have a good time. Lemon Bay, lined with bars and clubs, is a hotspot for those looking to kick off the night. The Roof Lounge Bar, perched atop Le Méridien Nouméa, is a stylish venue where you can savor handcrafted cocktails while enjoying panoramic views of the sunset.

For a more laid-back waterfront experience, Mondo Bar at Port Plaisance is a favorite among locals and visitors alike. With live music and a diverse drink menu, Mondo provides the perfect ambiance for a relaxing evening by the marina.

2. Local Vibes and International Tunes

To experience Nouméa's local music scene, head to La Bodega Del Mar. This vibrant venue often features live performances by local bands, showcasing the diversity of New Caledonia's music culture. The atmosphere is electric, and the dance floor beckons those with a passion for rhythm.

For those seeking a more international flair, The Jungle Bar is a haven for expats and travelers. With a playlist that spans genres and cultures, The Jungle Bar ensures that the party doesn't stop until the early hours of the morning.

Insider Tips

Reservations are Key: Given the popularity of Nouméa's dining scene, especially at fine-dining establishments, it's advisable to make reservations in advance to secure your spot.

Embrace Local Recommendations: Strike up conversations with locals to discover hidden gems and lesser-known eateries. Some of the best culinary experiences are found off the beaten path.

Dress the Part: While Nouméa's atmosphere is generally relaxed, some upscale dining establishments and clubs may have a dress code. It's always a good idea to check in advance and dress accordingly.

Nouméa's dining and nightlife scene is a tapestry woven with flavors and rhythms from around the world. From savoring French delicacies against the backdrop of the Pacific to dancing the night away in a local hotspot, Nouméa promises an unforgettable journey for the senses. So, whether you're a food connoisseur, a music enthusiast, or someone simply seeking a taste of the good life, Nouméa invites you to indulge in its culinary and nocturnal wonders.

III. Unveiling Nouméa's Finest: A Guide to the Best Hotels and Resorts

Nouméa, the vibrant capital city of New Caledonia, offers a harmonious blend of French sophistication and Pacific island charm. As you plan your visit to this tropical paradise, selecting the right accommodation is crucial. In this guide, we present an in-depth exploration of the best hotels and resorts that Nouméa has to offer, ensuring your stay is both luxurious and memorable.

1. Le Méridien Nouméa Resort & Spa

Nestled along Anse Vata Bay, Le Méridien Nouméa Resort & Spa is a haven of tranquility.

Highlights:

Oceanfront Luxury: With rooms offering breathtaking views of the turquoise waters, this resort sets the stage for an unforgettable experience.

Culinarian Delights: The resort boasts multiple restaurants serving a fusion of French and Pacific flavors, offering a gastronomic journey.

Wellness Oasis: Pamper yourself at the Deep Nature Spa, where traditional Kanak rituals and modern wellness practices collide.

2. Château Royal Beach Resort & Spa

An epitome of elegance, Château Royal Beach Resort & Spa is a beachfront gem in the heart of Nouméa.

Features:

Private Beach Access: Enjoy direct access to the pristine beaches, perfect for a relaxing day under the Pacific sun.

Contemporary Design: The rooms and suites are tastefully designed, marrying contemporary comforts with tropical aesthetics.

Diverse Dining Options: Indulge in a variety of cuisines at the resort's restaurants, each promising a culinary adventure.

3. Hilton Noumea La Promenade Residences

For those seeking a blend of luxury and homely comfort, Hilton Noumea La Promenade Residences is a premier choice.

Noteworthy Aspects:

Spacious Residences: Ideal for extended stays, the residences are equipped with full kitchens and private balconies.

Rooftop Pool and Bar: Unwind with panoramic views of the city and ocean at the rooftop pool and bar.

Proximity to Attractions: Strategically located, the Hilton provides easy access to Nouméa's attractions, making exploration effortless.

4. Ramada Hotel & Suites Noumea

Balancing affordability with quality, Ramada Hotel & Suites Noumea is a chic option for the savvy traveler.

Key Points:

Modern Accommodations: The hotel offers a range of contemporary rooms and suites, providing comfort at an accessible price point.

Central Location: Situated in the heart of Nouméa, guests can explore the city on foot, discovering local markets and cultural sites.

Rooftop Terrace: Take in panoramic views of the city and bay from the rooftop terrace, a perfect spot for relaxation.

5. Escapade Island Resort

For an exclusive island retreat, Escapade Island Resort, located on the nearby Îlot Maître, is a paradisiacal escape.

Highlights:

Overwater Bungalows: Indulge in luxury with overwater bungalows featuring direct access to the crystalline lagoon.

Water Activities: The resort offers a plethora of water-based activities, from snorkeling to paddleboarding, ensuring an active stay.

Secluded Paradise: Escape the bustle of Nouméa and enjoy the serenity of a private island, accessible by a short boat ride.

Nouméa's diverse selection of hotels and resorts caters to every type of traveler, from those seeking opulent luxury to budget-conscious adventurers. Whether you choose to bask in the sophistication of Le Méridien or revel in the tranquility of Escapade Island Resort, your stay in Nouméa is destined to be an extraordinary experience. Whatever your preference, the city's hospitality awaits, promising a blend of French elegance and Pacific warmth that is truly unique.

Le Méridien Nouméa Resort & Spa

Le Méridien Nouméa Resort & Spa stands as a testament to luxury and tranquility on the shores of Anse Vata Bay in Nouméa, New Caledonia. This exquisite resort is a harmonious blend of French sophistication and Pacific island charm, offering guests an unparalleled experience of opulence and relaxation.

Upon entering the premises, visitors are greeted by the resort's stunning architecture, a seamless fusion of contemporary design and traditional Melanesian influences. The lobby, adorned with vibrant artwork and intricate detailing, sets the tone for the aesthetic delights that await within.

The accommodation at Le Méridien Nouméa is nothing short of indulgent. Each room and suite is meticulously designed to provide a haven of comfort and elegance. Floor-to-ceiling windows offer panoramic views of the turquoise waters, creating a seamless connection between the interior and the breathtaking natural surroundings. Guests can choose from a variety of room categories, each exuding its own unique charm and character.

Culinary enthusiasts will find themselves in a gastronomic paradise at Le Méridien. The resort boasts a collection of restaurants and bars, each offering a distinctive culinary experience. La Pirogue Restaurant, overlooking the lagoon, serves a delectable array of international and local dishes, expertly crafted by the resort's renowned chefs. For a more casual setting, Latitude 22° Bar invites guests to savor a selection of tapas and refreshing cocktails in a relaxed ambiance.

Le Méridien Nouméa Resort & Spa is not merely a place to rest; it's a destination for rejuvenation. The Deep Nature Spa, nestled within the resort, is a sanctuary of wellness inspired by traditional Kanak healing rituals. Guests can indulge in a range of spa treatments and therapies, each designed to promote relaxation and balance. The spa's serene atmosphere, coupled with skilled therapists, ensures a holistic and transformative experience.

The resort's commitment to recreation is evident in its array of facilities and activities. Those seeking an active holiday can partake in water sports such as kayaking and paddleboarding, or dive into the resort's inviting swimming pool. The fitness center, equipped with state-of-the-art facilities, caters to the wellness needs of health-conscious guests.

Le Méridien Nouméa is also a popular choice for events and celebrations. The resort's conference and banquet facilities are equipped with modern technology and can accommodate a variety of functions, from business conferences to weddings. The picturesque surroundings provide a captivating backdrop for special occasions, creating lasting memories for guests and attendees.

Beyond the luxurious amenities, what truly sets Le Méridien Nouméa apart is its commitment to environmental sustainability. The resort actively engages in eco-friendly practices, from energy conservation to waste reduction. Guests can enjoy their stay with the knowledge that the resort is dedicated to minimizing its ecological footprint, contributing to the preservation of the pristine natural beauty that surrounds it.

The location of Le Méridien Nouméa adds another layer of allure to its already captivating offerings. Situated along Anse Vata Bay, guests have easy access to the white sandy beaches and crystal-clear waters. The nearby Lemon Bay and Duck Island provide additional opportunities for exploration and water-based activities.

In conclusion, Le Méridien Nouméa Resort & Spa is a destination that transcends the ordinary. It is a retreat where luxury meets authenticity, where the beauty of the Pacific merges with the sophistication of French-inspired design. Whether you seek a romantic getaway, a family vacation, or a rejuvenating spa experience, this resort promises an unforgettable sojourn in the heart of New Caledonia. Le Méridien Nouméa is more than a place to stay; it's a journey into elegance, tranquility, and the unspoiled beauty of the South Pacific.

Château Royal Beach Resort & Spa: A Haven of Luxury in Nouméa

Nouméa, the enchanting capital of New Caledonia, is renowned for its unique blend of French sophistication and Pacific island charm. Nestled along the shores of this tropical paradise is the Château Royal Beach Resort & Spa, a beacon of luxury and relaxation. In this comprehensive exploration, we delve into the intricacies of this distinguished establishment, unraveling the tapestry of experiences it offers to discerning travelers.

Château Royal Beach Resort & Spa stands as an epitome of elegance, seamlessly blending modern comforts with the serene beauty of its beachfront location. As guests step into the foyer, they are greeted by a sense of grandeur and refinement. The lobby, adorned with contemporary art pieces and ambient lighting, sets the tone for the luxurious experience that awaits.

Accommodations at Château Royal are nothing short of spectacular. The rooms and suites are tastefully designed, marrying contemporary aesthetics with tropical influences. Floor-to-ceiling windows invite the natural beauty of Nouméa indoors, providing panoramic views of the turquoise waters and white sandy beaches. Each accommodation option is a sanctuary of comfort, featuring plush furnishings, modern amenities, and a private balcony or terrace for guests to relish the sea breeze.

One of the standout features of Château Royal Beach Resort & Spa is its direct access to the pristine beaches that fringe the Anse Vata Bay. The resort takes full advantage of this privileged location by offering guests exclusive access to a stretch of powdery sands lapped by the crystal-clear waters of the Pacific. It's a haven for those seeking a tranquil escape or looking to engage in water sports right at their doorstep.

Culinary enthusiasts will find themselves spoiled for choice with the diverse dining options at Château Royal. The resort boasts a selection of restaurants, each offering a culinary journey that reflects the fusion of French and Pacific flavors. From gourmet seafood dishes prepared with locally sourced ingredients to exquisite pastries and desserts, the dining experiences here are designed to tantalize the taste buds.

The resort's commitment to holistic"well-being is evident at the Deep Nature Spa. Drawing inspiration from traditional Kanak rituals and incorporating modern wellness practices, the spa offers a rejuvenating escape. Guests can indulge in a range of treatments, from massages to facials, all aimed at fostering relaxation and harmony between body and mind.

Beyond the luxurious accommodations and world-class amenities, Château Royal stands out for its commitment to environmental sustainability. The resort has implemented eco-friendly practices, from waste reduction initiatives to energy-efficient technologies. This dedication to responsible tourism aligns seamlessly with the natural beauty that surrounds the resort, ensuring that guests can enjoy their stay with a clear conscience.

Château Royal Beach Resort & Spa is not only a haven for leisure travelers but also an ideal destination for corporate events and special occasions. The resort offers state-of-the-art conference facilities, event spaces with ocean views, and personalized services to cater to the needs of business travelers and those celebrating milestones in life.

The central location of Château Royal adds another layer of appeal. Situated in the heart of Nouméa, guests have easy access to the city's vibrant culture, shopping districts, and entertainment hubs. Whether strolling along the waterfront promenade or exploring the local markets, the resort serves as a convenient base for discovering the unique charm of Nouméa.

As the sun sets over Anse Vata Bay, Château Royal transforms into a magical realm. The resort's ambient lighting, combined with the soothing sounds of the ocean, creates an enchanting atmosphere. Guests can unwind at the rooftop bar, sipping on expertly crafted cocktails while enjoying panoramic views of the city and the bay.

In conclusion, Château Royal Beach Resort & Spa stands as a beacon of luxury in Nouméa, offering an unrivaled blend of French sophistication and Pacific tranquility. From the opulent accommodations and gourmet dining to the holistic spa experiences and commitment to sustainability, every aspect of this resort is crafted to provide an unforgettable stay. Whether seeking a romantic escape, a family retreat, or a venue for a special event, Château Royal beckons travelers to immerse themselves in the unparalleled beauty and hospitality of New Caledonia's capital.

Hilton Noumea La Promenade Residences

Nestled in the heart of Nouméa, New Caledonia, Hilton Noumea La Promenade Residences stands as a testament to luxury and comfort. This premier establishment offers a unique blend of sophistication and homely comfort, making it an ideal choice for both leisure and business travelers. From its spacious residences to its rooftop pool and bar, every aspect of Hilton Noumea La Promenade Residences is meticulously designed to provide guests with an unforgettable experience.

The first thing that captures your attention as you approach the Hilton Noumea La Promenade Residences is its strategic location. Situated in close proximity to Nouméa's major attractions, this hotel offers guests easy access to the vibrant pulse of the city. Whether you're interested in exploring local markets, immersing yourself in cultural experiences, or simply enjoying a leisurely stroll along the waterfront, the Hilton's central location ensures that all of Nouméa's charms are within arm's reach.

Upon entering the Hilton Noumea La Promenade Residences, guests are greeted by an atmosphere of contemporary elegance. The lobby, adorned with modern furnishings and tasteful décor, sets the tone for the luxurious experience that awaits within. The check-in process is seamless, with the hotel's attentive staff ensuring that guests feel welcomed from the moment they step through the doors.

Accommodations at Hilton Noumea La Promenade Residences are a highlight in themselves. The hotel offers a range of spacious residences, each meticulously designed to provide a comfortable and stylish retreat for guests. Whether you opt for a standard room or a suite, you can expect modern amenities, plush furnishings, and a soothing color palette that creates a serene and inviting atmosphere.

One notable feature of the residences at Hilton Noumea La Promenade is their functionality. Ideal for both short-term stays and extended visits, the residences are equipped with full kitchens, allowing guests the flexibility to prepare their meals. This is especially beneficial for those who prefer a more independent and self-sufficient travel experience. The inclusion of private balconies in many of the rooms provides an additional layer of luxury, offering guests a personal space to unwind and soak in the views of the city or the ocean.

As evening falls, guests can ascend to the Hilton Noumea La Promenade's rooftop to discover a true urban oasis. The rooftop pool and bar are undoubtedly among the hotel's standout features. The pool, surrounded by comfortable loungers and cabanas, invites guests to indulge in moments of relaxation while enjoying panoramic views of the city and the azure waters beyond. The rooftop bar complements the experience, offering a diverse menu of cocktails and refreshments that can be enjoyed against the backdrop of a breathtaking sunset.

For those who prioritize wellness and fitness, Hilton Noumea La Promenade Residences delivers with its well-equipped fitness center. The gym is outfitted with modern exercise equipment, allowing guests to maintain their fitness routines even while away from home. After a workout session, guests can unwind in the sauna, ensuring a holistic approach to well-being during their stay.

The hotel's commitment to providing a comprehensive experience extends to its dining options. Hilton Noumea La Promenade features on-site restaurants that cater to a variety of tastes. Whether guests crave local flavors or international cuisine, the hotel's culinary offerings are designed to satisfy discerning palates. The dining spaces are not only places to savor exquisite meals but also environments that enhance the overall ambiance of the hotel.

Beyond its physical offerings, the Hilton Noumea La Promenade Residences prides itself on its commitment to exceptional service. The staff, known for their professionalism and warmth, go the extra mile to ensure that every guest's needs are met. From concierge services that assist with travel arrangements to housekeeping that maintains impeccable standards, the attention to detail is evident in every interaction.

In conclusion, Hilton Noumea La Promenade Residences stands as a beacon of luxury in the heart of Nouméa. Its strategic location, well-appointed accommodations, rooftop oasis, and commitment to outstanding service make it a top choice for travelers seeking a refined and comfortable experience. Whether you're in Nouméa for business or leisure, the Hilton Noumea La Promenade Residences offers a haven where you can immerse yourself in the beauty and hospitality of New Caledonia's capital city.

Ramada Hotel & Suites Noumea

Ramada Hotel & Suites Noumea, nestled in the heart of the vibrant capital city of New Caledonia, stands as a testament to the perfect blend of modern comfort and affordability. The hotel, part of the globally recognized Ramada brand, offers a welcoming retreat for travelers seeking both convenience and style.

As you step into the lobby of Ramada Hotel & Suites Noumea, the atmosphere exudes contemporary elegance. The sleek design, adorned with subtle Pacific-inspired accents, sets the tone for a comfortable stay. The hotel's commitment to providing a modern and relaxed ambiance is evident in every corner.

Accommodations at Ramada Hotel & Suites Noumea cater to a diverse range of guests. From solo travelers to families and business professionals, the hotel offers a variety of rooms and suites, each thoughtfully designed to meet the needs of different travelers. The modern furnishings and neutral color palettes create a calming environment, providing a welcoming haven after a day of exploration in Nouméa.

One notable feature of Ramada Hotel & Suites Noumea is its central location. Situated strategically in the heart of the city, the hotel allows guests easy access to Nouméa's key attractions. Whether it's the vibrant local markets, cultural landmarks, or the picturesque beaches along Anse Vata Bay, everything seems just a stroll away. This convenience makes Ramada an ideal choice for those who wish to immerse themselves in the lively atmosphere of Nouméa.

The hotel's rooftop terrace is a hidden gem, offering panoramic views of the city and the glistening waters of the South Pacific. Guests can unwind in this elevated oasis, perhaps with a refreshing drink in hand, as they take in the breathtaking sunset over the horizon. The rooftop terrace not only provides a serene space for relaxation but also serves as an ideal spot for socializing or even some quiet reflection.

For culinary delights, Ramada Hotel & Suites Noumea boasts its own dining options. The on-site restaurant, with its diverse menu inspired by both French and Pacific cuisines, caters to the discerning palates of guests. Whether it's a hearty breakfast to kick-start the day or a leisurely dinner after exploring Nouméa's attractions, the hotel's restaurant offers a satisfying dining experience.

Beyond the gastronomic pleasures, the hotel takes pride in its commitment to guest well-being. The fitness center, equipped with modern exercise facilities, allows guests to maintain their health routines even while away from home. For those who prefer a more relaxed approach to wellness, the hotel's spa services provide an opportunity to rejuvenate both the body and the mind.

The allure of Ramada Hotel & Suites Noumea is not only in its facilities but also in the warmth of its hospitality. The attentive and friendly staff members contribute to creating a home away from home for guests. Whether it's offering local insights, assisting with travel arrangements, or ensuring a seamless check-in process, the hotel's staff goes the extra mile to enhance the overall guest experience.

For business travelers, the hotel provides meeting and conference facilities, equipped with modern technology to support a variety of events. The central location, coupled with these facilities, makes Ramada an attractive choice for those visiting Nouméa for business purposes.

As the day winds down, guests can retire to their comfortable rooms, where a restful night's sleep awaits. The thoughtfully designed accommodations, featuring contemporary amenities and plush bedding, ensure that guests wake up refreshed and ready for another day of exploration or business endeavors.

In conclusion, Ramada Hotel & Suites Noumea stands as a beacon of hospitality in the heart of Nouméa. Its combination of modern comfort, central location, and affordable luxury makes it a standout choice for travelers seeking a memorable stay in New Caledonia's capital city. Whether you're drawn to the vibrant street life, the cultural richness, or the pristine beaches, Ramada Hotel & Suites Noumea provides the perfect base for an enriching and fulfilling experience in this Pacific paradise.

Escapade Island Resort: A Tranquil Haven in Nouméa

Nestled within the crystalline waters of the Pacific, the Escapade Island Resort stands as a beacon of tranquility, offering an exclusive and luxurious retreat just a short boat ride away from Nouméa. This haven of opulence, situated on the pristine Îlot Maître, promises an escape from the ordinary, inviting guests to indulge in the beauty of New Caledonia's natural wonders while enjoying the height of comfort and sophistication.

As the boat approaches Îlot Maître, guests are greeted by a vision of paradise. The Escapade Island Resort, surrounded by the turquoise hues of the lagoon, emerges as an oasis of serenity. The resort's overwater bungalows, perched on stilts above the gentle waves, present a postcard-perfect image of luxury. Each bungalow is a private haven, offering unobstructed views of the expansive lagoon and the distant horizon.

The heart of Escapade Island Resort lies in its exceptional accommodations. The overwater bungalows, designed with a seamless blend of traditional Melanesian aesthetics and modern luxury, redefine the concept of tropical indulgence. Wooden floors, thatched roofs, and floor-to-ceiling windows characterize these abodes, creating an atmosphere of natural elegance.

Guests have the privilege of direct access to the lagoon from their private decks, allowing for a seamless transition between the comforts of their accommodations and the refreshing embrace of the Pacific waters. The experience of waking up to the gentle lapping of waves beneath the bungalow and witnessing the play of sunlight on the water's surface is nothing short of magical.

Dining at Escapade Island Resort is an exquisite affair. The resort features a selection of restaurants and bars, each offering a culinary journey that mirrors the diversity of New Caledonian flavors.

The Coral Restaurant, with its open-air setting overlooking the lagoon, serves a menu that showcases the freshest local ingredients. From succulent seafood to tropical fruits, every dish is a celebration of the region's rich gastronomic heritage.

For a more casual dining experience, the Sand Beach Grill offers a laid-back atmosphere right on the sandy shores. Guests can savor grilled specialties and refreshing cocktails while soaking in the sun-kissed ambiance.

Beyond its luxurious accommodations and delectable dining options, Escapade Island Resort beckons guests to explore the wonders of the surrounding marine environment. The lagoon, teeming with vibrant coral reefs and marine life, invites snorkelers and divers to discover its secrets.

The resort's water sports center provides equipment for kayaking, paddleboarding, and windsurfing, allowing guests to engage in exhilarating activities just steps away from their overwater abodes. Guided excursions, including boat trips and fishing expeditions, offer a deeper exploration of the ocean's treasures.

For those seeking relaxation and rejuvenation, the Deep Nature Spa at Escapade Island Resort is a sanctuary of wellness. Surrounded by lush tropical vegetation, the spa offers a range of treatments inspired by traditional Melanesian rituals and modern spa practices. From soothing massages to invigorating facials, each treatment is designed to harmonize mind, body, and spirit.

Guests can unwind in the spa's tranquil setting, complete with outdoor Jacuzzis and relaxation areas that capture the essence of the natural surroundings. The gentle rustle of palm leaves and the distant murmur of the lagoon provide a soothing soundtrack to the spa experience, creating an atmosphere of pure bliss.

As the day transforms into night, Escapade Island Resort continues to captivate its guests with mesmerizing sunsets that paint the sky in hues of orange, pink, and purple. The overwater bungalows offer front-row seats to this daily spectacle, allowing guests to witness the sun's descent into the Pacific in unparalleled comfort.

In the evening, the resort takes on a romantic ambiance, with soft lighting and the gentle murmur of the lagoon creating an enchanting atmosphere. The lack of light pollution on Îlot Maître also makes it an ideal location for stargazing. The night sky, unpolluted by city lights, reveals a celestial tapestry that adds a touch of magic to the secluded island experience.

Escapade Island Resort goes beyond being a mere vacation destination; it is also a venue for exclusive events and celebrations. From intimate weddings on the beach to corporate retreats surrounded by nature, the resort's event planning team ensures that every occasion is executed with precision and flair.

The island's seclusion adds a sense of exclusivity to events, making them truly special and memorable. The resort's staff, known for their warm hospitality and attention to detail, work tirelessly to create an atmosphere that reflects the unique charm of Îlot Maître.

As a custodian of the pristine environment that surrounds it, Escapade Island Resort is committed to sustainable and eco-friendly practices. The resort actively participates in coral conservation efforts and supports local initiatives aimed at preserving the delicate balance of the marine ecosystem.

Guests are encouraged to engage in responsible tourism practices during their stay, such as participating in beach clean-ups and respecting the natural habitat of the island. Through these initiatives, Escapade Island Resort seeks to ensure that future generations can continue to enjoy the unspoiled beauty of Îlot Maître.

In conclusion, Escapade Island Resort stands as a testament to the unparalleled beauty of New Caledonia and the epitome of luxury in the heart of the Pacific. Its overwater bungalows, gourmet dining options, and commitment to sustainability make it a destination that transcends the ordinary. For those seeking a retreat beyond imagination, where the lagoon becomes your playground and every sunset is a masterpiece, Escapade Island Resort awaits—an idyllic haven on Îlot Maître, where the spirit of the Pacific comes alive in every moment.

Isle of Pines

I. Isle of Pines: A Tapestry of Natural Wonders and Cultural Riches

The Isle of Pines, located in the heart of the South Pacific, stands as a testament to nature's artistic prowess and the vibrant tapestry of Kanak culture. This pristine island, part of New Caledonia, beckons travelers with its white sandy beaches, crystal-clear waters, and a wealth of cultural attractions. In this exploration, we delve into the exquisite natural wonders and the rich cultural tapestry that define the allure of the Isle of Pines.

Natural Wonders

1. Kanumera Bay: Paradise Found

Nestled along the southwestern coast, Kanumera Bay unfolds like a dream. The turquoise waters gently kiss the shores of powdery white sand, creating an idyllic setting for relaxation and water-based activities. Snorkeling enthusiasts are in for a treat as the bay is home to vibrant coral reefs teeming with marine life.

2. Natural Pool: Nature's Infinity Pool

Tucked away in Oro Bay, the Natural Pool is a mesmerizing geological formation. Surrounded by limestone rocks, this pool is a natural aquarium where tropical fish dance beneath the water's surface. The calm, clear waters make it a haven for snorkelers, providing an immersive encounter with the island's underwater wonders.

3. N'ga Peak: A Panoramic Vista

For those seeking a breathtaking view of the island, the summit of N'ga Peak is the answer. A moderate hike leads to the top, where panoramic views of the lush landscape and the surrounding turquoise sea await. The golden hour at N'ga Peak is a spectacle, with the sun painting the sky in hues of orange and pink.

4. Piscine Naturelle: Tranquil Lagoon

Piscine Naturelle, or the Natural Swimming Pool, is a secluded lagoon with tranquil waters protected by coral reefs. Accessible by boat or a scenic hike, it offers a serene escape surrounded by the island's lush greenery. The clarity of the water and the vibrant marine life make it an ideal spot for swimming and snorkeling.

Cultural Attractions

1. Vao Village: Kanak Heritage

At the heart of the Isle of Pines lies Vao Village, a cultural hub that provides a glimpse into the traditional lifestyle of the Kanak people. Visitors can explore traditional huts, learn about customary practices, and witness captivating dance performances that tell stories of the island's rich heritage.

2. St. Joseph's Catholic Church: Architectural Marvel

This iconic church, with its wooden structure and distinctive blue roof, is a blend of European and Kanak architectural styles. Built by the island's inhabitants in the late 1800s, St. Joseph's Catholic Church is not only a place of worship but also a symbol of cultural resilience and unity.

3. Grotte de la Reine Hortense: Cave of Legends

The Grotte de la Reine Hortense, or the Cave of Queen Hortense, is a sacred site with great cultural significance. Legend has it that Queen Hortense took refuge in this cave during tribal conflicts. Today, it serves as a spiritual site where visitors can appreciate the cultural and historical narratives woven into the island's fabric.

4. The Prison: Reliving History

A visit to the ruins of the old penal colony, known simply as "The Prison," provides a somber yet insightful look into the island's history. The preserved structures stand as a reminder of the penal history of the Isle of Pines, where indigenous Kanaks and political prisoners were once confined.

Harmony of Nature and Culture

As visitors traverse the Isle of Pines, they witness a harmonious blend of natural wonders and cultural treasures. The island's pristine beaches and lush landscapes serve as the backdrop to a vibrant tapestry of Kanak traditions, ensuring that every visitor leaves with not just memories of a tropical paradise but also a deep appreciation for the rich heritage that defines this jewel in the Pacific. The Isle of Pines beckons, inviting all to explore its shores and uncover the secrets of a destination where nature and culture dance in perfect harmony.

Kanumera Bay: Paradise Found

In the heart of the South Pacific, a jewel of unparalleled beauty graces the world—the Kanumera Bay. Nestled along the southwestern coast of the Isle of Pines in New Caledonia, this pristine haven beckons travelers with its ethereal charm and breathtaking scenery. As the sun casts its golden glow upon the powdery white sands and the turquoise waters gently lap against the shore, Kanumera Bay unfolds like a dream, captivating the hearts of those fortunate enough to experience its magic.

The allure of Kanumera Bay lies not only in its picturesque landscapes but also in the myriad of experiences it offers to those seeking solace, adventure, or simply a moment of pure tranquility. As one steps onto the soft sands that stretch along the bay, a sense of serenity envelopes the soul, setting the stage for a journey into a paradise found.

The sands of Kanumera Bay are not just grains beneath your feet; they are a canvas painted by the hands of nature. The powdery texture, almost like walking on clouds, creates an otherworldly sensation, inviting visitors to kick off their shoes and connect with the earth beneath. The pristine beach, fringed by swaying palm trees, sets the perfect scene for those seeking relaxation.

The crystal-clear waters of Kanumera Bay are an invitation to explore a vibrant underwater world. Snorkeling enthusiasts find themselves immersed in a kaleidoscope of colors as they encounter the thriving marine life beneath the surface. Coral reefs, alive with a myriad of fish species, create a natural aquarium where every fin movement tells a story of life in the South Pacific.

For those seeking more than a leisurely swim, Kanumera Bay offers a playground for water sports enthusiasts. Kayaking and paddleboarding are popular activities, allowing visitors to venture beyond the shore and witness the beauty of the bay from a different perspective. As the gentle waves carry the kayaks, the rhythmic sound becomes a melody echoing the harmony of nature.

The allure of Kanumera Bay extends beyond its shores. Just offshore lies a paradise for divers—an underwater realm that unveils the mysteries of the deep. The vibrant coral gardens, home to an array of marine creatures, create a surreal landscape where every dive is an exploration into a world untouched by time. Whether a seasoned diver or a novice, the underwater wonders of Kanumera Bay are an irresistible invitation to discover the secrets hidden beneath the surface.

As the day unfolds, Kanumera Bay transforms into a canvas painted with the hues of the setting sun. The sky blushes with shades of orange and pink, casting a warm glow over the bay. The transition from day to night is a spectacle in itself, inviting those on the shores to pause and witness nature's grand finale—a breathtaking sunset that leaves an indelible mark on the soul.

Beyond its natural beauty, Kanumera Bay is also a place of cultural significance. For the indigenous Kanak people, the bay is more than a picturesque landscape; it is a part of their history and identity. The connection between the Kanak culture and the land is palpable, and visitors are invited to appreciate the sacredness of this space.

Kanumera Bay is not just a destination; it is an experience that transcends the boundaries of time and space. It is a sanctuary for those seeking refuge from the hustle of the modern world and a canvas where nature and culture coalesce in a harmonious dance. In the embrace of Kanumera Bay, paradise is not a distant dream; it is a tangible reality—a place where the soul finds solace, and the spirit of adventure is awakened. As the waves continue to kiss the shores, Kanumera Bay remains an eternal testament to the wonders of the natural world and the profound connection between land, sea, and the human soul.

Natural Pool: Nature's Infinity Pool

The Isle of Pines, nestled in the heart of the South Pacific, is a canvas painted with nature's most exquisite hues. Among its many treasures, the Natural Pool stands as a testament to the island's unparalleled beauty. This hidden gem, tucked away in the embrace of Oro Bay, is nature's very own infinity pool, a place where the boundaries between the terrestrial and the aquatic blur into a seamless, mesmerizing panorama.

Upon reaching the Natural Pool, visitors are greeted by a landscape that seems almost surreal. Limestone rocks cradle the pool, creating a protective barrier against the rhythmic dance of the Pacific Ocean. The azure waters, kissed by the gentle caress of the island breeze, beckon travelers to immerse themselves in a world of serenity and wonder.

The journey to the Natural Pool is an adventure in itself. Whether arriving by boat, guided by the rhythmic strokes of an oar, or embarking on a scenic hike, the anticipation builds with each step. The island's lush greenery provides a scenic backdrop, a prelude to the aquatic paradise that awaits. As the pool comes into view, the senses are immediately captivated by the tranquility that pervades the atmosphere.

Stepping into the Natural Pool is like entering a liquid haven. The water, crystal clear and inviting, mirrors the azure sky above. The pool is a sanctuary where time seems to stand still, and the worries of the world dissolve into the gentle ripples created by the tide. It is a place where the mind finds solace, and the soul connects with the purity of nature.

What sets the Natural Pool apart is its unique blend of seclusion and openness. The encircling limestone rocks create a sense of intimacy, a private alcove carved by centuries of natural artistry. Yet, as one looks beyond the protective embrace of the rocks, the vastness of the Pacific unfolds—an infinite horizon that merges seamlessly with the sky. It is this juxtaposition of containment and boundlessness that gives the Natural Pool its character as nature's very own infinity pool.

As the sun traverses its daily arc, the Natural Pool undergoes a transformation that is nothing short of magical. The changing angles of sunlight play upon the water's surface, casting dancing reflections that shimmer like liquid diamonds. The play of light and shadow adds a dynamic element to the pool, creating a visual symphony that evolves throughout the day.

For those with an inclination for aquatic exploration, the Natural Pool offers a window into an underwater realm teeming with life. The clarity of the water unveils a vibrant ecosystem—coral formations, schools of colorful fish, and the occasional sea turtle gliding gracefully beneath the surface. Snorkeling in the Natural Pool is not just an activity; it's an immersion into an aquatic wonderland, an opportunity to witness the delicate balance of life in a pristine environment.

The Natural Pool is not merely a geological formation; it is a sanctuary for both the adventurous and the contemplative. It beckons those seeking adventure to plunge into its refreshing depths, to swim amid the wonders of the underwater world. Yet, it also extends an invitation to those yearning for serenity—to float on its surface, to be cradled by the embrace of nature, and to drink in the symphony of waves and wind.

As the day draws to a close, the Natural Pool transforms yet again. The golden hues of the setting sun cast a warm glow over the landscape, painting the rocks and water with a palette of oranges, pinks, and purples. It is a time for quiet reflection, a moment to appreciate the ephemeral beauty of a day well spent in communion with nature.

The Natural Pool is more than a destination; it is an experience—a journey into the heart of the Isle of Pines, where the elements conspire to create a haven for the weary traveler. It is a microcosm of the island's essence, where the natural and cultural narratives intertwine, and the spirit of the Pacific comes alive. Whether viewed through the lens of adventure, relaxation, or simple appreciation for the wonders of the world, the Natural Pool stands as a testament to the enduring allure of the Isle of Pines—a place where nature unfolds its beauty in a timeless, enchanting dance.

N'ga Peak: A Panoramic Vista

The Isle of Pines, a jewel in the South Pacific, boasts an array of natural wonders that captivate the hearts of travelers. Among these wonders, N'ga Peak stands as a majestic testament to the island's beauty. This towering summit, reaching towards the heavens, offers visitors a panoramic vista that transcends the ordinary and transports them into a realm of awe and wonder.

As the sun rises over the Isle of Pines, casting its warm embrace upon the landscape, the call of N'ga Peak beckons the adventurous souls seeking a higher perspective. This ascent is not merely a climb; it is a journey into the heart of the island's soul, where the convergence of land and sky paints an unparalleled masterpiece.

N'ga Peak is situated on the southern end of the Isle of Pines, and its prominence makes it a natural focal point for those exploring the island. Rising 262 meters above sea level, the peak provides an unrivaled viewpoint, offering a sweeping panorama of the surrounding turquoise waters, verdant landscapes, and distant horizons.

The journey to N'ga Peak begins with a trail that winds its way through the island's lush vegetation. As hikers ascend, the air becomes filled with the fragrance of exotic flora, and the sounds of native birds create a harmonious symphony. The trail, though challenging at times, rewards those who persevere with glimpses of the island's diverse ecosystems.

The ascent is a rhythmic dance between the natural and the human. The towering pine trees, endemic to the Isle of Pines, sway gently in the breeze, their branches whispering tales of centuries gone by. Moss-covered rocks, adorned with vibrant ferns, bear witness to the passage of time, inviting reflection on the island's geological history.

As hikers approach the summit, the landscape undergoes a transformative dance. The once-distant horizon draws nearer, and the vastness of the Pacific Ocean unfolds before the eyes like a canvas painted with hues of blue and green. The lagoon surrounding the Isle of Pines glistens in the sunlight, revealing coral reefs that weave intricate patterns beneath the surface.

Reaching the pinnacle of N'ga Peak is a triumphant moment, a communion with the elements and a celebration of the human spirit. The summit is crowned by a simple marker, a humble testament to the island's untouched beauty. From this vantage point, one can witness the sun as it casts its golden glow upon the landscape during sunrise or bids farewell in a spectacular display of colors during sunset.

The allure of N'ga Peak extends beyond its visual splendor. It is a place where the breeze carries whispers of tales untold, where the energy of the land resonates with those who pause to listen. The spiritual significance of the peak is not lost on the Kanak people, who regard it as a sacred site. This spiritual connection adds a profound layer to the experience, as visitors feel a sense of reverence in the presence of such natural majesty.

N'ga Peak is not merely a destination; it is a pilgrimage for those who seek communion with nature and a deeper understanding of the island's soul. It is a place where time seems to stand still, and the worries of the world below are momentarily forgotten. The panoramic vista from N'ga Peak is a gift to the senses, an invitation to contemplate the grandeur of creation and appreciate the delicate balance between earth and sky.

In every season and at every hour, N'ga Peak invites explorers, wanderers, and dreamers to ascend its slopes and partake in the silent conversation between the land and the heavens. It is a place where the tangible and the intangible converge, where the earth meets the sky, and where the human spirit finds solace in the embrace of nature's grandeur. N'ga Peak is not just a summit; it is a sanctuary, a living testament to the timeless beauty of the Isle of Pines.

Piscine Naturelle: A Tranquil Lagoon Retreat

The Isle of Pines, situated in the heart of the South Pacific, is a haven for nature enthusiasts and seekers of serenity. Amidst its myriad natural wonders, Piscine Naturelle stands out as a jewel in the crown of this idyllic island. This tranquil lagoon, with its crystal-clear waters and pristine surroundings, beckons travelers to experience a retreat into nature's embrace.

As the sun casts its golden glow on the Isle of Pines, visitors find themselves drawn to the allure of Piscine Naturelle. Tucked away from the bustling world, this secluded lagoon promises a sanctuary of calmness and natural beauty. Its name, translating to the "Natural Swimming Pool," is a testament to the peaceful and untouched character of this aquatic paradise.

Upon arrival, the first impression is one of awe. The lagoon is framed by a backdrop of lush greenery, a symphony of vibrant hues that mirror the untouched beauty of the island. The turquoise waters of Piscine Naturelle are striking, inviting visitors to step into a world where time seems to slow down.

The accessibility of Piscine Naturelle adds to its allure. While the lagoon can be reached by a picturesque hike through the island's verdant landscape, many opt for the alternative – a short boat ride from Kuto Bay. As the boat approaches the lagoon, the gradual reveal of its beauty is a prelude to the serenity that awaits.

Entering the waters of Piscine Naturelle is akin to stepping into a liquid oasis. The lagoon is protected by a natural barrier of coral reefs, ensuring calm waters that are perfect for swimming and snorkeling. The clarity of the water allows for a clear view of the vibrant marine life that calls the lagoon home. Schools of colorful fish dance beneath the surface, weaving through the coral gardens that add to the underwater spectacle.

Snorkelers find themselves immersed in a world of aquatic wonders, exploring the intricate formations of coral and encountering a kaleidoscope of marine life. The diversity of fish species, from the smallest shimmering damselfish to the majestic butterflyfish, creates a mesmerizing underwater tableau.

For those seeking a tranquil escape, the shallow and warm waters of Piscine Naturelle provide a soothing experience. The lagoon's sandy bottom is a natural cushion beneath the feet, and the gentle currents offer a therapeutic massage as visitors wade through the shallows. The absence of large waves and strong currents makes Piscine Naturelle suitable for visitors of all ages, creating an environment where families can share in the joy of the island's natural splendor.

The fringing vegetation surrounding Piscine Naturelle adds to its allure, providing shaded spots where visitors can relax and enjoy a picnic. Towering pine trees, endemic to the Isle of Pines, cast dappled shadows on the shore, creating a serene atmosphere that invites contemplation and relaxation.

As the day unfolds, the lagoon undergoes a transformation. The changing angles of sunlight cast a spectrum of colors on the water's surface, ranging from shades of turquoise to deep azure. The play of light and shadow enhances the already picturesque surroundings, creating a dynamic canvas that evolves with the passage of time.

The sense of tranquility at Piscine Naturelle extends beyond the water's edge. The surrounding landscape, characterized by the endemic flora of the Isle of Pines, is a testament to the island's commitment to preserving its natural heritage. Indigenous plants thrive along the shores, creating a seamless transition between land and water. Visitors are encouraged to explore the lush vegetation, discovering hidden pockets of biodiversity that contribute to the overall richness of the ecosystem.

The ecological significance of Piscine Naturelle is not lost on those who appreciate the delicate balance of nature. The coral reefs that protect the lagoon serve as a crucial habitat for marine life, contributing to the overall health of the surrounding waters. Conservation efforts on the Isle of Pines emphasize the importance of responsible tourism, ensuring that visitors can enjoy the wonders of Piscine Naturelle without compromising the delicate ecosystem.

As the sun begins its descent, casting a warm glow over the Isle of Pines, visitors to Piscine Naturelle find themselves reluctant to leave. The lagoon's tranquility and the harmony of nature create a profound sense of connection to the environment. Whether it's the first visit or a return to this aquatic sanctuary, the allure of Piscine Naturelle remains timeless.

In conclusion, Piscine Naturelle is more than a destination; it's an immersive experience in the untouched beauty of the Isle of Pines. This tranquil lagoon, with its pristine waters, vibrant marine life, and natural serenity, encapsulates the essence of the island's allure. In the heart of Piscine Naturelle, visitors discover not just a swimming pool of nature's making but a sanctuary that rejuvenates the spirit and leaves an indelible mark on the soul.

Vao Village: Embracing Kanak Heritage

Nestled at the heart of the Isle of Pines, Vao Village stands as a living testament to the rich cultural tapestry of the Kanak people. As visitors meander through this tranquil village, they are transported back in time, immersed in the traditions, customs, and daily life of a community deeply connected to its heritage.

The allure of Vao Village lies not just in its picturesque surroundings but in the authenticity with which it preserves and shares the Kanak way of life. From traditional huts to vibrant dance performances, every element of Vao Village tells a story—a story of resilience, unity, and the enduring spirit of the Kanak people.

Upon entering Vao Village, one is greeted by the sight of meticulously crafted traditional huts, known as "cases." These huts, made from local materials such as wood and thatch, serve as both homes and communal spaces. As you step inside, the warmth of the wooden interiors and the earthy aroma of thatch create an immediate connection to the natural elements that surround the village.

The heart of Vao Village is its communal meeting area, a space where villagers gather for ceremonies, celebrations, and important discussions. Here, elders share traditional tales, passing down the oral history of the Kanak people to younger generations. The sense of community is palpable, and visitors are often invited to partake in the communal activities, fostering a sense of inclusion and cultural exchange.

One of the most captivating aspects of Vao Village is its commitment to preserving and showcasing traditional Kanak dance and music. Performances are not merely staged for tourists; rather, they are integral to the fabric of daily life in the village. The rhythmic beats of traditional drums and the mesmerizing movements of the dancers convey stories of the land, the ancestors, and the spiritual connection that binds the Kanak people to their environment.

The significance of dance In Kanak culture goes beyond entertainment; it is a form of expression that encapsulates the community's values and history. Each movement, gesture, and costume holds symbolic meaning, and as the dancers weave through the village, they invite onlookers to join in the celebration of a cultural legacy that has endured for centuries.

The preservation of language is another vital aspect of Kanak heritage, and Vao Village plays a pivotal role in ensuring the survival of traditional languages. Elders, often the guardians of linguistic traditions, engage in language preservation efforts, teaching younger members of the community and, in some cases, interested visitors. The result is a harmonious blend of past and present, where ancient languages continue to echo through the village.

Beyond the communal spaces, Vao Village is surrounded by lush landscapes that further emphasize the deep connection between the Kanak people and the natural world. The village is often adorned with vibrant flora, and the gardens are not just sources of sustenance but also spaces that reflect the community's profound respect for the environment.

As one explores the outskirts of Vao Village, the landscape opens up to reveal ancestral burial grounds—a sacred space where the spirits of the departed are believed to reside. The significance of these grounds extends beyond the spiritual realm; they are a tangible link to the ancestors, a reminder of the enduring legacy that shapes the present and future of the Kanak people.

Vao Village, while welcoming tourists with open arms, remains steadfast in its commitment to preserving the authenticity of Kanak heritage. The village's leaders actively engage in sustainable tourism practices, ensuring that the influx of visitors contributes positively to the community without compromising its cultural integrity.

In conclusion, Vao Village is more than a tourist destination; it is a living, breathing testament to the resilience, unity, and cultural richness of the Kanak people. As visitors stroll through its pathways, engage with its residents, and witness the vibrant expressions of dance and music, they become participants in a narrative that transcends time—a narrative that celebrates the enduring spirit of a community deeply connected to its roots. Vao Village invites all who enter to not just observe but to immerse themselves in the embrace of Kanak heritage, where every step Is a dance, and every story is a thread woven into the vibrant tapestry of the Isle of Pines.

St. Joseph's Catholic Church: An Architectural Marvel on the Isle of Pines

The Isle of Pines, nestled in the South Pacific and part of New Caledonia, is renowned for its natural beauty and cultural richness. Among the treasures that adorn this idyllic island, St. Joseph's Catholic Church stands as an architectural marvel and a testament to the historical and cultural tapestry woven into the landscape.

St. Joseph's Catholic Church is not just a place of worship; it is a living testament to the fusion of European and Kanak architectural styles. Its wooden structure, adorned with a distinctive blue roof, draws visitors into a world where spirituality and craftsmanship converge in harmony. As we delve into the history and architectural significance of this iconic church, we uncover the layers of meaning embedded in its walls and foundations.

The roots of St. Joseph's Church stretch back to the late 19th century when Catholic missionaries arrived on the Isle of Pines. The church's construction began in 1870 under the guidance of the Marist Fathers, who sought to establish a spiritual refuge on this remote island. The labor for building the church was undertaken by the local Kanak people, adding a profound layer of community involvement to its construction.

What sets St. Joseph's Catholic Church apart is its unique blend of architectural styles. The church seamlessly combines European influences with traditional Kanak design elements. The wooden construction, a nod to European ecclesiastical architecture, is complemented by intricately carved wooden patterns that reflect the artistic heritage of the Kanak people. The fusion is a visual testament to the cultural exchange that occurred during a crucial period in the island's history.

The church's wooden construction is not merely practical but adds an elegant charm to the structure. The use of local timber not only resonates with sustainability but also creates a warm and inviting atmosphere within the church's walls. Visitors entering St. Joseph's find themselves surrounded by the comforting embrace of wood, a material that connects the spiritual space with the natural world outside.

The most striking feature of St. Joseph's Catholic Church is its distinctive blue roof. The vivid hue serves both aesthetic and symbolic purposes. Symbolically, blue is often associated with spirituality, symbolizing the infinite and the divine. Aesthetically, the blue roof stands out against the greenery of the surrounding landscape, creating a visual focal point that draws the eyes upward, inviting contemplation.

St. Joseph's Church is more than an architectural gem; it is a repository of cultural symbolism. The fusion of European and Kanak elements is a testament to the coexistence of diverse cultures on the Isle of Pines. The church becomes a symbol of unity, where different traditions converge in a shared space of worship. The carved patterns on the wooden pillars and beams tell stories of both religious significance and Kanak heritage.

Preserving St. Joseph's Catholic Church is not only a matter of architectural conservation but also a commitment to safeguarding the cultural and historical legacy of the Isle of Pines. Over the years, efforts have been made to ensure the structural integrity of the church while maintaining the authenticity of its design. The careful preservation of St. Joseph's speaks to the collective dedication of the community to honor its past.

Beyond its architectural splendor, St. Joseph's Catholic Church serves as a spiritual sanctuary for the island's residents and visitors. The tranquil interior, adorned with religious iconography and bathed in the soft glow of natural light, creates an atmosphere of reverence. The church's significance extends beyond its physical form, encompassing the spiritual experiences of those who gather within its walls.

St. Joseph's is not only a place of worship but also a focal point for community gatherings and events. The church, surrounded by lush greenery and overlooking the azure waters of the Pacific, becomes a communal space where celebrations, ceremonies, and cultural events unfold. It stands as a symbol of communal strength and resilience, echoing with the shared history of the Isle of Pines.

In the heart of the Isle of Pines, St. Joseph's Catholic Church stands tall as a testament to the confluence of cultures, a tangible representation of the island's history, spirituality, and architectural brilliance. As visitors marvel at its wooden elegance and distinctive blue roof, they partake in a journey through time, witnessing the harmonious blend of European and Kanak influences. St. Joseph's Catholic Church is not just a structure; it is a living embodiment of the Isle of Pines' rich heritage, inviting all who enter to be a part of its continuing story.

Grotte de la Reine Hortense: Cave of Legends

The Isle of Pines, a tranquil haven nestled in the heart of the South Pacific, is home to a multitude of natural wonders and cultural treasures. Among these, the Grotte de la Reine Hortense, or the Cave of Queen Hortense, stands as a testament to the rich tapestry of legends woven into the fabric of this pristine island.

The Grotte de la Reine Hortense is not merely a physical entity; it is a portal to the past, a repository of stories passed down through generations. Located on the Isle of Pines, part of the archipelago of New Caledonia, this cave is situated in the lush greenery of the island, hidden away from the bustling modernity that characterizes other parts of the world.

As visitors approach the cave, they are greeted by the sheer geological marvel of the site. The entrance to the Grotte de la Reine Hortense is framed by limestone formations, creating an otherworldly façade that beckons explorers to step into a realm where time seems to stand still. The cave's interior is a labyrinth of stalactites and stalagmites, forming intricate patterns that captivate the imagination.

Yet, it is not the geological features alone that make this cave a compelling destination. The Grotte de la Reine Hortense holds profound cultural significance for the indigenous Kanak people of the Isle of Pines. Legend has it that Queen Hortense, a revered figure in Kanak folklore, sought refuge in this cave during a period of tribal conflict.

Queen Hortense, whose name is synonymous with resilience and wisdom, played a pivotal role in the history of the Isle of Pines. Her story is interwoven with the struggles and triumphs of the

Kanak people. As the legend goes, during a time of conflict, Queen Hortense found solace and protection within the depths of the Grotte de la Reine Hortense.

The cave, beyond being a physical refuge, became a spiritual sanctuary for Queen Hortense. It is said that within the confines of the cave, she communed with the spirits of the island, seeking guidance and strength to lead her people through tumultuous times. The echoes of her prayers, some believe, still resonate within the cavernous expanse of the Grotte de la Reine Hortense.

The cave has become a site of pilgrimage for the Kanak people, who honor Queen Hortense through rituals and ceremonies held within its sacred chambers. These ceremonies, rooted in ancient traditions, connect the present generation with the cultural legacy passed down by their ancestors. The cave serves as a living testament to the enduring strength of Kanak identity.

Over the years, archaeological expeditions have uncovered artifacts within the Grotte de la Reine Hortense, shedding light on the historical authenticity of the legend. The remnants of ancient pottery and tools provide tangible links to the past, validating the cave's role not only as a shelter but as a witness to the ebb and flow of human existence on the Isle of Pines.

As the Grotte de la Reine Hortense gains recognition as a cultural and historical gem, efforts have been made to ensure its preservation. Conservation initiatives aim to protect both the natural formations within the cave and the cultural heritage it represents. Striking a delicate balance between tourism and preservation is crucial to maintaining the integrity of this sacred site.

For those fortunate enough to visit the Grotte de la Reine Hortense, the experience is transformative. The cave's cool, dimly lit chambers invite contemplation, and the sense of stepping into a living myth is palpable. The journey through the cave becomes a symbolic passage through time, connecting the present with the ancient narratives that define the identity of the Isle of Pines.

In the heart of the Isle of Pines, the Grotte de la Reine Hortense stands as more than a geological marvel; it is a testament to the resilience of a people and the enduring power of cultural narratives. As visitors explore the depths of this cave, they become part of a continuum, where the past and present converge, and the legends of Queen Hortense continue to echo through the chambers of time. The Grotte de la Reine Hortense is not just a cave; it is a living, breathing testament to the intertwined forces of nature and culture that shape the identity of this enchanting island in the South Pacific.

The Prison: Reliving History

The Isle of Pines, nestled in the cerulean embrace of the South Pacific, holds within its borders not only the pristine beauty of nature but also the haunting echoes of a historical past. Among the silent witnesses to bygone eras is a place simply known as "The Prison." Standing as a testament to a tumultuous history, the remnants of this penal colony offer a poignant journey into a time when the island's destiny was shaped by forces beyond its tranquil shores.

The story of The Prison Is not just one of incarceration but a narrative woven into the very fabric of the Isle of Pines. As visitors wander through the overgrown paths and moss-covered stones, they step into a world where hardship, resilience, and the inexorable march of time have etched indelible marks on the landscape.

The remnants of The Prison are scattered across a landscape that now seems to have absorbed the suffering and stories of its past. The dilapidated structures, with walls that once confined bodies and spirits, stand as solemn monuments to an era when the destiny of the Isle of Pines was entwined with the complex forces of colonialism and conflict.

The history of The Prison dates back to the late 19th century when France, seeking to assert control over its overseas territories, established penal colonies in remote corners of the world. The Isle of Pines, with its isolation and challenging terrain, became one such location. The idea was not only to punish but also to tame the land and its indigenous inhabitants.

As the first rays of sunlight pierced through the dense foliage, illuminating the ruins of The Prison, it becomes apparent that these walls once held the stories of hardship and defiance. The prisoners, a mix of indigenous Kanaks and political dissidents, faced not only the physical challenges of forced labor but also the psychological toll of being removed from their homes and families.

Walking through the remains of the cells, one can almost feel the weight of history pressing down. The cramped quarters, the rusting bars, and the overgrown courtyards tell a tale of deprivation and struggle. Yet, amid the ruins, there is also a sense of resilience—the spirit of those who endured, resisted, and found ways to survive in the face of adversity.

The Prison was not just a place of confinement; it was a microcosm of the broader historical forces at play during that era. The clash of cultures, the imposition of colonial rule, and the resistance of the Kanak people converge within these crumbling walls. The stories of those who suffered here are intertwined with the broader narrative of New Caledonia's complex history.

Exploring The Prison is not merely an encounter with ruins; it's an immersive experience that prompts reflection on the consequences of power dynamics, colonialism, and the indomitable human spirit. The silence that now envelops the site speaks louder than any words can convey, inviting visitors to contemplate the shared human experience of struggle and survival.

Among the ruins, one finds a stark contrast between the natural beauty that surrounds The Prison and the scars left by human endeavor. The juxtaposition of lush vegetation and decayed structures paints a poignant picture—one that encapsulates the dualities of the Isle of Pines, a place where paradise and pain coexist.

While The Prison stands as a somber reminder of a dark chapter in the island's history, it also serves as a catalyst for dialogue and remembrance. Efforts to preserve and interpret these historical sites are essential not only for acknowledging the past but also for fostering understanding and reconciliation in the present.

In the process of exploring The Prison, visitors may grapple with uncomfortable truths about the shared history of humanity. The echoes of confinement, the shadows of injustice, and the resilience of the human spirit all converge within these walls. The experience transcends mere historical curiosity; it becomes a meditation on the enduring impact of the past on the present.

As the sun begins its descent, casting long shadows across the ruins, one cannot help but feel a sense of gratitude for the passage of time. The Isle of Pines has evolved, and so too has the world around it. The remnants of The Prison, weathered by years and elements, stand as a reminder not only of the pain that once echoed through these corridors but also of the possibility of healing and renewal.

In the twilight hours, as the last rays of sunlight illuminate the weathered stones, The Prison on the Isle of Pines becomes more than a historical relic; it transforms into a symbol of resilience, a testament to the human capacity to endure, learn, and, ultimately, move forward. The Isle of Pines, with its natural wonders and historical echoes, invites all who visit to contemplate not only the beauty of the present but the complexities of the past that shape our collective journey.

II.   *Isle of Pines: A Paradise of Hotels and Resorts*

Nestled in the heart of the South Pacific, the Isle of Pines, also known as "Kunie" by the locals, stands as a pristine haven for travelers seeking tranquility, natural beauty, and a touch of luxury. This idyllic island, part of New Caledonia, is renowned for its crystal-clear waters, powdery white sands, and vibrant coral reefs. Accommodations on the Isle of Pines range from charming

boutique hotels to upscale resorts, each offering a unique blend of comfort and immersion in the island's natural wonders.

1. Kanua Hotel: Where Nature Meets Luxury

Nestled amidst lush greenery and overlooking the serene Kuto Bay, Kanua Hotel is a testament to luxury seamlessly blending with nature. The hotel offers a range of accommodations, from intimate bungalows to spacious suites, all designed with traditional Melanesian influences. Guests can wake up to the gentle rustling of palm trees and enjoy breathtaking views of the turquoise waters. The onsite restaurant serves a fusion of local and international cuisine, using fresh, locally sourced ingredients.

2. Le Méridien Ile des Pins: A Tropical Oasis

Le Méridien Ile des Pins stands as an epitome of elegance on the Isle of Pines. Situated along the pristine Oro Bay, this resort boasts overwater bungalows that offer direct access to the lagoon. The resort's architecture pays homage to the traditional Kanak culture, creating a harmonious blend of luxury and authenticity. Guests can indulge in a range of water activities, unwind at the Deep Nature Spa, or savor gourmet delights at the resort's restaurant, overlooking the serene waters.

3. Oure Tera Beach Resort: Secluded Serenity

For those seeking seclusion and tranquility, Oure Tera Beach Resort is an ideal choice. Located on the southern tip of the island, the resort offers exclusive access to the Oro Bay and Kuto Bay. The bungalows, adorned with traditional thatched roofs, provide a sense of intimacy and privacy. Guests can enjoy the resort's private beach, partake in water sports, or simply relax in a hammock, taking in the breathtaking views of the Coral Sea.

4. Hotel Kou Bugny: A Cultural Retreat

Hotel Kou Bugny is not just a place to stay; it's an immersive cultural experience. The hotel's architecture and décor pay homage to the Kanak heritage, with traditional wood carvings and woven artistry adorning the spaces. Situated near Vao village, guests have the opportunity to engage with the local community and learn about their customs. The hotel's restaurant offers a delightful journey into Kanak cuisine, featuring flavors inspired by the island's rich cultural tapestry.

5. Nouvata: Budget-Friendly Comfort

For travelers seeking a more budget-friendly option without compromising on comfort, Nouvata is a welcoming choice. Situated near the popular Kuto Bay, the hotel offers a range of room options, from standard to family-sized. Guests can relax by the pool, explore nearby hiking trails, and enjoy easy access to the island's attractions. The hotel's casual restaurant serves a mix of local and international dishes, catering to diverse tastes.

6. Gîte Nataiwatch: Homestay Charm

For a more intimate experience, Gîte Nataiwatch offers a charming homestay option. This family-run accommodation provides guests with a unique opportunity to immerse themselves in the local way of life. The bungalows are nestled amidst tropical gardens, creating a cozy and authentic atmosphere. Guests can savor homemade Kanak meals, participate in traditional activities, and forge genuine connections with the hospitable hosts.

The Isle of Pines, with its enchanting landscapes and warm hospitality, beckons travelers to experience a unique blend of luxury and authenticity. Whether indulging in the opulence of upscale resorts or opting for the cultural immersion of boutique hotels, the accommodations on this paradisiacal island offer a gateway to the natural wonders and rich heritage that define the Isle of Pines. As visitors unwind in the lap of tropical luxury, they are sure to carry with them cherished memories of this South Pacific gem.

Kanua Hotel: Where Nature Meets Luxury

Nestled in the heart of the South Pacific, the Kanua Hotel on the Isle of Pines stands as a testament to the seamless integration of luxury and nature. This boutique hotel, surrounded by lush greenery and overlooking the tranquil Kuto Bay, offers guests an unparalleled experience of serenity and sophistication. From its architectural design to its commitment to sustainable practices, Kanua Hotel embodies a harmonious connection between modern comfort and the natural beauty of its surroundings.

As you approach Kanua Hotel, the first thing that captures your attention is its architecture. The design of the hotel is a thoughtful fusion of contemporary elegance and traditional Melanesian influences. The buildings, adorned with traditional thatched roofs and local wood accents, seamlessly blend into the natural landscape. The use of sustainable materials reflects the hotel's commitment to preserving the authenticity of the environment.

The accommodations at Kanua Hotel are designed to immerse guests in the tranquility of nature. From intimate bungalows to spacious suites, every room provides a private sanctuary with panoramic views of the surrounding tropical paradise. The interiors are tastefully decorated with local artwork and crafts, creating a warm and inviting atmosphere that pays homage to the Kanak culture.

Kuto Bay, visible from the hotel's grounds, adds a touch of magic to the Kanua experience. The bay's turquoise waters gently lap against the shore, creating a soothing soundtrack for guests as they explore the hotel's surroundings. The lush tropical gardens that envelop Kanua Hotel not only enhance its natural beauty but also serve as a habitat for local flora and fauna.

Guests can take leisurely strolls through the gardens, discovering the vibrant colors of exotic flowers and the melodies of tropical birds. For those seeking relaxation, there are secluded spots where one can unwind with a book or simply absorb the serenity of the surroundings. Kanua Hotel's commitment to preserving the natural habitat is evident in every corner, fostering a deep connection between guests and the island's biodiversity.

The dining experience at Kanua Hotel is a journey into the flavors of New Caledonia. The onsite restaurant, overlooking the bay, serves a fusion of local and international cuisine. Guests can savor the freshness of locally sourced ingredients, including tropical fruits, seafood caught in the pristine waters, and a variety of aromatic herbs.

The culinary team at Kanua Hotel is dedicated to providing a gastronomic experience that reflects the diversity of New Caledonian cuisine. From traditional Kanak dishes to French-inspired delicacies, each meal is a celebration of flavors. The open-air setting of the restaurant allows guests to enjoy their meals while surrounded by the sights and sounds of nature, enhancing the overall dining experience.

Kanua Hotel goes beyond providing comfortable accommodations and delectable cuisine; it also caters to the well-being of its guests. The Deep Nature Spa, located within the hotel grounds, offers a range of rejuvenating treatments inspired by traditional Pacific wellness practices. Guests can indulge in massages, facials, and body treatments designed to harmonize the body and mind.

The spa's serene atmosphere, coupled with the skilled therapists, creates an oasis of relaxation. After a day of exploring the island or engaging in water activities, a visit to the Deep Nature Spa becomes a rejuvenating ritual. The spa's commitment to using natural, locally sourced products aligns with Kanua Hotel's overall dedication to sustainability and holistic well-being.

While Kanua Hotel provides a tranquil retreat within its grounds, it also serves as a gateway to the adventures awaiting guests on the Isle of Pines. The hotel's concierge can arrange a variety of activities and excursions, ensuring that visitors make the most of their time on the island.

From water sports, such as snorkeling and paddleboarding in the pristine waters of Kuto Bay, to land-based adventures like hiking through the island's lush interior, Kanua Hotel caters to diverse interests. The hotel's strategic location allows for easy access to some of the Isle of

Pines' most iconic attractions, including the stunning natural pool of Oro Bay and the enchanting N'Ga Peak.

Kanua Hotel takes pride in its commitment to sustainability. From its architectural design to its daily operations, the hotel strives to minimize its environmental impact while contributing to the preservation of the local ecosystem. Solar panels provide a significant portion of the hotel's energy needs, and water conservation practices are in place to protect the island's precious resources.

The hotel also engages in community initiatives, supporting local conservation projects and collaborating with nearby villages. By prioritizing eco-friendly practices, Kanua Hotel not only provides a luxurious retreat for its guests but also contributes to the long-term well-being of the Isle of Pines.

In essence, Kanua Hotel offers more than just a place to stay; it provides an immersive experience where guests can reconnect with nature, indulge in luxury, and explore the cultural richness of the Isle of Pines. The hotel's dedication to preserving the environment, combined with its commitment to providing exceptional hospitality, creates a symphony of luxury and nature that resonates long after guests have left this tropical haven. Whether seeking a romantic getaway, an adventurous exploration, or a tranquil retreat, Kanua Hotel beckons travelers to experience the beauty of the South Pacific in its purest form.

Le Méridien Ile des Pins: A Tropical Oasis

Nestled in the heart of the South Pacific, Le Méridien Ile des Pins stands as a testament to luxury and elegance on the Isle of Pines, a jewel in the archipelago of New Caledonia. This resort, with its idyllic location along the pristine Oro Bay, offers guests an immersive experience where the natural beauty of the surroundings harmoniously blends with world-class hospitality.

The Isle of Pines, known as "Kunie" by the locals, is celebrated for its turquoise waters, powdery white sands, and lush greenery. Le Méridien Ile des Pins takes full advantage of this breathtaking backdrop, situated in an enclave of natural beauty. As guests arrive, they are greeted by the scent of tropical flowers and the sound of gentle waves lapping against the shore.

The architecture of Le Méridien Ile des Pins pays homage to the traditional Kanak culture, creating a harmonious blend of modern luxury and island authenticity. The resort's design incorporates traditional thatched roofs, local woodwork, and indigenous artistry, offering a visual journey into the rich cultural tapestry of the region.

Walking through the resort feels like traversing a modern oasis seamlessly integrated with the natural surroundings. The use of natural materials and the incorporation of open spaces allow guests to feel a constant connection to the tropical paradise that envelops them.

Le Méridien Ile des Pins offers a variety of accommodations, each designed to provide a luxurious and comfortable retreat. The overwater bungalows are a highlight, perched above the crystal-clear lagoon and offering direct access to the water. These bungalows provide an intimate and exclusive experience, allowing guests to wake up to panoramic views of the Coral Sea.

In addition to the overwater bungalows, the resort offers spacious suites and rooms situated amidst lush gardens, providing a sense of privacy and tranquility. Each accommodation is thoughtfully appointed with modern amenities and adorned with local artwork, creating an atmosphere of refined island living.

Culinary experiences at Le Méridien Ile des Pins are a celebration of local flavors and international cuisine. The resort's restaurant, overlooking the serene waters of Oro Bay, invites guests on a gastronomic journey. Fresh, locally sourced ingredients are used to craft a menu that showcases the best of New Caledonian and French culinary traditions.

The bar at Le Méridien is a lively hub where guests can unwind with tropical cocktails while enjoying the sunset. The skilled bartenders often infuse local ingredients into their creations, providing a taste of the island's vibrant flavors in every sip.

While the beauty of the Isle of Pines is enough to captivate any visitor, Le Méridien Ile des Pins enhances the experience with a range of activities and recreational options. Water enthusiasts can explore the underwater wonders through snorkeling or embark on a kayak adventure in the tranquil lagoon.

For those seeking relaxation, the Deep Nature Spa offers a haven of serenity. The spa, nestled amidst tropical gardens, provides a range of treatments inspired by traditional Melanesian techniques, allowing guests to rejuvenate both body and mind.

Le Méridien Ile des Pins is not only a place of leisure but also a gateway to cultural exploration. The resort frequently organizes cultural events and activities, allowing guests to engage with the rich traditions of the Kanak people. From traditional dance performances to craft workshops, visitors have the opportunity to deepen their understanding of the local culture.

The enchanting surroundings of Le Méridien Ile des Pins make it a sought-after destination for weddings and special events. The resort offers wedding packages that include everything from the ceremony on the beach to a reception in a tropical garden. The professional event planning team ensures that every detail is taken care of, allowing couples and event organizers to focus on creating lasting memories.

In addition to providing a luxurious retreat, Le Méridien Ile des Pins is committed to environmental sustainability. The resort implements eco-friendly practices, from waste reduction initiatives to energy-efficient technologies. Guests are encouraged to participate in responsible tourism efforts, fostering a sense of environmental consciousness during their stay.

The heart of Le Méridien Ile des Pins lies in its dedicated and attentive staff. From the moment guests arrive, they are welcomed with warmth and genuine hospitality. The staff members, many of whom are locals, contribute to the sense of community within the resort, creating an atmosphere where guests feel not just like visitors but as part of a larger, welcoming family.

Le Méridien Ile des Pins stands as a timeless escape on the Isle of Pines, offering a perfect blend of luxury, natural beauty, and cultural immersion. Whether basking in the sun on the private beaches, indulging in gourmet cuisine, or exploring the vibrant marine life, guests at this tropical oasis are sure to find a harmonious balance between relaxation and adventure. Le Méridien Ile des Pins not only provides a haven for those seeking a luxurious getaway but also serves as a gateway to the enchanting allure of the Isle of Pines itself.

Oure Tera Beach Resort: Secluded Serenity

Nestled on the southern tip of the Isle of Pines, Oure Tera Beach Resort stands as a testament to the harmonious blend of natural beauty and secluded luxury. This idyllic resort, situated along the pristine shores of Oro Bay, offers an escape into a world of serenity and tranquility.

As one approaches Oure Tera Beach Resort, the first impression is one of awe-inspiring natural beauty. The resort is surrounded by lush tropical vegetation, with swaying palm trees and vibrant flowers creating a picturesque backdrop. The azure waters of Oro Bay gently lap against the sandy shores, inviting guests to immerse themselves in the tranquil embrace of the Coral Sea.

Oure Tera Beach Resort boasts a selection of accommodations designed to provide guests with a sense of intimacy and privacy. The bungalows, with their traditional thatched roofs, are strategically positioned to offer stunning views of the ocean or the verdant gardens. Each bungalow is a private oasis, equipped with modern amenities while maintaining a connection to the natural surroundings.

For those seeking the ultimate oceanfront experience, Oure Tera Beach Resort features overwater bungalows that extend gracefully into the lagoon. These bungalows not only offer direct access to the crystal-clear waters but also provide a sense of seclusion and exclusivity. Guests can wake up to panoramic views of the sunrise over the Coral Sea, creating a truly magical and romantic atmosphere.

The resort's dining experiences are a culinary journey that complements the natural beauty of the surroundings. The restaurant, with its open-air design, allows guests to dine while enjoying the gentle sea breeze and the soothing sound of waves. The menu showcases a fusion of local flavors and international cuisine, with an emphasis on fresh, locally sourced ingredients. From seafood delicacies to tropical fruits, every dish is a celebration of the island's bountiful offerings.

One of the highlights of Oure Tera Beach Resort is its private beach, a secluded stretch of powdery white sand where guests can unwind in solitude. Whether it's a leisurely stroll along the shoreline or a day spent basking in the sun, the resort's private beach provides an exclusive retreat. Additionally, the freshwater pool offers an alternative for those who prefer a refreshing swim in a tranquil setting surrounded by lush vegetation.

Oure Tera Beach Resort offers a range of activities that allow guests to connect with the island's natural wonders. Snorkeling in the coral-rich waters, kayaking along the coast, or simply enjoying a sunset cruise are among the many options available. The resort's staff, knowledgeable about the local ecosystems, can guide guests to the best spots for observing marine life or experiencing the island's diverse flora and fauna.

To enhance the sense of relaxation and rejuvenation, Oure Tera Beach Resort features the Deep Nature Spa. Nestled in a tranquil corner of the resort, the spa offers a range of treatments inspired by traditional healing practices and modern wellness techniques. Guests can indulge in massages, facials, and holistic therapies, all performed with a focus on promoting harmony between mind, body, and spirit.

Oure Tera Beach Resort is not just a luxury retreat; it's an opportunity to connect with the rich cultural heritage of the Kanak people. The resort organizes cultural experiences, including traditional dance performances, artisan workshops, and guided tours that provide insights into the island's history and traditions. Guests have the chance to engage with the local community and gain a deeper understanding of the Kanak way of life.

In addition to providing a luxurious escape, Oure Tera Beach Resort is committed to sustainable and eco-friendly practices. The resort actively engages in initiatives aimed at preserving the pristine environment of the Isle of Pines. From waste reduction measures to supporting local conservation projects, Oure Tera Beach Resort takes pride in being a responsible custodian of this natural paradise.

Oure Tera Beach Resort, with its secluded setting, luxurious accommodations, and commitment to preserving the natural beauty of the Isle of Pines, offers a retreat into tranquility. Whether guests seek a romantic getaway, a peaceful escape, or an adventure in harmony with nature, the resort provides an experience that goes beyond conventional luxury. Oure Tera Beach Resort invites visitors to immerse themselves in the serenity of Oro Bay, where time slows down, and the beauty of the Coral Sea becomes a constant companion.

Hotel Kou Bugny: A Cultural Retreat

Nestled in the heart of the Isle of Pines, Hotel Kou Bugny stands as more than just a place to rest; it is a cultural retreat that beckons travelers to immerse themselves in the rich heritage of the Kanak people. Surrounded by lush greenery and situated near the quaint Vao village, this unique accommodation offers an authentic experience, seamlessly blending traditional Kanak influences with modern comforts.

The moment one sets foot into Hotel Kou Bugny, the architectural homage to Kanak culture becomes evident. Traditional wood carvings, symbolic patterns, and woven artistry adorn the spaces, creating an ambiance that resonates with the island's history. The bungalows, with their thatched roofs and natural materials, not only provide a comfortable stay but also serve as a testament to the enduring traditions of the Kanak people.

Hotel Kou Bugny goes beyond being a mere accommodation; it is a portal to Kanak heritage. Guests have the unique opportunity to engage with the local community and learn about their customs. The hotel organizes cultural activities and workshops, allowing visitors to participate in traditional dances, art demonstrations, and storytelling sessions. This immersive approach fosters a deep connection between guests and the Kanak way of life.

The bungalows at Hotel Kou Bugny are not just rooms; they are sanctuaries that seamlessly blend comfort with tradition. Each bungalow is designed to provide a cozy retreat, with handcrafted furnishings and local artwork adorning the spaces. The use of natural materials ensures a harmonious connection with the surrounding environment, allowing guests to feel truly embraced by the Isle of Pines.

A stay at Hotel Kou Bugny is incomplete without savoring the culinary delights that showcase the flavors of Kanak cuisine. The hotel's restaurant serves a variety of dishes inspired by traditional recipes, using fresh, locally sourced ingredients. Guests can indulge in delicacies that reflect the island's cultural tapestry, offering a gastronomic journey that mirrors the authenticity of the Kanak lifestyle.

Hotel Kou Bugny actively promotes community engagement, encouraging guests to interact with the local residents. The hotel organizes visits to the nearby Vao village, where guests can witness traditional ceremonies, explore artisan markets, and gain insights into the daily life of the Kanak people. This commitment to community integration ensures that every guest leaves with not just memories of a place but also connections with the warm and welcoming Kanak community.

Beyond cultural preservation, Hotel Kou Bugny is committed to environmental sustainability. The hotel adopts eco-friendly practices to minimize its ecological footprint. From energy-efficient initiatives to waste reduction strategies, every effort is made to ensure that the natural beauty that surrounds the Isle of Pines is preserved for future generations. Guests are encouraged to participate in these initiatives, fostering a sense of responsibility towards the island's delicate ecosystem.

While Hotel Kou Bugny emphasizes cultural immersion, it also recognizes the importance of relaxation. The hotel's serene surroundings provide the perfect backdrop for unwinding. Guests can relax by the pool, surrounded by tropical gardens, or take a leisurely stroll through the nearby forests. The balance between cultural exploration and leisure ensures that visitors leave not only enriched with cultural experiences but also rejuvenated by the tranquil atmosphere.

At Hotel Kou Bugny, hospitality goes beyond service; it is a warm Kanak welcome that makes guests feel like part of the island's extended family. The staff, often drawn from the local community, are not just hosts but storytellers who share the narrative of the Isle of Pines. Their genuine smiles and willingness to connect create an atmosphere of genuine hospitality, turning a stay at the hotel into a memorable and heartwarming experience.

In the heart of the Isle of Pines, Hotel Kou Bugny stands as a cultural retreat, weaving the rich tapestry of Kanak heritage into the very fabric of its existence. From the architectural homage to traditional design to the immersive cultural experiences offered to guests, every aspect of the hotel reflects a commitment to preserving and sharing the unique identity of the Isle of Pines. A stay at Hotel Kou Bugny is not just a visit; it's a journey into the soul of the Kanak people and the timeless beauty of this South Pacific paradise.

Nouvata: A Budget-Friendly Oasis in Paradise

In the heart of the South Pacific, where turquoise waters meet the azure sky, lies the Isle of Pines, a haven for those seeking solace in nature's embrace. Among the various accommodations that dot this paradise, Nouvata stands as a beacon of budget-friendly comfort, inviting travelers to experience the beauty of the island without breaking the bank.

Nouvata, strategically situated near the picturesque Kuto Bay, opens its doors to visitors with the promise of a warm welcome and a comfortable stay. The hotel's architecture echoes the laid-back charm of the island, featuring a blend of modern design elements and traditional Pacific Island aesthetics. The inviting atmosphere is complemented by the lush tropical surroundings, creating a sense of tranquility from the moment guests step onto the premises.

One of Nouvata's key strengths lies in its ability to cater to a diverse range of travelers. Whether you're a solo adventurer, a couple seeking a romantic getaway, or a family on a tropical holiday, Nouvata offers a variety of room options to suit different needs and preferences.

From standard rooms with essential amenities to spacious family-sized accommodations, each room at Nouvata is designed with both comfort and practicality in mind. The interiors are tastefully decorated, reflecting the island's vibrant colors and creating a cozy retreat after a day of exploration.

One of the undeniable perks of choosing Nouvata as your base on the Isle of Pines is its proximity to some of the island's most stunning natural attractions. Kuto Bay, with its powdery white sands and crystal-clear waters, is just a leisurely stroll away. Guests can easily spend their days basking in the sun, swimming in the gentle waves, or simply marveling at the breathtaking views of the Coral Sea.

For those with an adventurous spirit, Nouvata serves as a convenient starting point for exploring the island's hiking trails and nature reserves. The hotel's staff is always ready to assist with information about the best spots to witness the island's unique flora and fauna.

After a day of island exploration, Nouvata welcomes guests back with the promise of relaxation by the poolside. The hotel features a spacious swimming pool surrounded by lush tropical gardens, providing the perfect setting for unwinding and rejuvenating. Guests can lounge on comfortable sunbeds, take refreshing dips in the pool, or simply enjoy the serenity of the surroundings.

Nouvata doesn't just offer a comfortable place to rest; it also caters to the culinary desires of its guests. The hotel's casual restaurant serves a diverse menu that combines local flavors with international cuisine. From freshly caught seafood to tropical fruits, guests can indulge in a gastronomic journey that reflects the richness of the island's culinary heritage.

The open-air dining area provides a laid-back ambiance, allowing guests to enjoy their meals while immersed in the natural beauty of the Isle of Pines. Whether it's a leisurely breakfast to kickstart the day or a romantic dinner under the stars, Nouvata ensures that every dining experience is a memorable one.

Beyond its role as a comfortable accommodation, Nouvata offers guests the opportunity to connect with the local culture. The hotel organizes cultural events and activities that provide insights into the traditions and customs of the Kanak people, the indigenous inhabitants of New Caledonia. From traditional dance performances to artisan markets, guests can get a glimpse of the vibrant cultural tapestry that defines the Isle of Pines.

Nouvata understands that a seamless travel experience goes beyond comfortable rooms and scenic surroundings. The hotel is equipped with practical amenities to ensure that guests have everything they need for a stress-free stay. From Wi-Fi connectivity to laundry services, Nouvata combines budget-friendly pricing with the conveniences that modern travelers expect.

While Nouvata provides a haven of relaxation within its premises, it also serves as a gateway to the numerous adventures awaiting travelers on the Isle of Pines. The hotel's staff can assist with arranging various excursions, including boat trips to secluded islets, snorkeling in vibrant coral gardens, and exploring the island's hidden gems.

For those who prefer to chart their own course, Nouvata provides rental services for bicycles and scooters, allowing guests the freedom to explore the island at their own pace. Whether you're drawn to the cultural sites of Vao village or the untouched beauty of Oro Bay, Nouvata ensures that the wonders of the Isle of Pines are easily accessible.

Nouvata takes pride in being more than just a place to stay; it actively engages with the local community and promotes responsible tourism practices. The hotel collaborates with local artisans and businesses, ensuring that guests have the opportunity to support the island's economy and take home authentic souvenirs.

Additionally, Nouvata is committed to sustainable and eco-friendly initiatives. From energy-efficient practices to waste reduction measures, the hotel strives to minimize its environmental impact and contribute to the preservation of the Isle of Pines' natural beauty.

In the realm of budget-friendly accommodations on the Isle of Pines, Nouvata emerges as a shining gem. It not only provides a comfortable retreat for travelers seeking affordability but also weaves an immersive experience that connects guests with the island's natural wonders and cultural richness. Whether you're lounging by the pool, savoring local delicacies, or

embarking on island adventures, Nouvata stands as a testament to the idea that paradise is not reserved for the privileged few—it's accessible to all who seek it.

Gîte Nataiwatch: Homestay Charm

Nestled in the heart of the South Pacific, the Isle of Pines, also known as "Kunie" by the locals, stands as a pristine haven for travelers seeking tranquility, natural beauty, and a touch of authenticity. Among the myriad accommodation options that dot the landscape of this tropical paradise, Gîte Nataiwatch emerges as a hidden gem, offering homestay charm that goes beyond the conventional notions of hospitality.

Gîte Nataiwatch is more than just a place to rest; it's an immersive cultural experience. As you step onto the grounds of this family-run homestay, you are greeted not just as a guest but as a participant in the rich tapestry of Kanak life. The warm smiles of the hosts, the traditional thatched-roof bungalows nestled amidst tropical gardens, and the inviting aroma of home-cooked Kanak meals create an atmosphere that resonates with authenticity.

The homestay is strategically located, providing guests with a unique vantage point to explore the natural wonders and cultural heritage of the Isle of Pines. The intimate setting of Gîte Nataiwatch allows for a personalized experience, forging genuine connections between guests and the local community.

The architecture of the homestay is a testament to Kanak traditions. The bungalows, adorned with intricate wood carvings and woven artistry, reflect the craftsmanship that has been passed down through generations. The design seamlessly blends with the natural surroundings, creating a harmonious balance between human habitation and the pristine beauty of the Isle of Pines.

Upon arrival, guests are not just given a room key; they are welcomed into the heart of Kanak hospitality. The hosts, often the members of the extended family, take pride in sharing their customs and way of life with visitors. It's not uncommon for guests to be invited to participate in traditional activities, whether it be weaving, cooking, or storytelling sessions that impart the wisdom of Kanak culture.

The communal spaces of Gîte Nataiwatch serve as focal points for interaction. The central gathering area, shaded by ancient trees, becomes a hub for conversations, cultural exchanges, and the sharing of stories under the warm embrace of the South Pacific sun. The homestay provides an opportunity for travelers to step away from the hurried pace of modern life and immerse themselves in the unhurried rhythm of island living.

Accommodations at Gîte Nataiwatch range from cozy single rooms to larger family-sized bungalows. The décor is simple yet authentic, with local artwork and handcrafted elements adding to the overall charm. Each bungalow opens up to the lush gardens, providing guests with a private retreat while maintaining a strong connection to nature.

One of the highlights of the Gîte Nataiwatch experience is undoubtedly the culinary journey. The hosts take pride in preparing traditional Kanak meals using locally sourced ingredients. Guests are treated to a feast of flavors that reflect the unique blend of Melanesian and French influences that define the cuisine of the Isle of Pines.

Meals are not just about sustenance at Gîte Nataiwatch; they are an integral part of the cultural exchange. The hosts often join guests at the communal dining area, sharing stories about the history of the island, the significance of certain dishes, and the cultural rituals associated with mealtime. It's a chance for guests to not only savor the delicious fare but also to gain a deeper understanding of the cultural nuances that shape Kanak identity.

Beyond the confines of Gîte Nataiwatch, the Isle of Pines beckons with its natural wonders. Guests can explore the pristine beaches, embark on hiking trails that lead to panoramic viewpoints, and engage in water activities in the crystal-clear lagoons. The homestay provides a gateway to the island's attractions while ensuring that guests return to the embrace of genuine hospitality.

As the sun sets over the Isle of Pines, guests at Gîte Nataiwatch often find themselves gathered around a bonfire, sharing laughter and stories under the starlit sky. It's a moment that encapsulates the essence of this homestay—the creation of memories that go beyond the ordinary, the forging of connections that transcend cultural boundaries.

In conclusion, Gîte Nataiwatch stands as a testament to the power of homestay hospitality in providing travelers with an authentic and immersive experience. It's not just a place to stay; it's an opportunity to become a part of the vibrant tapestry of Kanak life. For those seeking more than just accommodation, Gîte Nataiwatch offers a chance to unravel the layers of cultural richness that define the Isle of Pines, creating an indelible mark on the hearts of those who choose to embrace its homestay charm.

Lifou:

Beaches and Activities in Lifou: A Tropical Paradise Unveiled

Lifou, the largest and most populous island in the Loyalty Archipelago of New Caledonia, is a haven for those seeking sun-soaked beaches, crystal-clear waters, and a rich blend of cultural experiences. This tropical paradise, surrounded by the Coral Sea, boasts a diverse landscape that includes lush forests, limestone caves, and pristine coral reefs. In this guide, we'll explore the enchanting beaches and a myriad of activities that make Lifou a must-visit destination for travelers seeking both relaxation and adventure.

1. Easo Beach

Nestled along the western coast of Lifou, Easo Beach greets visitors with its powdery white sands and turquoise waters. The gently sloping shoreline makes it an ideal spot for swimming and snorkeling. The vibrant coral formations teem with marine life, offering a captivating underwater world for snorkelers of all skill levels. Coconut palms fringe the beach, providing natural shade for those seeking respite from the tropical sun.

3. Jinek Bay

For a tranquil escape, Jinek Bay stands out as a hidden gem. Its secluded location and calm, shallow waters make it perfect for families. Visitors can explore the vibrant marine life while snorkeling or simply unwind on the soft sands. The surrounding cliffs and lush vegetation add to the bay's secluded and intimate atmosphere.

4. Luengoni Beach

Stretching along the eastern coast, Luengoni Beach captivates with its long stretches of untouched white sand and stunning coral formations. This beach is a favorite among both sunbathers and water sports enthusiasts. The coral gardens just offshore are a snorkeler's paradise, offering a kaleidoscope of colors and a diverse array of marine species.

5. **Water Activities**

Lifou's marine playground extends beyond its beautiful beaches. Visitors can indulge in an array of water activities, from kayaking and paddleboarding to windsurfing. The gentle trade winds create ideal conditions for windsurfing, while the calm lagoons are perfect for kayaking and paddleboarding, allowing travelers to explore the coastlines at their own pace.

6. **Traditional Kanak Fishing**

Engage in an authentic cultural experience by joining local fishermen for a traditional Kanak fishing expedition. Accompanied by skilled locals, visitors can learn traditional fishing techniques, discover the art of crafting fish traps, and even try their hand at catching some of the abundant marine life found in Lifou's waters.

7. **Hiking Adventures**

Beyond the beaches, Lifou offers a network of hiking trails that lead to panoramic viewpoints and hidden treasures. Explore the dense forests and limestone caves, such as the iconic Jokin Cliffs. The panoramic views from the cliffs provide a breathtaking vantage point, especially during sunrise or sunset.

8. **Cultural Encounters**

Immerse yourself in the unique Kanak culture by participating in cultural activities organized by the local communities. Traditional dance performances, storytelling sessions, and visits to local villages offer insights into the rich cultural heritage of Lifou. Don't miss the chance to taste traditional Kanak cuisine prepared with local ingredients and flavors.

9. **Vanilla Plantations**

Lifou is renowned for its vanilla plantations, where visitors can witness the cultivation process of this precious spice. Take a guided tour to learn about the history of vanilla in Lifou, from cultivation to harvesting. The intoxicating aroma and lush greenery of the plantations provide a sensory experience that complements the island's natural beauty.

In conclusion, Lifou is a tropical paradise that beckons travelers with its pristine beaches, diverse marine life, and vibrant cultural experiences. Whether you seek relaxation on the shores or adventures beneath the waves, Lifou offers a perfect blend of natural beauty and cultural

richness, making it a destination that lingers in the hearts of those fortunate enough to experience its wonders.

Easo Beach: A Tranquil Haven on the Shores of Lifou

Lifou, a jewel in the South Pacific, is renowned for its picturesque landscapes and pristine beaches. Among the myriad of coastal wonders that adorn this tropical paradise, Easo Beach stands out as a tranquil haven, enticing travelers with its powdery white sands, crystal-clear waters, and the serene ambiance that defines the essence of Lifou. As we delve into the beauty of Easo Beach, we discover not just a stretch of coastline but a canvas painted with nature's finest strokes, inviting visitors to partake in the tranquility and marvels of this coastal gem.

Upon arriving at Easo Beach, one is immediately struck by the sheer beauty of the surroundings. The gentle rustling of palm leaves, the distant murmur of the waves, and the soft embrace of the ocean breeze create an atmosphere of calm and serenity. Easo Beach, situated along the western coast of Lifou, unfolds like a dream, with its expansive shoreline stretching as far as the eye can see.

The hallmark of Easo Beach is undoubtedly its pristine sands, which rival the finest flour in texture. The powdery, white grains invite barefoot strolls and cast a radiant glow in the sunlight. The beach's gentle slope into the ocean makes it an ideal spot for swimmers of all ages. The water, in hues ranging from turquoise to deep blue, reflects the clear skies above, inviting visitors to immerse themselves in its refreshing embrace.

As the coral-fringed waters lap against the shore, a mesmerizing underwater world reveals itself. Easo Beach is not merely a place to bask in the sun; it's a gateway to a marine paradise. Snorkelers are treated to a kaleidoscope of colors beneath the surface, where vibrant coral formations provide a habitat for an array of marine life. Schools of fish dance through the underwater gardens, and curious sea creatures become companions in this aquatic symphony.

For those who prefer to stay ashore, Easo Beach offers ample opportunities for relaxation. The coconut palms that line the beach provide natural shade, creating inviting spots for picnics, reading, or simply gazing out at the horizon. The rhythmic swaying of the palms adds a tropical melody to the air, completing the sensory experience of being in this idyllic setting.

Easo Beach is more than just a destination for sunbathing and swimming; it's a canvas for water sports enthusiasts. The gentle waves and steady trade winds make it an ideal location for kayaking and paddleboarding. Adventurous souls can rent equipment locally and explore the coastline at their own pace, discovering hidden coves and inlets that add an extra layer of mystique to the beach.

As the day unfolds, Easo Beach undergoes a subtle transformation. The sun, a golden orb in the sky, begins its descent, casting warm hues across the landscape. Sunset at Easo is a spectacle of nature, a time when the beach is bathed in a soft, amber glow. The changing colors of the sky reflect on the calm waters, creating a serene and romantic atmosphere that captivates those fortunate enough to witness this daily ritual.

The allure of Easo Beach extends beyond its physical beauty. It is a place where time seems to slow down, allowing visitors to escape the hustle and bustle of everyday life. The gentle lull of the waves and the pristine surroundings create a therapeutic environment, inviting introspection and a deep connection with nature.

For those seeking a more immersive experience, Easo Beach is not just a destination but a gateway to Lifou's cultural richness. Local communities often organize events and gatherings on the beach, providing visitors with the opportunity to engage with the vibrant Kanak culture. Traditional dance performances, storytelling sessions, and cultural exchanges unfold against the backdrop of the setting sun, creating memories that linger long after the journey back home.

As night falls, Easo Beach undergoes yet another transformation. The star-studded sky above, unobscured by city lights, becomes a celestial tapestry. Strolling along the beach under the moonlit sky is a magical experience, with the sound of the waves and the cool night air adding to the enchantment of the surroundings.

In conclusion, Easo Beach is a testament to the natural beauty and tranquility that define Lifou. Its powdery sands, clear waters, and the harmonious coexistence of land and sea create a destination that transcends the typical beach experience. Easo Beach is not just a location; it's a sanctuary where travelers can find solace, adventure, and a profound connection with the beauty of the South Pacific. It beckons those in search of an idyllic escape to step into its embrace and discover the timeless allure of Lifou's coastal wonders.

Jinek Bay: A Tranquil Oasis on Lifou's Eastern Coast

Lifou, the largest island in the Loyalty Archipelago of New Caledonia, is renowned for its breathtaking landscapes and pristine beaches. Among its many gems, Jinek Bay stands out as a tranquil oasis on the island's eastern coast. This secluded haven, with its powdery white sands and calm, azure waters, offers visitors a serene escape from the hustle and bustle of everyday life.

Jinek Bay is situated along the rugged eastern shoreline of Lifou, embraced by lush vegetation and cliffs that add to its secluded charm. The bay's pristine beauty and untouched natural surroundings make it a favorite among travelers seeking a peaceful retreat. Let's embark on a journey to discover the enchanting allure of Jinek Bay, exploring its landscapes, marine life, and the unique experiences it has to offer.

As the sun rises over the Coral Sea, Jinek Bay is bathed in a soft morning light that casts a magical glow over its sandy shores. The rhythmic lapping of gentle waves against the beach sets a tranquil soundtrack for the day ahead. The bay's pristine stretch of white sand invites visitors to take leisurely strolls along the water's edge or simply relax and soak in the natural beauty that surrounds them.

The waters of Jinek Bay are known for their clarity and calmness, creating an inviting environment for swimming and snorkeling. The bay's shallow depths make it an ideal spot for families and those looking to explore the underwater world at a leisurely pace. Snorkelers can revel in the vibrant marine life that thrives in the coral gardens just offshore, where an array of colorful fish and intricate coral formations create a mesmerizing underwater tableau.

Surrounded by cliffs adorned with indigenous flora, Jinek Bay provides a sense of seclusion that enhances its tranquil ambiance. The cliffs not only serve as a natural backdrop but also as vantage points for breathtaking panoramic views of the bay and the Coral Sea beyond. Visitors can climb these vantage points to witness the changing hues of the sea and sky during sunrise or sunset, creating moments of pure serenity.

Beyond the pristine sands and crystal-clear waters, Jinek Bay offers opportunities for exploration and adventure. Hiking enthusiasts can venture into the surrounding lush vegetation, discovering hidden trails that lead to elevated viewpoints and secluded coves. The juxtaposition of dense foliage against the turquoise waters creates a striking contrast, emphasizing the untouched beauty of this coastal haven.

For those seeking cultural enrichment, Jinek Bay provides a gateway to the unique traditions of the Kanak people, the indigenous inhabitants of Lifou. Local communities often organize cultural events, such as traditional dance performances and storytelling sessions, allowing visitors to gain insights into the rich cultural heritage that is an integral part of Lifou's identity.

The tranquility of Jinek Bay is not only found in its natural beauty but also in the absence of crowds and commercial developments. Unlike more popular tourist destinations, Jinek Bay has managed to preserve its unspoiled charm, offering an authentic and immersive experience for those fortunate enough to discover its hidden shores.

As the day transitions into evening, Jinek Bay undergoes a transformation, with the fading sunlight casting a warm glow over the landscape. The sound of waves becomes a gentle lullaby, creating a serene atmosphere that encourages introspection and relaxation. It's during these moments that visitors truly appreciate the untouched beauty and sense of seclusion that Jinek Bay provides.

In conclusion, Jinek Bay is a testament to the unassuming elegance of Lifou's eastern coast. Its powdery white sands, calm azure waters, and surrounding cliffs create a picturesque setting that embodies the untouched beauty of a tropical paradise. Whether you seek a quiet retreat, a snorkeling adventure, or a cultural immersion, Jinek Bay welcomes you with open arms, promising a tranquil escape and an unforgettable connection with the natural wonders of Lifou.

Luengoni Beach: A Tranquil Haven on Lifou's Eastern Coast

Lifou, the largest island in the Loyalty Archipelago of New Caledonia, is a treasure trove of natural beauty, cultural richness, and idyllic beaches. Among its many pristine coastal gems, Luengoni Beach stands out as a true embodiment of tropical paradise. Located along the island's eastern coast, Luengoni Beach captivates visitors with its long stretches of untouched white sand, crystal-clear waters, and stunning coral formations. In this exploration, we delve into the allure of Luengoni Beach, unraveling its unique charm and the experiences it offers to those fortunate enough to grace its shores.

As the morning sun paints the sky with hues of orange and pink, Luengoni Beach awakens to reveal a scene of unparalleled beauty. The soft sands, untouched by the footprints of the night, stretch for miles, inviting wanderers to tread upon their warmth. The turquoise waters gently lap against the shore, creating a soothing melody that harmonizes with the rustle of the palm leaves overhead. The atmosphere is one of tranquility and serenity, where time seems to slow down, and the worries of the world fade away.

Luengoni Beach boasts a coastline adorned with the purest of white sands, a testament to the untouched beauty that defines Lifou. The powdery texture invites barefoot strolls along the water's edge, where the warm embrace of the sand contrasts with the refreshing touch of the gentle waves. Unlike some busier tourist destinations, Luengoni retains a sense of pristine wilderness, allowing visitors to connect with nature in its purest form.

The waters that caress Luengoni's shores are a translucent shade of turquoise, reminiscent of a watercolor painting. The clarity of the sea unveils a world beneath the surface, where vibrant coral gardens and a kaleidoscope of marine life await exploration. Snorkelers and swimmers find themselves immersed in a living aquarium, surrounded by schools of colorful fish, intricate coral formations, and the occasional sea turtle gracefully gliding through the clear waters.

One of the defining features of Luengoni Beach is its captivating coral gardens. Just a short swim from the shore, a submerged world of wonder awaits. Snorkelers don their masks and fins, eager to discover the intricate dance of life beneath the surface. The coral formations come alive with a myriad of colors – a vibrant mosaic of reds, blues, and greens. Schools of tropical fish navigate through the coral, creating a spectacle that rivals even the most elaborate of underwater documentaries.

The coral gardens of Luengoni are not only a visual feast but also a haven for marine biodiversity. Diverse species of fish, from the flamboyant parrotfish to the elusive clownfish, call these waters home. The delicate balance of the ecosystem is evident as each creature plays its role in the intricate web of life. It's a reminder of the importance of preserving such pristine environments for future generations.

What sets Luengoni Beach apart is not just its natural beauty but also the sense of seclusion it offers. Unlike more crowded tourist hotspots, Luengoni retains an unspoiled charm, allowing visitors to bask in the serenity of the surroundings. Whether one seeks a quiet spot to read a book, meditate to the rhythmic sounds of the waves, or simply gaze at the horizon in contemplation, Luengoni provides the perfect backdrop for moments of introspection and connection with nature.

The absence of large crowds enhances the feeling of exclusivity, as if stumbling upon a secret paradise known only to a fortunate few. This seclusion makes Luengoni Beach an ideal destination for those seeking a romantic retreat or a peaceful escape from the demands of modern life.

As the day gracefully transitions into evening, Luengoni Beach undergoes a transformation bathed in the warm hues of the setting sun. The sky becomes a canvas painted with shades of orange, pink, and purple, casting a magical glow over the landscape. Sunset at Luengoni is a spectacle that transcends description – a moment where time seems to stand still, and the beauty of nature takes center stage.

Visitors often gather on the beach to witness this daily masterpiece. Couples walk hand in hand along the shore, silhouetted against the radiant sky. Families build sandcastles as the last rays of sunlight dance on the water's surface. The air is filled with a sense of gratitude, as onlookers marvel at the privilege of experiencing such a breathtaking display of nature's artistry.

While the beach itself is a mesmerizing attraction, the allure of Luengoni extends beyond its sandy shores. The surrounding landscape beckons adventurers to explore the natural wonders that define Lifou's eastern coast. Lush vegetation and coconut palms fringe the beach, providing shade for those seeking respite from the sun. A leisurely walk inland unveils hidden gems such as freshwater springs and indigenous flora, adding layers to the overall experience of Luengoni.

For the more adventurous souls, the exploration of nearby caves and cliffs adds an adrenaline rush to the tranquil beach experience. Journeys to places like the iconic Jokin Cliffs reveal panoramic views of the surrounding seascape, creating lasting memories for those who dare to venture beyond the comfort of the sand.

As visitors succumb to the allure of Luengoni, the importance of responsible tourism becomes evident. The delicate balance of this pristine ecosystem relies on the mindfulness of those who partake in its beauty. Local initiatives and community-led conservation projects aim to preserve the natural integrity of Luengoni Beach, ensuring that future generations can also revel in its unspoiled magnificence.

Visitors are encouraged to adhere to guidelines that prioritize the preservation of the environment. This includes respecting designated paths, refraining from disturbing wildlife, and properly disposing of waste. By embracing sustainable practices, travelers become stewards of Luengoni's beauty, contributing to the longevity of this natural paradise.

Beyond its natural splendor, Luengoni is intertwined with the rich cultural heritage of Lifou. Traditional Kanak customs and practices are deeply rooted in the island's identity, and visitors have the opportunity to engage with the local community. Traditional dance performances, storytelling sessions, and interactions with the residents offer a glimpse into the unique fusion of nature and culture that defines Lifou.

Local artisans often showcase their craft near Luengoni Beach, providing an opportunity for travelers to acquire authentic souvenirs and support the island's economy. The symbiotic relationship between culture and nature is evident, as the islanders draw inspiration from the surrounding beauty to craft their traditional art and share their stories with visitors.

Practical Tips for Visiting Luengoni

For those eager to experience the magic of Luengoni Beach, some practical tips can enhance the overall journey:

Timing is Key: The beach experiences different facets throughout the day. Early mornings offer tranquility, while evenings boast spectacular sunsets. Plan your visit based on personal preferences.

Snorkeling Gear: Bring your snorkeling gear to explore the underwater wonders. The coral gardens are easily accessible from the shore, providing an immersive experience for snorkelers of all levels.

Comfortable Attire: The beach is an inviting canvas for relaxation. Pack comfortable attire, sunscreen, and a hat to shield from the sun.

Cultural Respect: When engaging with the local community, approach with respect and a willingness to learn. Understanding and appreciating the local customs enriches the overall experience.

Conservation Awareness: Support local conservation efforts by adhering to responsible tourism practices. Leave only footprints and contribute to the preservation of Lifou's natural treasures.

Luengoni Beach, with its untouched beauty, vibrant coral gardens, and cultural richness, encapsulates the essence of Lifou. It is a destination where time seems to stand still, allowing visitors to connect with nature in its purest form. Whether drawn by the allure of underwater wonders, the tranquility of pristine sands, or the cultural tapestry woven into the island's identity, those who step onto Luengoni find themselves immersed in a timeless paradise.

As the sun dips below the horizon, casting a golden glow over the landscape, Luengoni Beach remains a testament to the enduring beauty of the natural world. In its seclusion and splendor, Luengoni invites travelers to leave behind the hustle of daily life and embrace the serenity of a beach that transcends the ordinary—a beach that, in its timeless allure, becomes etched in the memories of those fortunate enough to experience its magic.

Water Activities in Lifou: A Paradise for Aquatic Enthusiasts

Lifou, an island gem nestled in the heart of the South Pacific, is renowned for its breathtaking beauty and diverse marine ecosystems. Surrounded by the azure waters of the Coral Sea, Lifou stands as a haven for aquatic enthusiasts seeking an array of water activities. From tranquil lagoons to vibrant coral reefs, the island offers a spectrum of experiences that cater to both leisurely beachgoers and thrill-seeking adventurers.

The crystalline waters that embrace Lifou are a playground for water lovers, providing the canvas for a myriad of activities that showcase the island's natural wonders. Whether you're drawn to the serenity of a leisurely paddle or the exhilaration of windsurfing, Lifou invites you to immerse yourself in its aquatic offerings.

Lifou's coral reefs are a mesmerizing underwater world waiting to be explored. The island's fringing reefs and coral gardens boast a kaleidoscope of colors and host a diverse array of marine life. Snorkeling enthusiasts can don their masks and fins to discover the vibrant coral formations that house a symphony of tropical fish. The clarity of the water allows for unparalleled visibility, making each snorkeling excursion a journey into a living, breathing aquatic wonderland.

For those seeking a deeper connection with the underwater realm, Lifou's scuba diving opportunities are unparalleled. Certified divers can explore the island's drop-offs, caves, and underwater canyons. The dive sites around Lifou cater to all levels of expertise, from novice divers to seasoned professionals. The encounters with sea turtles, rays, and vibrant coral species create unforgettable memories that linger long after resurfacing.

The gentle lagoons of Lifou provide an ideal setting for kayaking enthusiasts. Whether paddling solo or in tandem, kayakers can glide over calm waters, exploring the coastline at their own pace. The tranquil bays and hidden coves reveal the island's natural beauty, and the rhythmic sound of paddles dipping into the water creates a serene soundtrack for the journey.

Paddleboarding has become a popular water activity, and Lifou's sheltered lagoons offer an idyllic setting for this tranquil pursuit. Novices can enjoy the ease of gliding across calm waters, while experienced paddleboarders may venture into more challenging areas, testing their balance against the gentle currents. The elevated vantage point from a paddleboard provides a unique perspective of Lifou's coastal landscapes.

Lifou's trade winds create perfect conditions for windsurfing enthusiasts. The island's bays and lagoons become a canvas for windsurfers to showcase their skills. Beginners can take advantage of the steady winds to learn the basics, while experienced riders can revel in the thrill of skimming across the water, propelled by the forces of nature.

Engage in a cultural and recreational experience by joining local fishermen on a traditional Kanak fishing expedition. Lifou's waters are teeming with a variety of fish, providing an opportunity to learn traditional fishing techniques handed down through generations. The camaraderie of the experience and the chance to savor the day's catch make this activity a memorable blend of adventure and cultural immersion.

Exploring Lifou's neighboring islands and islets by boat adds an extra layer of adventure to your aquatic experience. Charter a boat to visit secluded beaches, hidden lagoons, and untouched coral reefs. The journey between islands unveils the diversity of the Loyalty Archipelago, allowing travelers to appreciate the unique charm of each destination.

As the day draws to a close, embark on a sunset cruise to witness the kaleidoscope of colors painting the sky. Many operators offer dolphin-watching excursions during the golden hours, providing a chance to observe these playful creatures in their natural habitat. The magical combination of a vibrant sunset and the joyful presence of dolphins creates an enchanting finale to a day filled with water adventures.

In conclusion, Lifou's allure extends far beyond its pristine beaches and lush landscapes; it is a paradise for those who find solace and excitement in the embrace of the ocean. Whether you're floating atop serene lagoons, exploring vibrant coral reefs, or chasing the wind on a windsurfing board, Lifou invites you to immerse yourself in a world where water activities become not just pastimes but profound connections with nature's aquatic wonders. Each ripple in Lifou's waters tells a story, and every splash echoes the island's invitation to discover the beauty beneath the surface.

Traditional Kanak Fishing

Traditional Kanak fishing in Lifou is a captivating journey into the heart of Melanesian culture, where the ocean is not just a source of sustenance but a profound element intertwined with spiritual beliefs and communal practices. As one explores the shores of this enchanting island in the Loyalty Archipelago of New Caledonia, the rhythmic dance of traditional fishing techniques comes to life, passed down through generations and deeply rooted in the identity of the Kanak people.

The traditional fishing methods of the Kanak people reflect a harmonious relationship with the sea, honoring the balance between taking from and giving back to the ocean. For the Kanak, fishing is not merely a means of acquiring food but a cultural practice that carries a profound spiritual significance. The methods employed are often simple, sustainable, and demonstrate a deep understanding of the local marine ecosystem.

At the heart of traditional Kanak fishing lies the outrigger canoe, a vessel perfectly adapted to the coastal waters surrounding Lifou. Crafted with precision from native materials, these canoes are not just modes of transportation but extensions of the Kanak way of life. The outrigger provides stability, allowing fishermen to navigate the often unpredictable currents and waves with ease.

Timing is everything in traditional Kanak fishing. The Kanak people have an intimate understanding of the tides and moon phases, knowledge passed down through generations. These factors influence when and where fishing expeditions take place. The close connection to nature's rhythms ensures that the catch is not only plentiful but also sustainable, respecting the natural cycles of marine life.

One of the most distinctive aspects of traditional Kanak fishing is the use of fish traps and weirs, ingenious structures designed to corral fish into easily accessible areas. Crafted from local materials such as bamboo and vines, these traps showcase the Kanak people's resourcefulness and ingenuity. Fishermen carefully position these traps in areas known for abundant marine life, allowing them to efficiently harvest the ocean's bounty.

Casting nets is an art form in traditional Kanak fishing. The design and construction of these nets are specific to the types of fish being targeted. Fishermen skillfully throw their nets, creating a mesmerizing dance of intricate movements. The success of a cast depends on a deep understanding of the ocean currents and the behavior of the fish, acquired through years of experience and observation.

Traditional Kanak fishing is inherently communal. It's a collaborative effort where knowledge is shared, and experiences are passed down from elders to the younger generation. Fishing expeditions are often community events, bringing together families and neighbors. The collective energy fosters a sense of unity and strengthens the ties that bind the Kanak people to their cultural heritage.

In the vast expanse of the Pacific Ocean, traditional Kanak fishermen navigate not only by the patterns of the waves but also by the celestial bodies above. The stars serve as a celestial compass, guiding the canoes during both day and night. This intimate knowledge of the night sky allows fishermen to venture far from the shores, ensuring a diverse and plentiful catch.

The act of fishing in Kanak culture extends beyond the physical realm; it is a spiritual engagement. Fishermen often perform rituals and make offerings to the sea spirits before embarking on a fishing expedition. This connection to the spiritual world reflects a deep respect for the natural forces that sustain life on the island. It is a reminder that, in the Kanak worldview, the ocean is not just a provider of food but a sacred entity deserving of reverence.

While traditional Kanak fishing methods have endured for centuries, the Kanak people also face the challenges of a rapidly changing world. Modernization, environmental changes, and global fishing practices present new obstacles. The delicate balance between preserving tradition and adapting to the demands of the contemporary world is a nuanced dance that the Kanak people navigate with care.

Efforts are underway to preserve and promote traditional Kanak fishing practices. Cultural initiatives and educational programs aim to pass on the knowledge and skills essential to this

ancient art form. The hope is that by ensuring the continuity of traditional fishing, the Kanak people can maintain a vital connection to their roots, even in the face of evolving landscapes.

Traditional Kanak fishing in Lifou is not just a method of catching fish; it's a tapestry woven with threads of culture, spirituality, and environmental stewardship. The rhythmic dance of casting nets, the silent communion with the stars, and the deep respect for the sea are all part of a heritage that defines the Kanak people. As visitors explore the shores of Lifou, witnessing these time-honored practices is an invitation to delve into the soul of a community whose identity is inseparable from the ebb and flow of the Pacific Ocean.

Hiking Adventures

Lifou, the largest island in the Loyalty Archipelago of New Caledonia, is a destination blessed with not only stunning beaches and crystalline waters but also a lush interior that beckons adventurers and nature enthusiasts. The island's diverse topography, characterized by dense forests, limestone caves, and panoramic cliffs, provides an ideal setting for a myriad of hiking adventures. In this exploration, we embark on a journey through the untamed landscapes of Lifou, uncovering the hidden trails, natural wonders, and cultural encounters that await those who seek to traverse its paths.

Lifou's hiking trails offer a gateway to the heart of the island's natural beauty. As you lace up your hiking boots and venture into the wilderness, you'll discover a tapestry of landscapes that range from dense rainforests to open savannas, each with its unique charm and allure.

A highlight of Lifou's hiking adventures is the iconic Jokin Cliffs, towering limestone formations that offer breathtaking panoramic views of the surrounding seascape. The trek to the cliffs takes you through dense forests and meandering trails, gradually unveiling the sheer grandeur of these natural wonders. Whether you choose to embark on a sunrise hike to witness the first light kissing the cliffs or prefer the tranquility of a sunset expedition, the Jokin Cliffs promise a spectacle that will etch itself into your memory.

Lifou's interior is crisscrossed with a network of trails that wind through lush forests, revealing hidden waterfalls, pristine creeks, and an abundance of endemic flora and fauna. These trails cater to hikers of all levels, from easy strolls suitable for families to challenging routes that beckon seasoned trekkers.

Beyond the natural beauty, Lifou's hiking adventures provide a unique opportunity to connect with the island's rich Kanak culture. Many trails lead to traditional villages where visitors can interact with locals, witness traditional dance performances, and gain insights into the island's cultural heritage. These cultural encounters add a layer of depth to the hiking experience, creating a holistic journey that blends the beauty of nature with the richness of tradition.

Lifou's coastal trails offer a different perspective, guiding hikers along rugged cliffs and pristine shorelines. The rhythmic sound of waves crashing against the rocks provides a soothing soundtrack as you navigate these paths, often leading to hidden coves, sea caves, and other seaside wonders. These treks offer a chance to witness the raw power and beauty of the ocean while immersing yourself in the tranquility of the island's coastal landscapes.

As you traverse Lifou's hiking trails, you'll encounter a diverse array of plant and animal life. The island is home to numerous endemic species, and keen-eyed hikers may spot colorful birds, unique insects, and vibrant plant species that thrive in this tropical paradise. The biodiversity adds an educational element to the hikes, as nature enthusiasts can learn about the delicate ecosystems that exist within Lifou's boundaries.

Practical Tips for Hiking in Lifou

Before embarking on your hiking adventure in Lifou, it's essential to be well-prepared. Here are some practical tips to enhance your experience:

Guided Tours: Consider joining guided hiking tours led by local experts. They not only provide valuable insights into the flora, fauna, and cultural aspects but also enhance the overall safety of the experience.

Footwear and Clothing: Wear sturdy hiking boots with good traction, as trails can vary from soft forest paths to rocky terrain. Dress in lightweight, breathable clothing suitable for tropical climates, and don't forget to apply sunscreen.

Water and Snacks: Carry an ample supply of water to stay hydrated, especially during the warmer parts of the day. Pack energy-boosting snacks to keep you fueled throughout the hike.

Respect Nature and Culture: Practice responsible hiking by sticking to designated trails, avoiding littering, and respecting the natural and cultural heritage of Lifou.

In conclusion, Lifou's hiking adventures offer a kaleidoscope of experiences, from the lofty heights of Jokin Cliffs to the serene beauty of hidden waterfalls in the heart of the island. The trails weave a narrative that combines the raw beauty of nature with the cultural richness of the Kanak people, creating an immersive experience that transcends the ordinary. As you traverse Lifou's paths, you'll not only conquer peaks and explore forests but also forge a connection with an island that holds the essence of adventure and tranquility in equal measure.

Cultural Encounters

Lifou, the largest and most populous island in the Loyalty Archipelago of New Caledonia, is not merely a tropical destination blessed with pristine beaches and azure waters. It's a cultural tapestry woven with the rich threads of Kanak traditions and influences from its colonial past. As travelers step onto this idyllic island, they find themselves immersed in a world where cultural encounters are not just events but transformative experiences.

The heart of Lifou beats to the rhythm of Kanak culture, an intricate tapestry of customs, beliefs, and practices that have withstood the test of time. The Kanak people, the indigenous inhabitants of Lifou, take great pride in preserving and sharing their heritage with visitors.

Walking through local villages, visitors may witness traditional Kanak huts, characterized by their conical roofs made from local materials. These villages are not merely static exhibits but living entities where daily life unfolds amidst the echoes of ancient traditions.

One of the most captivating ways to delve into the Kanak culture is through traditional dance performances. These dances are not mere spectacles but living expressions of stories, myths, and rituals passed down through generations. The rhythmic beats of drums and the graceful movements of the dancers convey narratives that span the island's history, from ancient tales to stories of resistance during colonial times.

During cultural events and celebrations, such as the popular "Fête du Têt" or Feast of the Head, visitors have the opportunity to witness these mesmerizing performances. Dancers adorned in traditional costumes move with a grace that transcends time, inviting spectators to share in the spiritual and cultural significance of each movement.

In the oral traditions of the Kanak people, storytelling is a sacred art. Elders pass down myths, legends, and histories through spoken word, ensuring that each generation carries the collective wisdom of its ancestors. Travelers fortunate enough to engage with local storytellers gain insights into the island's lore, understanding how ancient stories continue to shape Lifou's present.

These storytelling sessions often take place in communal areas, under the shade of ancient trees or within the confines of traditional meeting places. Visitors find themselves transported to a different era, where the spoken word becomes a conduit for cultural transmission and understanding.

For those seeking a more immersive experience, spending time in local villages is a must. Lifou's villages are not only showcases of traditional architecture but vibrant hubs where the pulse of

daily life can be felt. From communal cooking sessions where traditional Kanak dishes are prepared to communal ceremonies marking significant events, village life provides an authentic and unfiltered encounter with the Kanak way of life.

Visitors might be invited to participate in customary practices, such as the preparation of "bougna," a traditional Kanak feast cooked in an earth oven. These communal activities foster a sense of camaraderie and offer a deeper understanding of the values that bind the community together.

The culinary scene in Lifou is a testament to the island's cultural richness. Traditional Kanak cuisine, influenced by the bounty of the land and sea, is a gastronomic journey that reflects the symbiotic relationship between the Kanak people and their natural surroundings.

Visitors can indulge in delicacies like "ignames" (yams), fresh seafood prepared with local herbs and spices, and tropical fruits that tantalize the taste buds. Dining experiences often extend beyond the mere act of eating; they become opportunities for cultural exchange as locals share stories behind each dish.

Throughout the year, Lifou comes alive with a calendar of ceremonies and celebrations that mark important milestones in the lives of the Kanak people. From weddings and births to harvest festivals, each event is a manifestation of cultural identity and a testament to the resilience of Kanak traditions.

Participating in these ceremonies offers visitors a profound connection to the community and a firsthand experience of the rituals that define Kanak life. The beating of drums, the singing of traditional chants, and the vibrant display of traditional attire create an atmosphere that is both festive and deeply rooted in cultural significance.

The Kanak language, Drehu, is more than a means of communication; it's a vessel for preserving the nuances of cultural expression. Engaging with locals in their native language is a bridge to understanding the depth of their perspectives, values, and traditions.

While French is the official language of New Caledonia, Drehu remains a vital part of daily life in Lifou. Visitors who take the time to learn a few basic phrases find that the effort is reciprocated with warmth and a sense of appreciation from the locals.

The artistic expression of the Kanak people extends beyond dance and oral traditions to the realm of visual arts and crafts. Intricate wood carvings, woven baskets, and traditional masks are not just artifacts but living representations of cultural identity and craftsmanship.

Local artisans often welcome visitors into their workshops, providing insights into the creative process and the symbolism embedded in each piece. Purchasing these handcrafted items becomes not just a souvenir but a tangible connection to the cultural heritage of Lifou.

Religion plays a significant role in the cultural fabric of Lifou. The Kanak people practice a syncretic form of Christianity that harmoniously integrates traditional beliefs with Christian teachings. Visiting local churches, adorned with traditional Kanak art, offers a glimpse into the spiritual dimensions of Kanak culture.

The sounds of hymns sung in the Drehu language resonate through the air, creating a unique blend of sacred and cultural expressions. Visitors attending church services during their stay in Lifou find themselves welcomed into a community that finds spiritual solace in both traditional and Christian practices.

For the Kanak people, the environment is not merely a backdrop but a sacred entity woven into the fabric of their cultural identity. Traditional ecological knowledge and sustainable practices are intrinsic to the Kanak way of life.

Engaging in discussions with locals about their relationship with the land and sea provides insights into age-old practices of resource management and conservation. From traditional fishing techniques to the use of medicinal plants, visitors discover a holistic approach to environmental stewardship that has sustained the Kanak people for centuries.

In Lifou, cultural encounters are not confined to scheduled performances or designated heritage sites; they permeate every aspect of daily life. The island invites visitors to partake in a cultural odyssey that transcends the superficial and delves into the essence of Kanak identity.

The warmth of the people, the vibrancy of their traditions, and the seamless integration of ancient customs into contemporary life create an immersive experience that leaves an indelible mark on those who have the privilege of stepping onto the shores of Lifou. Beyond the beaches and beneath the swaying palms, Lifou unfolds as a living testament to the resilience, creativity, and spirit of the Kanak people.

Vanilla Plantations

Lifou, nestled within the Loyalty Archipelago of New Caledonia, is a captivating island that goes beyond its azure waters and sandy shores. Amidst its lush landscapes, one particular treasure stands out – the vanilla plantations. Lifou's vanilla, renowned for its exquisite flavor and fragrance, is cultivated with care and tradition, creating a sensory journey for those fortunate enough to explore the island's vanilla-scented realms.

The story of vanilla in Lifou is a tale that intertwines nature, culture, and history. The island's climate, with its warm temperatures and high humidity, provides the ideal conditions for vanilla cultivation. As visitors step onto the vanilla plantations, they are greeted by a symphony of scents and sights, setting the stage for an immersive experience.

The journey of Lifou's vanilla begins with the delicate vanilla orchid, a climbing plant that requires meticulous care. The farmers, often belonging to local communities, nurture the plants from seedlings to maturity. The art of pollination, a delicate process performed by hand, is essential for the development of the vanilla pods. This hands-on approach not only ensures the quality of the vanilla but also reflects the deep connection between the Kanak people and the land.

As the vanilla orchids bloom, signaling the arrival of the precious pods, the harvesting season commences. Skilled hands carefully pluck the green vanilla beans from the vines, marking the culmination of months of attentive cultivation. The vanilla pods undergo a curing process, a critical stage where the pods are blanched, sweated, and dried. This process intensifies the flavor and aroma, transforming the green vanilla into the prized dark brown pods that are synonymous with quality vanilla.

Lifou's vanilla plantations often embrace sustainable and eco-friendly practices. The cultivation methods prioritize environmental conservation, ensuring the longevity of the delicate ecosystems that support vanilla growth. Traditional agricultural wisdom, passed down through generations, coexists with modern sustainability principles, creating a harmonious balance between tradition and innovation.

Walking through a vanilla plantation in Lifou is a sensorial experience like no other. The air is permeated with the intoxicating fragrance of vanilla, creating an olfactory symphony that envelops visitors. The sight of rows of vanilla vines, their lush green leaves contrasting with the dark brown pods, is a visual feast. The journey into the heart of Lifou's vanilla plantations allows individuals to witness not just the cultivation of a spice but the preservation of a cultural heritage.

The cultivation of vanilla in Lifou is deeply intertwined with the lives and traditions of the local communities. Many vanilla plantations are run by families or cooperatives, each contributing to the island's economy and cultural resilience. Visitors have the opportunity to engage with these communities, gaining insights into the significance of vanilla beyond its culinary applications. The stories shared by the farmers, often passed down through generations, add layers of meaning to the vanilla experience.

The journey into Lifou's vanilla plantations extends beyond the fields. Culinary enthusiasts can partake in workshops and tastings that showcase the versatility of Lifou's vanilla. From traditional desserts to contemporary culinary creations, the aromatic pods find their way into a myriad of dishes. The experience of savoring vanilla-infused delicacies against the backdrop of the plantations adds another dimension to the overall immersion.

As global demand for vanilla continues to rise, Lifou faces the delicate task of balancing commercial viability with environmental sustainability. Conservation efforts are underway to protect the biodiversity of the island and ensure that the cultivation of vanilla remains a harmonious practice. These endeavors often involve collaboration between local communities, government bodies, and environmental organizations, showcasing a commitment to responsible agricultural practices.

Beyond its economic and culinary significance, vanilla holds cultural importance in Lifou. The vanilla plantations, woven into the fabric of daily life, become not just sources of income but symbols of identity and continuity. The Kanak people, with their deep connection to the land, view the cultivation of vanilla as a sacred tradition, a link between past and present.

In the heart of Lifou's vanilla plantations, a fragrant legacy unfolds. The story of vanilla here is more than an agricultural process; it is a testament to the symbiotic relationship between the people, the land, and the aromatic orchid. As visitors stroll through the verdant fields, inhaling the sweet perfume that lingers in the air, they become part of a narrative that transcends time—a narrative where tradition, nature, and community converge to create an enduring legacy. Lifou's vanilla plantations stand as not just producers of a prized spice but as guardians of a fragrant heritage, inviting travelers to immerse themselves in the essence of Lifou.

II. Exploring the Culinary Delights of Lifou: A Gastronomic Journey into Local Cuisine

Lifou, an idyllic island in the heart of the Pacific, is not only renowned for its pristine beaches and vibrant culture but also for its rich and diverse culinary offerings. The island's cuisine is a delectable fusion of traditional Kanak flavors, French influences, and a touch of tropical freshness. In this gastronomic journey, we delve into the local cuisine of Lifou, uncovering the unique dishes, culinary traditions, and the essence of the island's food culture.

1. **Kanak Gastronomy: A Symphony of Indigenous Flavors**

Lifou's cuisine is deeply rooted in Kanak traditions, reflecting the island's indigenous culture. Traditional dishes often feature staple ingredients like yams, taro, coconut, and seafood. Bougna, a ceremonial dish, stands as a testament to Lifou's Kanak heritage. It involves wrapping a combination of root vegetables, fish, and meats in banana leaves, then slow-cooking them in an earth oven, infusing the ingredients with a distinctive smoky flavor.

2. **French Influences: A Culinary Blend**

As a French overseas territory, Lifou's cuisine bears the unmistakable influence of French gastronomy. Boulangeries dot the island, offering an array of freshly baked baguettes and pastries. Crepes, both sweet and savory, are a popular snack among locals and visitors alike. French culinary techniques have also found their way into traditional dishes, creating a harmonious blend of flavors that is uniquely Lifouan.

3. **Seafood Extravaganza: Fresh Catches from Azure Waters**

Surrounded by crystal-clear waters teeming with marine life, Lifou is a seafood lover's paradise. Locally sourced fish, lobster, and prawns take center stage in many dishes. Grilled lobster with coconut milk, a delicacy often enjoyed during festive occasions, exemplifies the island's commitment to celebrating its maritime bounty.

4. Tropical Delights: Fruits of the Island

The tropical climate of Lifou blesses the island with an abundance of exotic fruits. Visitors can savor the sweetness of juicy pineapples, papayas, and passion fruits. Coconut, omnipresent in both sweet and savory dishes, adds a refreshing and tropical touch to many culinary creations.

5. Culinary Traditions: Celebrating Life through Food

Food is not merely sustenance on Lifou; it is a celebration of life, community, and tradition. The act of sharing meals holds great cultural significance, and communal feasts are common during special occasions. These gatherings showcase the diversity of Lifouan cuisine and the warmth of its people.

6. Local Markets: A Kaleidoscope of Colors and Flavors

Exploring Lifou's local markets is a sensory adventure. Vibrant displays of fresh produce, spices, and handmade crafts paint a vivid picture of the island's culinary and artisanal heritage. Visitors can engage with local vendors, learning about traditional ingredients and even tasting unique snacks like coconut candy and cassava chips.

7. Culinary Festivals: A Feast for the Senses

Lifou hosts various culinary festivals throughout the year, where locals and tourists alike come together to celebrate food, music, and dance. These festivals offer a fantastic opportunity to sample a wide array of Lifou's culinary delights, from street food to elaborate traditional dishes.

In Lifou, the heart of the Pacific beats in rhythm with the island's culinary traditions. The fusion of Kanak and French influences, the abundance of fresh seafood, the tropical fruits, and the communal spirit that surrounds food create a culinary landscape that is as diverse as the island itself. Lifou's cuisine is not just a part of its identity; it is a journey through history, culture, and the vibrant flavors of the Pacific. For those seeking a true taste of paradise, Lifou's local cuisine is a symphony of delight waiting to be savored.

III. Exploring Paradise: A Comprehensive Guide to Hotels and Resorts in Lifou, New Caledonia

Nestled in the heart of the South Pacific, Lifou, the largest island in the Loyalty Archipelago of New Caledonia, is a haven of natural beauty and cultural richness. Travelers seeking an escape to pristine beaches, vibrant coral reefs, and the warm embrace of Kanak culture will find Lifou to be an enchanting destination. To make the most of your stay, it's crucial to choose accommodation that complements the island's unique charm. In this guide, we'll delve into the top hotels and resorts on Lifou, ensuring your experience is nothing short of extraordinary.

1. Drehu Village Hotel

Situated near the picturesque Easo village, the Drehu Village Hotel is a beacon of tranquility. This boutique hotel seamlessly blends modern comfort with traditional Melanesian aesthetics. Guests can choose from a range of bungalows surrounded by lush gardens, providing an intimate and immersive experience. The on-site restaurant showcases the island's culinary delights, featuring fresh seafood and locally sourced produce.

2. Lifou Hotel

For those seeking a centrally located accommodation option, Lifou Hotel is an excellent choice. Overlooking the Baie du Santal, this hotel offers breathtaking views of the turquoise waters. The rooms are tastefully decorated, providing a cozy retreat after a day of exploration. The hotel's

restaurant serves a fusion of French and Kanak cuisine, offering a delightful gastronomic experience.

3. Jokin Apart Hotel

Ideal for travelers who prefer self-catering options, Jokin Apart Hotel provides well-appointed apartments equipped with kitchen facilities. Located in We, the cultural capital of Lifou, Jokin Apart Hotel is close to markets, allowing guests to immerse themselves in the vibrant local life. The personalized service and homely atmosphere make it a popular choice for both short and extended stays.

4. Chez Odile et Michel

For a more authentic experience, consider staying at a guesthouse like Chez Odile et Michel. This charming establishment is run by a local family, offering guests a glimpse into everyday Lifouan life. The guesthouse is surrounded by tropical gardens and is just a short walk from the beach. Odile and Michel's warm hospitality and personalized recommendations create a home away from home.

5. Noujoum Hotel

Noujoum Hotel, perched on a cliff overlooking the crystalline waters, provides a luxurious retreat for discerning travelers. The hotel's architecture seamlessly integrates with the natural surroundings, and each room boasts a private balcony with panoramic views. The spa facilities, infinity pool, and gourmet dining options contribute to an indulgent stay, making Noujoum Hotel a haven for relaxation.

6. Ecolodge L'Escape

For eco-conscious travelers, Ecolodge L'Escape is a shining example of sustainable tourism. Nestled in the heart of a tropical forest, this eco-friendly retreat offers a range of bungalows with minimal environmental impact. Guests can engage in guided nature walks, bird watching, and other eco-friendly activities, providing a unique and immersive experience in harmony with nature.

7. Les Koghis – Lifou Hotel & Spa

Situated on the stunning Chateaubriand Bay, Les Koghis is a resort and spa that caters to those seeking a luxurious escape. The resort features elegant overwater bungalows, allowing guests to wake up to the gentle lapping of waves beneath their rooms. The spa offers a range of traditional Melanesian treatments, providing a holistic approach to relaxation and rejuvenation.

8. Hotel Santal Bay

Perched on the edge of Santal Bay, Hotel Santal Bay is a beachfront paradise. The resort offers a range of accommodations, from garden bungalows to beachfront suites. The on-site water sports center provides opportunities for snorkeling, kayaking, and paddleboarding, ensuring that guests can make the most of Lifou's stunning marine life.

9. Oasis de Kiamu

For a more intimate and secluded experience, Oasis de Kiamu is a hidden gem. This boutique resort is nestled in a private cove, surrounded by lush vegetation. The individually designed bungalows provide a sense of exclusivity, and the on-site restaurant showcases the best of local and international cuisine.

Lifou, with its natural wonders and cultural richness, is a destination that beckons the discerning traveler. Choosing the right accommodation is paramount to ensuring an unforgettable experience. Whether you opt for a boutique hotel, a beachfront resort, or a cozy guesthouse, the options in Lifou cater to a variety of preferences. Immerse yourself in the island's beauty, and let your choice of accommodation enhance the magic of your Lifouan adventure.

Drehu Village Hotel

Nestled amidst the lush landscapes of Lifou, the Drehu Village Hotel stands as a testament to the seamless fusion of modern comfort and traditional Melanesian aesthetics. This boutique hotel, situated near the picturesque Easo village, offers a retreat into tranquility and cultural richness. As we embark on a journey to explore the essence of the Drehu Village Hotel, we find ourselves immersed in the allure of this unique destination.

From the moment guests arrive, the Drehu Village Hotel welcomes them with open arms. The architecture itself is a harmonious blend of contemporary design and indigenous elements, creating a setting that reflects the rich cultural tapestry of Lifou. The use of traditional materials, such as wood and thatch, imparts a warm and inviting atmosphere, inviting visitors to experience the island's spirit from the very first step.

Accommodation at the Drehu Village Hotel is a journey into comfort and serenity. The hotel boasts a range of well-appointed bungalows, each surrounded by lush gardens that provide an intimate and immersive experience. Whether opting for a garden view or a more private bungalow nestled in the heart of tropical flora, guests are treated to an oasis of tranquility.

The interior design of the bungalows at Drehu Village Hotel is a testament to attention to detail. Local artwork adorns the walls, and the furnishings reflect both modern sensibilities and traditional craftsmanship. The rooms are thoughtfully arranged to maximize comfort, and large windows invite natural light while offering views of the verdant surroundings.

As the day unfolds, guests can indulge in the culinary delights that Drehu Village Hotel has to offer. The on-site restaurant showcases the island's vibrant flavors, with a menu featuring fresh seafood and locally sourced produce. Whether savoring a leisurely breakfast or a romantic dinner under the stars, the dining experience at the Drehu Village Hotel is a celebration of Lifouan cuisine.

Beyond the confines of the bungalows, the Drehu Village Hotel provides a range of facilities to enhance the guest experience. The swimming pool, surrounded by tropical gardens, offers a refreshing respite, while the spa provides a haven for relaxation and rejuvenation. The attentive and friendly staff contribute to the overall ambiance, ensuring that every guest feels not just accommodated but truly cared for.

Drehu Village Hotel is more than a place to stay; it's a gateway to the cultural richness of Lifou. The hotel organizes cultural activities and excursions that allow guests to immerse themselves in the traditions of the island. From traditional dance performances to guided tours of nearby villages, visitors have the opportunity to connect with the vibrant heritage of Lifou.

For those seeking a venue for special events or conferences, Drehu Village Hotel offers modern meeting facilities in a setting that inspires creativity and collaboration. The natural surroundings and the hotel's commitment to sustainability make it an ideal choice for those who wish to host events in an eco-friendly and culturally rich environment.

As the sun sets over Lifou, the Drehu Village Hotel takes on a magical quality. The evening brings a different kind of charm, with the gentle rustle of palm leaves and the distant sounds of the ocean creating a soothing symphony. Guests can choose to unwind in the comfort of their bungalows or gather at communal spaces to share stories and experiences.

In conclusion, the Drehu Village Hotel is more than a place to stay; it's a destination within a destination. It captures the essence of Lifou, providing a retreat that combines luxury with

cultural immersion. Whether seeking relaxation, adventure, or a bit of both, guests at Drehu Village Hotel find themselves in a haven where the spirit of Lifou comes alive in every detail. From the moment of arrival to the lingering memories after departure, the Drehu Village Hotel stands as a testament to the beauty and hospitality that Lifou has to offer.

Lifou Hotel: A Comprehensive Exploration of Paradise

Lifou, the largest island in the Loyalty Archipelago of New Caledonia, is a tropical haven that beckons travelers seeking natural beauty, cultural richness, and a serene escape from the ordinary. Amidst the turquoise waters, lush landscapes, and vibrant local life, Lifou Hotel stands as a testament to luxury, comfort, and the harmonious integration of modernity with the island's indigenous charm.

Nestled near the pristine Baie du Santal, Lifou Hotel is a jewel on the island's coastline. As the gentle waves of the South Pacific Ocean lap against the shores, guests are welcomed into a world where relaxation meets adventure, and luxury coexists with the simplicity of island living.

The architecture of Lifou Hotel seamlessly blends with its natural surroundings. The design draws inspiration from traditional Melanesian aesthetics, creating a space that feels both contemporary and deeply connected to the island's cultural heritage. The use of natural materials, such as wood and stone, reflects a commitment to sustainability and an eco-conscious approach to hospitality.

Accommodations at Lifou Hotel cater to diverse preferences, offering a range of rooms and suites designed to provide comfort and luxury. Whether you choose a room with a view of the azure waters, a suite with a private balcony, or an overwater bungalow that allows you to wake up to the sounds of the ocean, each space is meticulously crafted to ensure a restful and rejuvenating stay.

The dining experience at Lifou Hotel is a gastronomic journey that celebrates the fusion of French and Kanak cuisine. The on-site restaurant sources fresh, local ingredients to create a menu that tantalizes the taste buds. Guests can indulge in seafood caught from the nearby waters, tropical fruits plucked from the island's orchards, and a variety of dishes that showcase the culinary diversity of Lifou.

Beyond the luxurious accommodations and delectable dining options, Lifou Hotel offers a range of amenities and activities to enhance the guest experience. The infinity pool, overlooking the bay, invites guests to unwind under the warm Pacific sun. The spa facilities provide a sanctuary for relaxation, offering a selection of traditional Melanesian treatments that incorporate local herbs and techniques.

The location of Lifou Hotel is strategic, allowing guests easy access to the island's attractions and activities. Whether you wish to explore the vibrant markets of We, immerse yourself in the cultural richness of the Lifouan people, or embark on water adventures to discover the underwater wonders of the coral reefs, Lifou Hotel serves as a perfect base for your island exploration.

For those seeking a romantic getaway or a picturesque setting for special occasions, Lifou Hotel offers event and wedding planning services. The backdrop of the turquoise waters and the lush greenery creates a dreamlike atmosphere that adds a touch of magic to any celebration.

Lifou Hotel's commitment to sustainability extends beyond its architectural design. The hotel actively engages in eco-friendly practices, from waste reduction initiatives to energy-efficient technologies. Guests can take pride in choosing accommodation that aligns with principles of responsible tourism, allowing them to enjoy the beauty of Lifou while minimizing their ecological footprint.

As the sun sets over the Loyalty Archipelago, casting hues of orange and pink across the sky, Lifou Hotel transforms into a serene retreat where the sounds of nature harmonize with the gentle hum of contented guests. Whether you choose to spend your evenings strolling along the beach, sipping cocktails at the bar, or simply relaxing on your private balcony, Lifou Hotel offers an ambiance of tranquility that defines the essence of island living.

In conclusion, Lifou Hotel is not just a place to stay; it is an experience that encapsulates the spirit of Lifou itself. With its blend of luxury, cultural sensitivity, and environmental consciousness, Lifou Hotel stands as a beacon of hospitality in the heart of the South Pacific. For those seeking an unforgettable journey to a tropical paradise, Lifou Hotel awaits, promising a stay that transcends the ordinary and leaves an indelible mark on the soul.

Jokin Apart Hotel: A Comprehensive Exploration

In the heart of Lifou, the largest island in the Loyalty Archipelago of New Caledonia, Jokin Apart Hotel stands as a testament to the seamless blend of comfort and cultural immersion. This unassuming yet charming accommodation option caters to a diverse range of travelers, offering well-appointed apartments that provide a home away from home. In this comprehensive exploration, we delve into the essence of Jokin Apart Hotel, uncovering the details that make it a preferred choice for those seeking a unique and personalized Lifouan experience.

The location of Jokin Apart Hotel Is strategic, situated in We, the cultural capital of Lifou. This central positioning allows guests to immerse themselves in the vibrant local life, with markets, traditional ceremonies, and community activities just a stone's throw away. For travelers seeking not just a place to stay but an opportunity to engage with the cultural tapestry of Lifou, Jokin Apart Hotel proves to be an ideal base.

Upon entering the premises of Jokin Apart Hotel, guests are greeted with a sense of tranquility. The architecture seamlessly integrates with the surroundings, creating a serene atmosphere that reflects the island's natural beauty. The use of local materials and traditional design elements in the construction of the hotel pays homage to the Kanak heritage, providing visitors with an authentic experience from the moment they arrive.

Accommodations at Jokin Apart Hotel are designed to cater to different preferences and needs. The well-appointed apartments offer a range of amenities, including fully equipped kitchen facilities. This feature is particularly appreciated by those who prefer the flexibility of preparing their meals, perhaps incorporating locally sourced ingredients from Lifou's markets. The apartments are spacious and thoughtfully decorated, ensuring a comfortable retreat after a day of exploration.

The personalized service at Jokin Apart Hotel is a standout feature that sets it apart from more conventional accommodations. The staff, often composed of locals, goes the extra mile to make guests feel at home. From offering insider tips on the best places to explore on the island to arranging cultural experiences, the hospitality at Jokin Apart Hotel extends beyond the standard expectations, creating lasting memories for visitors.

The communal areas of Jokin Apart Hotel are designed to foster a sense of community among guests. The shared spaces, such as gardens or common lounges, provide opportunities for travelers to connect, share stories, and forge new friendships. This communal aspect is especially appreciated by solo travelers or those who seek a more sociable atmosphere during their stay.

In addition to its cultural and communal aspects, Jokin Apart Hotel prioritizes sustainability. As the global travel industry increasingly recognizes the importance of responsible tourism, Jokin Apart Hotel takes steps to minimize its environmental impact. From eco-friendly practices in daily operations to initiatives that support local conservation efforts, the hotel aims to contribute positively to both the local community and the broader ecosystem.

The culinary experience at Jokin Apart Hotel is a delightful journey into the flavors of Lifou. The on-site restaurant showcases a fusion of traditional Kanak cuisine and international dishes. Guests are treated to a gastronomic adventure that reflects the island's rich culinary heritage. The emphasis on using locally sourced ingredients not only enhances the freshness of the dishes but also supports the sustainability initiatives of the hotel.

For those who prefer a more independent exploration, Jokin Apart Hotel's proximity to local markets and eateries provides an array of dining options. Guests can venture out to sample authentic Lifouan dishes, engage with local vendors, and immerse themselves in the island's culinary scene. The hotel's staff is always on hand to offer recommendations and insights, ensuring that guests can savor the best of Lifou's flavors.

Beyond the confines of Jokin Apart Hotel, the surrounding area offers a myriad of activities for visitors to explore. From the vibrant markets of We to the cultural exhibitions that showcase the island's artistic traditions, guests can easily navigate the rich tapestry of Lifou's offerings. The hotel's strategic location serves as a gateway to the island's natural wonders, historical sites, and cultural landmarks.

In conclusion, Jokin Apart Hotel stands as a testament to the evolving landscape of travel preferences. It caters to those who seek more than just a place to stay – it offers an immersive experience that embraces the cultural, natural, and communal aspects of Lifou. Whether you're a solo traveler yearning for connections, a couple seeking a romantic retreat, or a family eager to explore, Jokin Apart Hotel welcomes you to Lifou with open arms, ensuring that your stay is not just a moment in time but a chapter in your lifelong travel memories.

Chez Odile et Michel: A Journey into Lifouan Hospitality

Nestled on the pristine shores of Lifou, the largest island in the Loyalty Archipelago of New Caledonia, Chez Odile et Michel stands as a testament to the genuine warmth of Kanak hospitality. In this remote corner of the South Pacific, where turquoise waters meet verdant landscapes, this charming guesthouse beckons travelers with the promise of an authentic and immersive experience.

As you approach Chez Odile et Michel, the first thing that captures your attention is not the grandeur of a luxury resort but the simplicity and serenity of island life. The guesthouse, embraced by tropical gardens, exudes a sense of tranquility that sets the tone for a laid-back escape from the hustle and bustle of everyday life.

Odile and Michel, the gracious hosts, welcome guests with open hearts and sincere smiles. Their genuine warmth is not just a formality; it's a reflection of Lifou's rich cultural heritage, where hospitality is deeply ingrained in the way of life. The couple, born and raised on the island, take pride in sharing their love for Lifou and its traditions with those who cross their doorstep.

Accommodations at Chez Odile et Michel are simple yet comfortable. The guest rooms, adorned with local artwork and traditional crafts, offer a cozy retreat. The emphasis here is on authenticity, with furnishings crafted from local materials, reflecting the island's commitment to sustainable living.

The communal spaces at the guesthouse are designed to encourage interaction among guests. The communal dining area, where Odile prepares and serves home-cooked meals, becomes a gathering place for sharing stories and experiences. The aromatic scents of traditional Kanak dishes waft through the air, enticing guests to savor the flavors of Lifouan cuisine.

As night falls, the atmosphere at Chez Odile et Michel takes on a magical quality. Under the starlit sky, guests often gather around a bonfire, exchanging tales of their adventures or simply relishing the tranquility of the moment. The rhythmic sounds of the ocean serve as a soothing soundtrack, creating an ambiance that is both enchanting and rejuvenating.

One of the unique aspects of staying at Chez Odile et Michel is the opportunity to participate in local activities. From guided hikes through lush tropical forests to immersive cultural experiences, the hosts go above and beyond to ensure that guests have a holistic understanding of Lifouan life. Traditional dance performances and storytelling sessions provide insights into the island's rich heritage, allowing visitors to connect with the soul of Lifou.

The nearby beach, just a short walk from the guesthouse, offers a serene escape. Guests can spend lazy afternoons basking in the sun, swimming in the crystal-clear waters, or exploring the vibrant marine life through snorkeling. The beach becomes a canvas for the vibrant hues of the sunset, creating a mesmerizing spectacle that lingers in the memory.

What truly sets Chez Odile et Michel apart is the sense of community that permeates the guesthouse. Beyond being a place to stay, it becomes a home away from home. Odile and Michel's personalized attention to each guest, their willingness to share local insights, and their genuine care for the well-being of visitors create an atmosphere that fosters connections and friendships.

The ethos of Chez Odile et Michel aligns with the concept of "slow travel," inviting guests to savor the moments, appreciate the nuances of island life, and forge connections with the local community. It's not just about ticking off tourist attractions but about immersing oneself in the rhythm of Lifou, where time seems to slow down, allowing for a deeper appreciation of the natural beauty and cultural richness that surround.

As you bid farewell to Chez Odile et Michel, it's not just a departure from a guesthouse; it's a parting from newfound friends and a slice of Lifouan paradise. The memories of shared laughter, the taste of traditional dishes, and the echoes of ocean waves will linger, inviting you to return to this haven of hospitality whenever the need for a genuine escape arises.

In the heart of Lifou, Chez Odile et Michel stands as a testament to the fact that sometimes, the most enriching journeys are not measured in miles traveled but in the depth of connections made and the authenticity of experiences lived.

Noujoum Hotel: A Paradise of Luxury and Tranquility in Lifou, New Caledonia

Lifou, the largest island in the Loyalty Archipelago of New Caledonia, is a destination known for its pristine beaches, vibrant coral reefs, and rich Kanak culture. Amidst this natural paradise, Noujoum Hotel stands as a beacon of luxury and tranquility, offering guests a unique and indulgent experience in one of the most enchanting corners of the South Pacific.

Perched on a cliff overlooking the crystalline waters surrounding Lifou, Noujoum Hotel enjoys a privileged location that seamlessly integrates with the island's natural beauty. The architectural design of the hotel is a testament to thoughtful planning, with each room strategically positioned to provide panoramic views of the ocean. The setting is nothing short of breathtaking, with lush greenery and the sound of waves creating a serene atmosphere that invites relaxation.

Noujoum Hotel offers a range of accommodations, each designed with a perfect blend of comfort and elegance. The rooms and suites are tastefully decorated, featuring modern amenities and traditional Melanesian touches. The use of local materials in the furnishings creates an authentic sense of place, connecting guests to the island's cultural heritage.

One of the highlights of Noujoum Hotel is its overwater bungalows. These exclusive accommodations provide a unique experience, allowing guests to wake up to the gentle lapping of waves beneath their rooms. The design is both luxurious and environmentally conscious, with sustainable practices in place to ensure minimal impact on the surrounding marine ecosystem.

The culinary experience at Noujoum Hotel is a journey of flavors that reflects the diversity of Lifou. The on-site restaurant serves a fusion of French and Kanak cuisine, curated with a focus on fresh, locally sourced ingredients. Guests can indulge in gourmet meals while enjoying breathtaking views of the ocean, creating a dining experience that is both sensory and visually delightful.

The culinary team at Noujoum Hotel takes pride in showcasing the unique flavors of Lifouan cuisine. From freshly caught seafood to tropical fruits and vegetables, each dish is a celebration of the island's bounty. The restaurant's commitment to sustainability is evident in its efforts to support local farmers and fishermen, contributing to the community's well-being.

Noujoum Hotel goes beyond providing a place to stay; it offers a holistic approach to well-being. The resort features a spa that draws inspiration from traditional Melanesian healing practices. Guests can indulge in a range of treatments, from massages using local oils to rejuvenating facials featuring natural ingredients sourced from the island.

The spa's serene ambiance, coupled with the skillful hands of experienced therapists, creates an oasis of relaxation. Whether guests seek to unwind after a day of exploration or simply want to pamper themselves, the spa at Noujoum Hotel offers a sanctuary for rejuvenation.

While Lifou's natural beauty is a major draw, Noujoum Hotel complements the island experience with a range of recreational activities. The resort has its own water sports center, providing guests with the opportunity to explore the vibrant marine life that surrounds Lifou. Snorkeling, kayaking, and paddleboarding are just a few of the activities available, allowing guests to immerse themselves in the azure waters of the South Pacific.

For those who prefer to stay on land, Noujoum Hotel organizes guided nature walks and cultural excursions. Guests can explore the island's hidden gems, from secluded beaches to traditional Kanak villages, gaining insights into Lifou's unique heritage and customs.

Noujoum Hotel is not only a destination for leisure travelers but also a sought-after venue for weddings and events. The romantic setting, combined with the impeccable service provided by the hotel's events team, makes it an ideal location for couples seeking a memorable wedding in paradise.

The resort's facilities can be tailored to accommodate a range of events, from intimate ceremonies to grand celebrations. The dedicated events staff at Noujoum Hotel ensures that every detail is taken care of, allowing guests to focus on creating lasting memories.

As a luxury resort, Noujoum Hotel is committed to environmental sustainability. The management recognizes the importance of preserving the pristine ecosystems that make Lifou a unique destination. The resort implements eco-friendly practices, from waste reduction initiatives to energy-efficient technologies.

Noujoum Hotel actively engages with local conservation efforts, supporting initiatives that aim to protect the island's flora and fauna. Through community partnerships, the resort contributes to the sustainable development of Lifou, ensuring that future generations can continue to enjoy the island's natural beauty.

Noujoum Hotel stands as a testament to the seamless integration of luxury, cultural authenticity, and environmental sustainability. For travelers seeking an unparalleled experience in Lifou, this resort provides a haven of comfort and elegance. From the moment guests arrive at the cliffside retreat to the time they spend indulging in gourmet meals and rejuvenating spa treatments, Noujoum Hotel offers a sensory journey that complements the island's natural wonders. In choosing Noujoum Hotel, guests embark on a voyage where luxury meets tradition, and where the spirit of Lifou is captured in every detail.

Ecolodge L'Escape: A Sustainable Haven in the Heart of Lifou

Nestled in the heart of Lifou, the largest island in the Loyalty Archipelago of New Caledonia, Ecolodge L'Escape stands as a testament to sustainable tourism. As travelers seek more responsible and eco-friendly options, this unique retreat offers an immersive experience in harmony with nature. From its minimal environmental impact to the guided nature walks that unveil the island's biodiversity, Ecolodge L'Escape beckons those who yearn for a meaningful connection with both the environment and the local culture.

The design of Ecolodge L'Escape reflects a commitment to sustainability. Bungalows, seamlessly integrated into the tropical forest surroundings, utilize eco-friendly materials and energy-efficient features. The architecture aims to minimize the ecological footprint while providing guests with comfortable and immersive accommodations. Each bungalow, with its natural color palette and locally inspired décor, becomes a tranquil haven where guests can connect with the pristine surroundings.

The emphasis on sustainable practices extends beyond architecture. Ecolodge L'Escape prioritizes responsible waste management, recycling initiatives, and water conservation. Guests are encouraged to participate in these efforts, fostering a sense of environmental stewardship during their stay. The lodge serves as a model for how tourism can coexist with nature without compromising the delicate balance of Lifou's ecosystems.

One of the highlights of Ecolodge L'Escape is its dedication to education and awareness. Guided nature walks, led by knowledgeable local guides, offer guests an opportunity to explore the diverse flora and fauna of Lifou. These walks, conducted with the utmost respect for the environment, provide insights into the delicate ecosystems and the importance of biodiversity conservation. Guests leave not only with fond memories of the island's natural beauty but also with a deeper understanding of the need to protect it.

The lodge's commitment to cultural immersion is equally noteworthy. Traditional Melanesian activities, such as weaving and storytelling, are woven into the guest experience. Visitors have the chance to engage with local artisans, gaining insights into the rich cultural tapestry of Lifou.

This cultural exchange fosters a connection between guests and the community, breaking down barriers and promoting mutual understanding.

Ecolodge L'Escape also takes pride in its culinary offerings. The on-site restaurant features a menu that celebrates locally sourced and organic ingredients. The culinary team crafts dishes that showcase the flavors of Lifou, providing a gastronomic journey that complements the overall experience. Guests can savor fresh, sustainable seafood and tropical fruits, contributing to the local economy and minimizing the carbon footprint associated with food sourcing.

The lodge's commitment to sustainability is not limited to its operations; it extends to the community. Ecolodge L'Escape actively engages in community development projects, supporting local initiatives that enhance the well-being of Lifou's residents. This approach ensures that the benefits of tourism are shared equitably, creating a positive impact on both the environment and the local population.

Ecolodge L'Escape, as a beacon of sustainable tourism, inspires a new way of experiencing travel. It challenges the conventional notion that luxury and environmental responsibility are mutually exclusive. Instead, it demonstrates that a stay can be both indulgent and ecologically sensitive. The lodge invites guests to be conscious consumers, making choices that align with their values and contribute to the preservation of Lifou's natural and cultural heritage.

In conclusion, Ecolodge L'Escape stands as a shining example of how tourism can be a force for good. As travelers increasingly seek destinations that prioritize sustainability, this eco-friendly retreat offers not just a place to stay but an opportunity to make a positive impact. Ecolodge L'Escape invites guests to step into a world where the beauty of Lifou is preserved, celebrated, and shared responsibly.

Les Koghis – Lifou Hotel & Spa

Les Koghis – Lifou Hotel & Spa is not just a destination; it's an experience that transcends the ordinary. Perched on the pristine shores of Chateaubriand Bay on the largest island of the Loyalty Archipelago, Lifou, this luxurious retreat beckons travelers with promises of unrivaled comfort, breathtaking views, and a holistic approach to relaxation.

Upon entering the grounds of Les Koghis, guests are greeted by a sense of tranquility. The resort's architecture seamlessly integrates with the natural beauty of its surroundings. The warm, earthy tones of the buildings harmonize with the lush greenery, creating an ambiance that is both inviting and calming.

Accommodations at Les Koghis are a testament to luxury. The resort boasts elegant overwater bungalows, each carefully designed to provide an immersive experience. These spacious retreats offer not only a comfortable stay but also panoramic views of the azure waters beneath. The gentle lapping of the waves against the stilts becomes a soothing soundtrack to the guest's stay, creating an atmosphere of serenity.

The interiors of the bungalows are a blend of modern sophistication and traditional Melanesian aesthetics. Local artworks adorn the walls, and the furnishings are crafted from native materials, infusing each space with a sense of place. The rooms are equipped with modern amenities, ensuring that guests have everything they need at their fingertips.

One of the highlights of Les Koghis is its spa, a sanctuary of wellness nestled within the resort. The spa offers a range of treatments inspired by traditional Melanesian healing practices. Guests can indulge in massages, body scrubs, and facials, each designed to rejuvenate both the body and the soul. The spa's expert therapists use locally sourced ingredients, such as fragrant tropical flowers and nourishing coconut oil, to enhance the therapeutic experience.

The infinity pool at Les Koghis is a visual masterpiece. Overlooking the bay, the pool seems to merge seamlessly with the horizon, creating a mesmerizing effect. Guests can lounge by the pool, taking in the breathtaking views, or take a refreshing dip to escape the tropical heat. The poolside bar offers a selection of refreshing beverages, allowing guests to savor a cocktail while basking in the sun's warm embrace.

Dining at Les Koghis is a culinary journey that reflects the diverse influences of the region. The resort's restaurant serves a fusion of French and Kanak cuisine, showcasing the best of local flavors. Fresh seafood, tropical fruits, and aromatic herbs are expertly combined to create dishes that are as visually appealing as they are delicious. Guests can choose to dine indoors or al fresco, with each option providing a unique ambiance.

Les Koghis is not just a destination for relaxation; it's also a hub for adventure. The resort offers a range of water-based activities, allowing guests to explore the vibrant marine life of Chateaubriand Bay. Snorkeling excursions reveal a kaleidoscope of coral formations and colorful fish, while kayaking provides a unique perspective of the coastline. The resort's water sports center can arrange guided tours and equipment rental, ensuring that guests can make the most of Lifou's stunning natural assets.

The attentive and friendly staff at Les Koghis contribute to the overall sense of well-being that permeates the resort. From the moment guests arrive, they are met with genuine hospitality and a commitment to making their stay memorable. Whether it's arranging excursions, providing recommendations for exploring Lifou, or attending to special requests, the staff at Les Koghis goes above and beyond to ensure a seamless and enjoyable experience for every guest.

As the sun sets over Chateaubriand Bay, Les Koghis takes on a magical quality. The resort is illuminated by soft, ambient lighting, creating a romantic and intimate atmosphere. Guests can enjoy a leisurely stroll along the beach or savor a candlelit dinner, serenaded by the gentle sounds of the ocean.

In conclusion, Les Koghis – Lifou Hotel & Spa is a jewel in the crown of Lifou's hospitality offerings. It seamlessly combines luxury, natural beauty, and cultural authenticity to create an experience that lingers in the memory long after the journey home. Whether seeking a romantic getaway, a wellness retreat, or a base for exploring the wonders of Lifou, Les Koghis stands as a testament to the art of hospitality in one of the most enchanting corners of the South Pacific.

Hotel Santal Bay: A Tranquil Beachfront Paradise in Lifou, New Caledonia

Nestled on the pristine shores of Santal Bay in Lifou, New Caledonia, Hotel Santal Bay stands as a testament to luxury, tranquility, and the natural beauty that defines this enchanting island. Lifou, the largest island in the Loyalty Archipelago, is renowned for its crystal-clear waters, vibrant coral reefs, and rich cultural heritage. Hotel Santal Bay seamlessly combines modern sophistication with the laid-back charm of island life, offering guests a haven where they can unwind, explore, and create lasting memories.

As you approach Hotel Santal Bay, the azure hues of the Pacific Ocean welcome you to a place where time seems to slow down. The resort's architecture is a fusion of contemporary design and traditional Melanesian elements, creating a harmonious blend with the natural surroundings. The open-air lobby provides an immediate connection to the island, offering panoramic views of the bay and a refreshing sea breeze.

Hotel Santal Bay offers a range of accommodations, each thoughtfully designed to provide comfort and serenity. From the garden bungalows nestled amidst tropical foliage to the beachfront suites with private balconies, every room offers a unique perspective of Lifou's beauty. The interiors are elegantly furnished, drawing inspiration from the island's natural palette, and are equipped with modern amenities to ensure a luxurious stay.

Culinary excellence is a hallmark of Hotel Santal Bay. The resort boasts an on-site restaurant that caters to diverse tastes, combining local flavors with international cuisine. Guests can savor fresh seafood caught from the surrounding waters, tropical fruits, and exquisite French-inspired dishes. Dining at Hotel Santal Bay is not just a gastronomic experience but a journey into the rich culinary traditions of Lifou.

To enhance the holistic experience, Hotel Santal Bay features the Santal Spa—a sanctuary of relaxation overlooking the bay. Indulge in a range of traditional Melanesian spa treatments, each crafted to rejuvenate the body and soothe the soul. From massages using local oils to therapeutic treatments inspired by ancient healing practices, the spa offers a tranquil escape for those seeking wellness and renewal.

For those with a spirit of adventure, Hotel Santal Bay provides an array of recreational activities to explore the natural wonders of Lifou. The on-site water sports center offers snorkeling, kayaking, and paddleboarding, allowing guests to discover the vibrant marine life just steps away from their accommodation. Guided tours to nearby attractions, such as the Jinek Bay and the cliffs of Xodre, provide a deeper understanding of Lifou's unique geography and cultural heritage.

Hotel Santal Bay's prime location on Santal Bay ensures that guests have direct access to the island's most beautiful beaches. Whether you choose to bask in the sun on the powdery white sand, take a leisurely stroll along the shoreline, or enjoy a romantic dinner by the water's edge, the beach becomes an integral part of your stay. The resort's commitment to sustainability is reflected in its efforts to preserve the natural beauty of the beach and surrounding marine ecosystems.

As the sun begins its descent over Santal Bay, Hotel Santal Bay transforms into a magical realm of colors. The resort's design takes full advantage of this natural spectacle, providing unobstructed views of the sunset from various vantage points. Guests can unwind with a cocktail in hand, watching as the sky is painted in hues of orange and pink—a daily spectacle that encapsulates the serenity of Lifou.

Hotel Santal Bay recognizes the importance of connecting guests with the island's cultural heritage. The resort often hosts traditional Kanak performances, allowing visitors to experience the vibrant dance, music, and storytelling that are integral to Lifouan identity. Additionally, guests can participate in cultural workshops, gaining insights into local customs and craftsmanship.

Environmental stewardship is a core value of Hotel Santal Bay. The resort has implemented various sustainability initiatives to minimize its ecological footprint. From energy-efficient practices to waste reduction measures, the commitment to preserving Lifou's natural beauty is evident throughout the resort. Guests are encouraged to participate in eco-friendly activities and support local conservation efforts.

What sets Hotel Santal Bay apart is its commitment to personalized service. The staff, known for their warmth and attentiveness, go the extra mile to ensure that each guest's needs and preferences are met. Whether it's arranging a private beachfront dinner, organizing a customized tour, or providing insights into the best local experiences, the team at Hotel Santal Bay strives to create a tailor-made experience for every visitor.

Hotel Santal Bay encapsulates the essence of Lifou—a destination where luxury meets nature in perfect harmony. From the moment you arrive, you are enveloped in a sense of tranquility and beauty that defines this island paradise. Whether you seek relaxation by the beach, thrilling adventures in the water, or a cultural immersion into Lifou's traditions, Hotel Santal Bay is the gateway to a truly unforgettable experience. As you bid farewell to this tranquil haven, the memories of Santal Bay will linger, inviting you to return and create new chapters in your Lifouan journey.

Oasis de Kiamu

Nestled in the heart of Lifou, the largest island in the Loyalty Archipelago of New Caledonia, Oasis de Kiamu stands as a testament to the island's allure. This boutique resort, cocooned in a private cove, is a hidden gem that beckons travelers seeking an intimate and secluded escape.

As you step into the oasis, a sense of tranquility washes over you. The resort is surrounded by lush vegetation, creating a natural barrier that enhances the feeling of exclusivity. The individual bungalows, thoughtfully designed to blend with the environment, offer a harmonious balance between modern comfort and traditional Melanesian aesthetics.

Accommodations at Oasis de Kiamu range from cozy retreats for couples to spacious family bungalows. Each bungalow is a sanctuary of privacy, with its own veranda overlooking the tropical landscape. The interiors are adorned with local artwork and handcrafted furnishings, creating an atmosphere that reflects the island's vibrant culture.

The resort's commitment to sustainability is evident in its eco-friendly practices. From solar-powered energy sources to water conservation initiatives, Oasis de Kiamu strives to minimize its environmental impact. This dedication to responsible tourism aligns seamlessly with the natural beauty that surrounds the resort, creating a retreat that is not only luxurious but also environmentally conscious.

Culinary delights at Oasis de Kiamu are a celebration of local flavors and international cuisine. The on-site restaurant sources fresh produce locally, ensuring that guests experience the authentic tastes of Lifou. Whether indulging in a leisurely breakfast on the veranda or savoring a romantic dinner under the stars, the dining experience at Oasis de Kiamu is a journey into the gastronomic wonders of the island.

The resort's commitment to guest satisfaction extends beyond accommodations and dining. The staff at Oasis de Kiamu are not just service providers; they are storytellers and guides, eager to share the secrets of Lifou with every visitor. From arranging personalized excursions to providing insights into the island's traditions, the hospitality at Oasis de Kiamu goes beyond expectations.

As the day unfolds, guests have a myriad of activities to choose from. The private beach, fringed with swaying palm trees, invites leisurely strolls and sun-soaked afternoons. The clear, azure waters are perfect for snorkeling, allowing guests to discover the vibrant marine life that inhabits the surrounding coral reefs. For those seeking adventure, the resort offers guided hikes into the island's interior, where dense forests conceal hidden waterfalls and indigenous flora.

For moments of pure relaxation, the spa at Oasis de Kiamu is a sanctuary within a sanctuary. Here, traditional Melanesian treatments are administered with expertise, using locally sourced ingredients to rejuvenate the body and soul. The sound of waves lapping against the shore serves as a soothing backdrop, enhancing the overall sense of serenity.

As the sun dips below the horizon, the resort comes alive with the warm glow of torchlight. Evenings at Oasis de Kiamu are a celebration of Lifouan culture, with traditional performances and music creating an enchanting ambiance. Guests are invited to immerse themselves in the rhythms and dances of the island, forging connections that transcend language.

Oasis de Kiamu is not merely a place to stay; it's a holistic experience that captures the essence of Lifou. The resort's dedication to preserving the island's natural beauty, combined with its commitment to providing a luxurious yet authentic experience, makes it a destination within a destination. Whether you seek quiet moments of reflection, thrilling adventures, or cultural immersion, Oasis de Kiamu stands ready to craft a personalized and unforgettable Lifouan journey for every guest.

Ouvéa

Title: Relaxing in Paradise: A Serene Escape to Ouvéa

Nestled in the heart of the South Pacific, Ouvéa, a small and idyllic island in New Caledonia, offers a serene escape for those seeking tranquility and natural beauty. Known for its pristine beaches, crystal-clear lagoons, and rich cultural heritage, Ouvéa is a paradise for travelers looking to unwind in a peaceful and untouched environment.

Ouvéa boasts some of the most enchanting beaches in the world. The powdery white sands stretch for miles, gently kissed by the turquoise waters of the Pacific. Mouli Beach, often referred to as the "Loyalty Islands' most beautiful beach," is a prime example. Imagine strolling along the shoreline, feeling the soft sand between your toes, and marveling at the stunning contrast between the lush greenery and the azure sea.

For an unparalleled experience, Ouvéa offers overwater bungalows that allow guests to wake up to the sound of gentle waves and panoramic views of the surrounding lagoon. These luxurious accommodations blend seamlessly with the island's natural beauty, providing an intimate and exclusive retreat. Imagine sipping your morning coffee on a private deck as you watch the sunrise over the tranquil waters.

Beyond its breathtaking beaches, Ouvéa is a haven for nature enthusiasts. The island is home to lush forests, unique flora, and diverse wildlife. Take a leisurely hike through the tropical landscapes, where the air is filled with the sweet fragrance of exotic flowers. Birdwatchers will delight in the opportunity to spot endemic species, adding a touch of adventure to the overall sense of relaxation.

Ouvéa is not only a feast for the senses but also a place to immerse oneself in the rich cultural heritage of the Kanak people. Engage in cultural experiences, such as traditional dance performances and handicraft workshops, where locals share their customs and stories. This connection with the island's heritage adds depth to the relaxation, providing a meaningful cultural context to your visit.

Savor the flavors of Ouvéa through its unique culinary offerings. Fresh seafood, coconut-infused dishes, and tropical fruits are staples of the local cuisine. Dining on the beach with the sound of the waves as your background music is an experience that encapsulates the island's laid-back atmosphere and contributes to the overall sense of relaxation.

While relaxation is key on Ouvéa, the island also offers a range of water activities for those seeking a bit of adventure. Snorkeling and diving enthusiasts can explore vibrant coral reefs teeming with marine life. The clear waters provide excellent visibility, making it a memorable experience for both novice and experienced divers.

As the day draws to a close, Ouvéa's sunsets are nothing short of magical. The sky transforms into a canvas of warm hues, casting a golden glow over the lagoon. Whether you choose to watch the sunset from the beach, a boat, or your overwater bungalow, the tranquil beauty of Ouvéa's evenings is the perfect conclusion to a day of pure relaxation.

Ouvéa, with its pristine beaches, overwater bungalows, cultural richness, and untouched landscapes, provides a haven for those seeking a truly relaxing escape. This slice of paradise in New Caledonia invites travelers to unwind, recharge, and connect with the beauty of nature and the warmth of Kanak hospitality. In Ouvéa, relaxation isn't just a state of mind; it's a way of life.

Local Traditions in Ouvéa: Embracing Culture and Heritage

Nestled in the heart of the South Pacific, Ouvéa stands as a jewel within the archipelago of New Caledonia. This serene island not only boasts breathtaking natural beauty but also preserves a rich tapestry of local traditions that reflect the vibrant cultural heritage of its people, primarily the Kanak community. In this exploration, we delve into the unique and fascinating local traditions that define life on Ouvéa.

1. **Kanak Culture: A Tapestry of Traditions**

Ouvéa is predominantly inhabited by the Kanak people, an indigenous Melanesian group with a history deeply rooted in their connection to the land and the sea. Traditional practices and rituals play a significant role in their daily lives, shaping the island's cultural landscape.

2. **The Art of Storytelling: Oral Traditions**

One of the most captivating aspects of Kanak culture on Ouvéa is the art of storytelling. Elders pass down tales of ancient times, weaving narratives that carry the wisdom, beliefs, and history of the community. These oral traditions are not just stories but living conduits that connect the present generation with their ancestors.

3. **Dance and Music: Expressions of Identity**

Dance and music hold a special place in Kanak ceremonies and celebrations. The rhythmic beats of traditional drums echo through the air as locals, adorned in vibrant customary attire, perform intricate dances that convey stories of love, war, and spirituality. These artistic expressions are more than performances; they are celebrations of identity and heritage.

4. **Customary Ceremonies: Rituals of Significance**

Customary ceremonies punctuate the life on Ouvéa, marking milestones such as births, marriages, and deaths. Each ceremony is a meticulous affair, guided by age-old customs and presided over by community leaders. These rituals serve as a testament to the resilience of traditions in the face of modernization.

5. The Kanak Way of Life: Living in Harmony with Nature

The Kanak people have a profound connection with nature, and this connection is reflected in their daily lives. Traditional agricultural practices, fishing techniques, and hunting methods are passed down through generations, ensuring a sustainable coexistence with the island's ecosystem. Visitors to Ouvéa often witness this harmonious relationship during guided tours that showcase the island's natural and cultural heritage.

6. Symbolism in Art and Craftsmanship

Art and craftsmanship play a pivotal role in expressing Kanak traditions. Intricate wood carvings, vibrant tapa cloth, and symbolic sculptures are not just artifacts; they are embodiments of cultural symbolism. Local artisans continue to practice age-old techniques, infusing modern designs with traditional motifs, preserving the legacy of their ancestors.

7. Language as a Cultural Keystone

The Kanak language, Drehu, is an essential part of Ouvéan identity. Beyond being a means of communication, the language carries the nuances of cultural expressions, with specific words embodying unique concepts tied to local traditions. Efforts to preserve and promote the Kanak language are underway, recognizing its role in safeguarding the cultural heritage of Ouvéa.

8. Rituals of Mourning: Honoring Ancestors

In times of sorrow, the Kanak people of Ouvéa engage in rituals of mourning that are deeply rooted in tradition. These ceremonies, marked by symbolic gestures and communal support, exemplify the importance of collective mourning and the belief that the spirits of the departed continue to influence the lives of the living.

9. Festivals and Celebrations: Showcasing Cultural Riches

Throughout the year, Ouvéa comes alive with vibrant festivals and celebrations. These events provide an opportunity for locals and visitors alike to immerse themselves in the colors, sounds, and flavors of Kanak culture. From the lively energy of the Yam Festival to the spiritual significance of the Canala Cross Festival, each celebration is a testimony to the resilience of Ouvéa's traditions.

10. The Future of Tradition: Balancing Preservation and Progress

As Ouvéa embraces modernity, the delicate balance between preserving traditions and adapting to change becomes increasingly crucial. Community-led initiatives, cultural education programs, and collaborative efforts with government agencies aim to ensure that future generations inherit a legacy that is both rooted in tradition and resilient in the face of evolving times.

In conclusion, Ouvéa's local traditions stand as a testament to the resilience, creativity, and deep-rooted spirituality of the Kanak people. As visitors explore this enchanting island, they are not just witnessing traditions; they become part of a living narrative, where the past, present, and future are intricately woven together in the vibrant tapestry of Ouvéan culture.

Unveiling the Paradise: Hotels and Resorts in Ouvéa, New Caledonia

Nestled in the heart of the South Pacific, the captivating island of Ouvéa in New Caledonia is a pristine gem that beckons travelers seeking an escape into nature's embrace. Blessed with powdery white sand beaches, crystal-clear waters, and a vibrant cultural tapestry, Ouvéa is a haven for those who yearn for tranquility and adventure. In this guide, we unveil the best hotels and resorts on this enchanting island, ensuring that your stay is as remarkable as the destination itself.

Before delving into accommodation options, it's essential to understand the allure of Ouvéa. This slender, 54-kilometer-long island is renowned for its immaculate beaches, surrounded by the world's largest enclosed lagoon. Ouvéa's rich cultural heritage, influenced by the indigenous Kanak people, adds a distinctive charm to the island. From vibrant coral reefs to traditional Melanesian villages, Ouvéa promises an immersive experience for every traveler.

Luxurious Retreats: Ouvéa's Premier Resorts

1. **Ouvéa Paradise Resort**

Location: Saint-Joseph Village

Nestled on the western coast of Ouvéa, the Ouvéa Paradise Resort stands as an epitome of luxury. Surrounded by lush tropical gardens, this resort offers spacious bungalows with private balconies overlooking the turquoise lagoon. The resort's architecture seamlessly blends with the natural surroundings, providing an authentic island experience.

The Ouvéa Paradise Resort is celebrated for its top-notch amenities, including a spa that offers traditional Kanak massages and rejuvenating treatments. Guests can also indulge in exquisite dining at the resort's beachfront restaurant, savoring a fusion of French and Melanesian flavors.

2. **Le Méridien Ouvéa Beach Resort**

Location: Anawa Bay

Perched on the pristine Anawa Bay, Le Méridien Ouvéa Beach Resort presents a harmonious blend of sophistication and island charm. The overwater bungalows provide direct access to the coral gardens below, offering a surreal underwater spectacle.

The resort's commitment to sustainability is commendable, with eco-friendly initiatives and local community engagement. From water sports to cultural performances, Le Méridien ensures a holistic experience for its guests.

Boutique Escapes: Charming Hotels in Ouvéa

1. **Tieti Hotel**

Location: Fayaoué

Tieti Hotel, located in the heart of Fayaoué, offers a more intimate setting for travelers seeking a blend of comfort and local authenticity. The hotel's design reflects traditional Kanak architecture, creating a cozy ambiance.

Guests at Tieti Hotel can explore nearby villages, engage in water activities arranged by the hotel, and unwind in well-appointed rooms. The on-site restaurant introduces visitors to Kanak culinary delights, creating a sensorial journey through the island's flavors.

2. L'Oasis de Kiamu

Location: Kiamu Village

For a secluded retreat, L'Oasis de Kiamu is a charming choice situated near Kiamu Village. This boutique hotel offers a handful of private bungalows nestled amid tropical gardens, providing an intimate connection with nature.

L'Oasis de Kiamu prides itself on personalized service, curating bespoke experiences for guests. From guided nature walks to intimate beachside dinners, the hotel caters to individual preferences, ensuring an unforgettable stay.

Practical Considerations: Booking Your Stay in Ouvéa

1. Best Time to Visit Ouvéa

Ouvéa enjoys a tropical climate, making it an appealing destination year-round. However, the dry season from July to September is considered the best time to visit, with pleasant temperatures and lower humidity.

2. Booking Tips

Given Ouvéa's popularity, especially during peak tourist seasons, it's advisable to book your accommodation well in advance. Many resorts and hotels offer package deals that include airport transfers, meals, and guided activities.

3. Transportation on the Island

Ouvéa is a relatively small island, and transportation is primarily facilitated by rental cars, bicycles, or hotel-provided shuttles. Exploring the island at a leisurely pace allows travelers to discover hidden gems and interact with the friendly local community.

As you plan your sojourn to Ouvéa, the accommodation options outlined here serve as gateways to the island's natural beauty and cultural richness. Whether you opt for the opulence of a beachfront resort or the charm of a boutique hotel, each lodging choice promises a unique experience on this idyllic slice of paradise. Ouvéa, with its pristine landscapes and warm hospitality, invites you to immerse yourself in a journey that transcends the ordinary, leaving indelible memories etched in the sands of time.

Ouvéa Paradise Resort

Nestled on the western coast of the slender and enchanting island of Ouvéa in New Caledonia, the Ouvéa Paradise Resort stands as a testament to luxury and tranquility. This resort is more than just a place to stay; it's an immersive experience that seamlessly blends modern comforts with the natural wonders of the South Pacific.

As you approach the resort, you're greeted by lush tropical gardens that frame the entrance. The foliage hints at the paradise that awaits within, creating a sense of anticipation and wonder. The architecture of the resort is designed to harmonize with its surroundings, with bungalows that seem to emerge organically from the landscape.

The heart of Ouvéa Paradise Resort lies in its accommodations. The spacious bungalows are a haven of comfort, offering a perfect blend of traditional charm and contemporary amenities. Each bungalow is strategically positioned to provide guests with privacy while maximizing the breathtaking views of the turquoise lagoon.

The overwater bungalows are a particular highlight, extending above the lagoon and creating a connection with the vibrant underwater world. Imagine waking up to the gentle lapping of waves beneath your private balcony or enjoying a sunset that paints the sky in hues of orange and pink, casting a magical glow over the water.

What sets Ouvéa Paradise Resort apart is its commitment to providing a holistic experience. The resort is not just a place to sleep; it's a destination in itself. The spa, nestled amidst the tropical greenery, beckons guests to indulge in a world of relaxation and rejuvenation. Traditional Kanak massages and wellness treatments draw inspiration from the island's rich cultural heritage, offering a unique and authentic experience.

For those seeking culinary delights, the beachfront restaurant at Ouvéa Paradise Resort is a culinary haven. Here, French and Melanesian flavors dance on the taste buds, creating a symphony of tastes that reflects the island's diverse influences. Guests can savor fresh seafood, tropical fruits, and other local delicacies while enjoying the panoramic views of the lagoon.

While the luxurious accommodations and spa provide ample reasons to linger within the confines of the resort, Ouvéa's natural wonders beckon adventurers to explore. The resort organizes various activities, from snorkeling in the coral-rich waters to guided nature walks that unveil the island's hidden treasures.

Water sports enthusiasts can revel in the vibrant marine life that Ouvéa is known for. The resort's proximity to the beach makes it easy for guests to partake in activities like paddleboarding, kayaking, or simply lounging on the pristine sands. The coral reefs surrounding the island are a snorkeler's paradise, offering a kaleidoscope of colors and marine life.

Ouvéa Paradise Resort goes beyond providing a luxurious escape; it is committed to sustainability and responsible tourism. The resort actively engages with the local community, incorporating aspects of Kanak culture into its operations. Guests have the opportunity to participate in cultural activities, fostering a deeper understanding of the island's heritage.

From eco-friendly initiatives to community-driven projects, Ouvéa Paradise Resort is a model of responsible tourism. The resort's commitment to minimizing its environmental impact is reflected in everything from waste reduction programs to energy-efficient practices.

As the sun sets over Ouvéa, casting a warm glow over the lagoon, guests at Ouvéa Paradise Resort find themselves immersed in a sense of tranquility and fulfillment. It's more than a luxurious retreat; it's a sanctuary where nature and modernity coexist in perfect harmony.

Ouvéa Paradise Resort transcends the conventional boundaries of a hotel stay. It is an experience that leaves an indelible mark on those who have the privilege of wandering its grounds and indulging in its offerings. In this corner of the South Pacific, where the sea meets the sky and culture intertwines with luxury, Ouvéa Paradise Resort stands as a testament to the timeless allure of this island paradise.

Le Méridien Ouvéa Beach Resort

Le Méridien Ouvéa Beach Resort is a sublime haven nestled on the shores of Anawa Bay, an ethereal escape that seamlessly blends luxury with the natural splendor of Ouvéa, New Caledonia. This resort stands as a testament to the harmonious coexistence of sophistication and island charm, offering an unparalleled experience for those seeking a retreat in the heart of the South Pacific.

Upon entering the Le Méridien Ouvéa Beach Resort, guests are welcomed by a captivating panorama of crystal-clear waters, powder-white sandy beaches, and vibrant coral reefs. The resort's design is a celebration of the natural beauty that surrounds it, with overwater bungalows providing direct access to the mesmerizing underwater world beneath.

The accommodations at Le Méridien Ouvéa Beach Resort are a symphony of elegance and comfort. The overwater bungalows, perched on stilts above the azure lagoon, offer a sense of seclusion and intimacy. Each bungalow is meticulously designed to maximize views of the surrounding landscape, with floor-to-ceiling windows that frame the breathtaking scenery.

Inside, guests are treated to a blend of modern amenities and traditional Kanak influences. The décor reflects the rich cultural heritage of Ouvéa, with indigenous artworks and locally inspired furnishings adorning the rooms. The seamless integration of luxury and authenticity creates a haven where guests can unwind in style while immersing themselves in the island's unique ambiance.

Le Méridien Ouvéa Beach Resort is not just a place to stay; it's a destination in itself. The resort's commitment to sustainability is evident in its eco-friendly initiatives and community engagement programs. Guests can participate in coral reef conservation efforts or learn about traditional Kanak practices, adding a meaningful dimension to their stay.

For those seeking relaxation, the resort's spa is a sanctuary of serenity. Nestled amid tropical gardens, the spa offers a range of rejuvenating treatments, including traditional Kanak massages that draw on ancient healing techniques. The soothing sounds of the ocean and the fragrant scent of local flowers create an immersive wellness experience.

Culinary delights at Le Méridien Ouvéa Beach Resort are a journey through the flavors of Ouvéa. The resort's beachfront restaurant serves a fusion of French and Melanesian cuisine, with fresh, locally sourced ingredients taking center stage. Guests can savor exquisite dishes while enjoying panoramic views of the bay, creating a dining experience that transcends the ordinary.

The resort's commitment to providing a holistic experience extends to its array of activities and amenities. From water sports such as snorkeling and kayaking to cultural performances that showcase the island's traditions, there is no shortage of things to do. The attentive and friendly staff can assist guests in crafting personalized itineraries, ensuring that every moment spent at Le Méridien Ouvéa Beach Resort is tailored to individual preferences.

As the sun sets over Anawa Bay, the resort comes alive with a magical ambiance. Guests can unwind at the beachside bar, sipping on signature cocktails while the colors of the sky mirror the hues of the lagoon. Evening entertainment, ranging from traditional dance performances to stargazing sessions, adds a touch of enchantment to the Ouvéa nights.

Beyond the confines of the resort, Ouvéa beckons with its own treasures. Le Méridien Ouvéa Beach Resort facilitates guided excursions, allowing guests to explore the island's natural wonders and cultural landmarks. From guided nature walks to visits to traditional Kanak villages, these excursions offer insights into the authentic charm of Ouvéa.

The booking process at Le Méridien Ouvéa Beach Resort is seamless, with the option to choose from various packages that include airport transfers, meals, and curated experiences. The resort's dedication to guest satisfaction is evident in the attention to detail, ensuring that every aspect of the stay exceeds expectations.

In conclusion, Le Méridien Ouvéa Beach Resort stands as a beacon of luxury in the heart of Ouvéa. From the opulence of its accommodations to the eco-conscious initiatives that underscore its commitment to sustainability, every facet of the resort reflects a dedication to providing an exceptional experience. For those seeking an escape to a paradise where luxury meets nature, Le Méridien Ouvéa Beach Resort is an unrivaled destination, inviting guests to create memories that linger like the gentle lapping of the Ouvéa waves.

Tieti Hotel: A Tranquil Haven in the Heart of Ouvéa

Ouvéa, the jewel of the Pacific, is renowned for its pristine beaches, crystal-clear waters, and vibrant cultural heritage. Among the accommodation options that grace this enchanting island, Tieti Hotel stands out as a tranquil haven that seamlessly blends comfort with local authenticity. In this comprehensive exploration, we delve into the allure of Tieti Hotel, uncovering the nuances that make it a cherished retreat for travelers seeking a genuine Ouvéan experience.

Tieti Hotel is strategically located in the heart of Fayaoué, a central village on Ouvéa. As you step into this boutique establishment, you are greeted by the warm embrace of traditional Kanak architecture. The hotel's design pays homage to the indigenous people of New Caledonia, creating an ambiance that reflects the island's cultural richness.

Accommodations at Tieti Hotel are a testament to the commitment to guest comfort. The rooms, adorned with local artwork and crafted with natural materials, provide a cozy and inviting retreat. Whether you choose a garden-view room or an option with a balcony overlooking the azure waters, each accommodation is a sanctuary that invites relaxation.

The charm of Tieti Hotel extends beyond its architecture. The hotel's intimate size fosters a sense of community, allowing guests to connect with fellow travelers and the friendly local staff. The personalized service at Tieti Hotel is a hallmark of the Ouvéan hospitality, where every guest is treated not as a visitor but as an integral part of the island's narrative.

As the sun rises over Ouvéa, guests at Tieti Hotel awaken to a world of possibilities. The hotel offers a range of activities that showcase the island's natural beauty and cultural heritage. Guided nature walks provide insights into the unique flora and fauna of Ouvéa, while excursions to nearby villages offer a glimpse into the daily lives of the Kanak people.

For those seeking a more relaxed pace, Tieti Hotel's proximity to Fayaoué's beach allows for leisurely strolls along the shore or moments of contemplation as the waves gently lap at the sand. The hotel provides bicycles for guests to explore the village and its surroundings at their own pace, adding a touch of adventure to the Ouvéan experience.

Culinary delights at Tieti Hotel are a fusion of traditional Kanak flavors and French influences. The on-site restaurant introduces guests to a gastronomic journey that mirrors the cultural diversity of New Caledonia. Fresh, locally sourced ingredients are transformed into dishes that tantalize the taste buds, creating a culinary symphony that complements the island's natural beauty.

Tieti Hotel's commitment to sustainability is evident in its eco-friendly initiatives. The hotel embraces responsible tourism practices, aiming to minimize its environmental impact and contribute to the preservation of Ouvéa's pristine ecosystems. From energy-efficient lighting to waste reduction strategies, Tieti Hotel aligns with the principles of sustainable travel, ensuring that guests can enjoy the beauty of Ouvéa without compromising its future.

As the day transitions into night, Tieti Hotel transforms into a haven of tranquility. Guests can unwind in the hotel's communal spaces, sharing stories of their Ouvéan adventures or simply enjoying the serenity of the surroundings. The night sky over Ouvéa, free from light pollution, unveils a celestial spectacle that adds a touch of magic to the evenings at Tieti Hotel.

Tieti Hotel's connection to the local community goes beyond providing employment opportunities. The hotel actively engages with nearby villages, supporting cultural initiatives and fostering a sense of pride in Ouvéa's heritage. Guests are encouraged to participate in cultural activities, from traditional dance performances to handicraft workshops, creating meaningful interactions that transcend the boundaries of tourism.

Practical considerations for guests at Tieti Hotel include convenient access to transportation options on Ouvéa. The hotel can arrange airport transfers and provide information on rental cars or bicycles for independent exploration. The staff at Tieti Hotel serves as knowledgeable guides, offering insights into the best attractions, hidden gems, and cultural experiences that Ouvéa has to offer.

In conclusion, Tieti Hotel stands as a testament to the essence of Ouvéa – a place where natural beauty, cultural heritage, and warm hospitality converge. Whether you seek adventure, relaxation, or a cultural immersion, Tieti Hotel is a gateway to the authentic Ouvéan experience. As you savor the moments of your stay at this tranquil haven, you become part of the narrative of Ouvéa, where every wave that kisses the shore whispers tales of a paradise discovered.

L'Oasis de Kiamu: A Tranquil Haven on the Shores of Ouvéa

Nestled in the heart of Ouvéa, the pristine jewel of New Caledonia, L'Oasis de Kiamu stands as a testament to the island's tranquility and natural beauty. This boutique hotel, situated near the charming Kiamu Village, offers a retreat from the ordinary, inviting travelers into a world where lush tropical gardens meet the azure waters of the Pacific. As we embark on a journey to explore L'Oasis de Kiamu, let us unravel the layers of this enchanting haven and discover why it has become a sought-after destination for those seeking an intimate connection with Ouvéa's serene landscape.

At the heart of L'Oasis de Kiamu lies a harmonious blend of nature and thoughtful architecture. The hotel's design is a celebration of Ouvéa's indigenous roots, with traditional Kanak influences seamlessly woven into the fabric of its aesthetic. Bungalows, adorned with thatched roofs and surrounded by vibrant flora, create an ambiance that is both inviting and authentic.

The choice of materials and construction reflects a commitment to sustainability, a theme that resonates with the island's eco-conscious ethos. As guests step into this oasis, they are greeted not only by the warm hospitality of the staff but also by the gentle whispers of the surrounding nature—the rustling leaves, the melody of tropical birds, and the distant murmur of the waves.

L'Oasis de Kiamu embraces the concept of exclusive seclusion, offering a limited number of private bungalows that dot the landscape like hidden gems. Each bungalow is a cocoon of comfort, designed to provide a sanctuary for guests to unwind and immerse themselves in the tranquil surroundings.

The interiors are a reflection of modern elegance infused with island charm. Clean lines and neutral tones create a soothing atmosphere, allowing the natural beauty outside to take center stage. Large windows and private terraces open up vistas of the lush gardens, inviting the outdoors in and blurring the lines between the interior and the exterior.

The bungalows are equipped with modern amenities, ensuring that guests enjoy a seamless blend of luxury and convenience. Air-conditioning provides respite from the tropical warmth, while Wi-Fi connectivity allows travelers to stay connected with the outside world, should they choose to do so.

What sets L'Oasis de Kiamu apart is its unwavering commitment to providing a personalized and immersive experience. From the moment guests arrive, they are welcomed not merely as visitors but as honored guests in a private residence. The attentive staff, with their genuine

warmth, go above and beyond to ensure that every aspect of a guest's stay is tailored to their preferences.

For those seeking exploration, the hotel offers curated experiences that showcase the best of Ouvéa. Guided nature walks through the island's verdant landscapes, snorkeling adventures in the coral-rich waters, and intimate beachside dinners under the starlit sky are just a few examples of the bespoke experiences awaiting guests.

No journey is complete without a culinary adventure, and L'Oasis de Kiamu excels in delivering a gastronomic experience that mirrors the diversity of Ouvéa itself. The on-site restaurant introduces guests to the rich tapestry of Kanak cuisine, where traditional flavors are artfully combined with modern culinary techniques.

Fresh, locally sourced ingredients form the backbone of the menu, ensuring that each dish is a celebration of Ouvéa's bountiful offerings. From grilled seafood that pays homage to the island's coastal abundance to vibrant tropical fruits that add a sweet note to desserts, every meal becomes a sensorial journey through the flavors of the South Pacific.

As travelers become increasingly conscious of their environmental footprint, L'Oasis de Kiamu takes pride in its commitment to sustainable practices. The hotel actively engages with the local community, sourcing produce and materials locally to support the island's economy. Efforts to minimize waste and energy consumption are seamlessly integrated into the daily operations, aligning with Ouvéa's dedication to preserving its natural treasures.

Understanding the practical aspects of planning a stay at L'Oasis de Kiamu enhances the overall experience. Ouvéa's climate, characterized by warm temperatures and occasional rainfall, necessitates packing lightweight clothing and adequate sun protection. Travelers are encouraged to book their stay well in advance, especially during peak seasons when the demand for this intimate retreat is high.

Transportation on the island is typically facilitated by rental cars or hotel-provided shuttles, allowing guests the freedom to explore Ouvéa at their own pace. Whether it's a leisurely drive to discover hidden beaches or a visit to the nearby Kiamu Village, the hotel's staff is always ready to assist in crafting memorable excursions.

In the heart of Ouvéa, L'Oasis de Kiamu stands not just as a hotel but as a gateway to the essence of the island. Here, amid the rustling palms and the gentle lull of the ocean, guests find not only a retreat but an immersion into the soul of Ouvéa. From the personalized service to the sustainable ethos, every facet of L'Oasis de Kiamu is a testament to the commitment to preserving the beauty and spirit of this island paradise. As travelers seek moments of serenity and connection, L'Oasis de Kiamu remains an idyllic haven—a tranquil oasis on the shores of Ouvéa, where time slows down, and nature's melody takes center stage.

CHAPTER 3: ACTIVITIES

Water Sports

New Caledonia, a jewel in the heart of the Pacific, offers a playground for water enthusiasts that is as diverse as it is breathtaking. The azure waters surrounding this archipelago are not just a visual feast; they beckon adventure-seekers from around the globe. From vibrant coral reefs to hidden lagoons, New Caledonia's aquatic wonders are a testament to the richness of its marine ecosystem.

The vast expanse of the Pacific Ocean that cradles New Caledonia provides the perfect canvas for an array of water sports. Snorkeling is an obvious starting point, with crystal-clear waters allowing a glimpse into the mesmerizing underwater world. The intricate coral formations harbor an astonishing variety of marine life, making every snorkeling expedition an exploration of vibrant colors and exotic species.

For those seeking a more immersive experience, scuba diving is an unparalleled adventure. The Great South Lagoon, a UNESCO World Heritage site, is a haven for divers. Beneath the surface, intricate coral gardens teem with life, and the shadows of passing schools of fish create an otherworldly ballet. Diving in New Caledonia is not merely a sport; it's a rendezvous with the sublime.

The archipelago's waters are also a canvas for windsurfers and kiteboarders. The trade winds that sweep across the Pacific create ideal conditions for these exhilarating activities. The lagoons of Nouméa, in particular, have become a magnet for those who revel in the marriage of wind and waves. Beginners and experts alike can be seen mastering the art of harnessing the elements for an adrenaline-fueled ride.

Kayaking and paddleboarding offer a more serene communion with the sea. Whether gliding along the mangrove-lined shores or paddling through the tranquil waters of Isle of Pines, these activities allow for a more contemplative exploration of New Caledonia's aquatic wonders. The sheer variety of landscapes, from sheltered bays to open seas, ensures that kayakers and paddleboarders can tailor their experiences to match their preferences.

Deep-sea fishing enthusiasts will find their paradise in the waters surrounding New Caledonia. The Pacific Ocean here is teeming with prized catches such as tuna and marlin. Local charters cater to both novice anglers and seasoned professionals, providing an opportunity to engage in the age-old pursuit of reeling in the big one while surrounded by the stunning vistas of the Pacific.

Surfing aficionados are not left wanting either. The outer reefs of New Caledonia, exposed to the full force of the Pacific swells, offer challenging breaks that attract surfers from around the world. The waves here are a force of nature, providing an adrenaline rush that only the most dedicated surfers can truly appreciate.

New Caledonia's water sports scene is not confined to the open sea. The numerous rivers and waterways that meander through the islands beckon kayakers and rafters. The untamed beauty of these inland watercourses is a stark contrast to the tranquil lagoons, presenting a different but equally enchanting facet of the archipelago.

In conclusion, New Caledonia is a water sports haven that transcends the conventional. It is not merely about riding waves or exploring coral reefs; it is a holistic immersion in the elemental beauty of the Pacific. Whether you seek the thrill of windsurfing, the meditative joy of kayaking, or the awe-inspiring depths of scuba diving, New Caledonia invites you to plunge into an aquatic adventure that will leave an indelible mark on your soul. The archipelago's waters are not just a playground; they are a sanctuary where nature reveals its most sublime secrets to those willing to explore its depths.

Hiking and Nature Trails

New Caledonia, a pristine archipelago nestled in the heart of the Pacific, is a haven for nature enthusiasts and hiking aficionados. Its diverse landscapes, ranging from lush forests to coastal trails, offer a plethora of options for those seeking an immersive experience in the great outdoors.

The hiking trails in New Caledonia cater to all levels of expertise, providing opportunities for both novice trekkers and seasoned hikers to explore the breathtaking beauty of this unique destination. One notable trail is the GR NC1, a long-distance path that spans the main island, Grande Terre. This trail takes adventurers through a tapestry of landscapes, from dense jungles to mountainous terrains, offering a comprehensive journey into the heart of the island's natural wonders.

For those who prefer coastal scenery, the Cap N'Dua Nature Trail is a captivating option. Located on the Isle of Pines, this trail winds through pristine beaches and dense vegetation, providing hikers with panoramic views of turquoise waters and limestone formations. The diverse

ecosystems along this trail showcase the rich biodiversity of New Caledonia, with unique plant and animal species waiting to be discovered.

Venturing into the heart of the islands, the Dumbea River Trails offer a refreshing escape into the wilderness. The network of trails follows the meandering Dumbea River, passing through dense forests and leading to cascading waterfalls. Hikers can revel in the serenity of nature, surrounded by the melodious sounds of birdlife and the soothing rush of water.

The hiking experience in New Caledonia goes beyond the terrestrial realm. The Blue River Provincial Park boasts trails that traverse landscapes adorned with unique flora, including the iconic Kaori trees. As hikers delve deeper into the park, they may encounter the ethereal Blue River, a natural pool with crystal-clear azure waters, inviting a refreshing dip amidst the natural splendor.

In the Northern Province, the Hienghene – Pouebo trail beckons with its dramatic landscapes, showcasing the colossal limestone cliffs of Lindéralique and the enchanting beauty of the Tao Waterfalls. This trail combines challenging ascents with rewarding vistas, providing hikers with a sense of accomplishment as they conquer the diverse terrains.

The commitment to conservation is evident in New Caledonia's nature trails. Efforts to preserve the unique flora and fauna have led to the establishment of protected areas and the implementation of sustainable tourism practices. Hikers are encouraged to embrace the principles of responsible trekking, ensuring minimal impact on the delicate ecosystems that make these trails so enchanting.

As the sun sets over the horizon, casting a warm glow on the landscapes, hikers in New Caledonia are treated to a spectacle of colors. The diverse trails, each with its own character and charm, create lasting memories for those who embark on this adventure. Whether it's the challenging mountainous paths or the serene coastal walks, the hiking and nature trails of New Caledonia promise an immersive journey into the heart of one of the Pacific's most remarkable destinations.

Cultural Experiences

New Caledonia, nestled in the heart of the South Pacific, is not just a tropical paradise known for its pristine beaches and azure waters but is also a rich tapestry of diverse cultures. The cultural experiences in this unique archipelago offer a fascinating blend of indigenous Kanak traditions, French influences, and a cosmopolitan lifestyle. As you embark on a journey through

New Caledonia, be prepared to immerse yourself in a world where ancient customs coexist harmoniously with contemporary influences.

The Kanak people, the original inhabitants of New Caledonia, have a deep connection to the land. Their cultural experiences are rooted in a profound respect for nature and a spiritual bond with the environment. Traditional Kanak huts, known as "case," dot the landscape, serving as a testament to a way of life that has endured for centuries. Visiting these villages provides an opportunity to witness age-old rituals, storytelling, and the mesmerizing sound of traditional music echoing through the air.

One of the highlights of cultural exploration in New Caledonia is participating in a "custom ceremony," a significant aspect of Kanak culture. These ceremonies, often centered around important life events or community celebrations, involve intricate dances, chanting, and the exchange of symbolic gifts. Witnessing or taking part in a custom ceremony is a profound experience that offers a glimpse into the spiritual and social fabric of the Kanak society.

The French influence in New Caledonia is unmistakable, adding a layer of sophistication to the cultural milieu. Nouméa, the capital city, is a vibrant hub where French and Melanesian cultures seamlessly coalesce. Stroll through the city's charming neighborhoods, and you'll encounter French-inspired architecture, stylish boutiques, and an array of bistros offering delectable French cuisine.

Cultural fusion is particularly evident in the gastronomic scene. The markets in Nouméa are a sensory delight, where the aroma of freshly baked baguettes mingles with the fragrance of tropical fruits. Indulge in a culinary adventure by sampling "bougna," a traditional Kanak dish made with chicken, root vegetables, and coconut milk, or savor the delicate flavors of French pastries in a local patisserie.

Art enthusiasts will find New Caledonia to be a treasure trove of creativity. The Tjibaou Cultural Centre, an architectural masterpiece set against a lush backdrop, is dedicated to preserving and showcasing Kanak art and heritage. The center's galleries feature a diverse collection of sculptures, paintings, and installations that provide insight into the Kanak people's artistic expression.

For a more hands-on experience, consider participating in a local art workshop. Learn traditional weaving techniques, create your own Tapa cloth, or try your hand at sculpting under the guidance of skilled artisans. These immersive activities not only allow you to express your creativity but also foster a deeper appreciation for the craftsmanship integral to Kanak culture.

Music and dance play a central role in Kanak ceremonies and festivities. The sounds of traditional instruments, such as the slit drum and conch shell, resonate in the air during cultural events. Attending a live performance, whether a mesmerizing dance accompanied by rhythmic drumming or a melodic serenade, offers a chance to feel the heartbeat of Kanak culture.

As you venture beyond the urban landscapes, the Loyalty Islands beckon with their untouched beauty and authentic cultural experiences. Lifou, Mare, and Ouvéa each have their distinct traditions and ceremonies. Take a guided tour to discover sacred sites, ancient petroglyphs, and the intricate craftsmanship of local artisans.

In conclusion, the cultural experiences in New Caledonia are a captivating journey through time and tradition. Whether you find yourself in the bustling streets of Nouméa, attending a custom ceremony in a remote village, or exploring the artistic expressions at the Tjibaou Cultural Centre, you'll encounter a harmonious blend of indigenous heritage and French sophistication. New Caledonia's cultural tapestry is a living testament to the resilience of traditions in the face of modernity, inviting travelers to embark on a voyage of discovery and appreciation for the diverse cultures that call this Pacific paradise home.

Wildlife Encounters

New Caledonia, nestled in the heart of the Pacific Ocean, is not just a haven for sun-seekers; it's also a treasure trove for wildlife enthusiasts. The archipelago's unique biodiversity, influenced by its isolation and varied ecosystems, offers a remarkable array of wildlife encounters that captivate the hearts of all who venture here.

The coral reefs surrounding New Caledonia are a testament to nature's artistry. Beneath the crystal-clear waters, a kaleidoscope of marine life awaits. Snorkeling or diving in the world's second-largest barrier reef provides a front-row seat to an underwater ballet. Vibrant corals, home to an incredible diversity of fish, beckon explorers into a realm where parrotfish, clownfish, and rays glide gracefully through an aquatic wonderland. Lucky visitors might even spot a sea turtle majestically cruising through the cerulean depths.

Beyond the reefs, New Caledonia's islands are home to unique avian species, some found nowhere else on Earth. The Kagu, with its elegant, gray plumage and distinctive long legs, is a bird watcher's delight. Endemic to the archipelago, this flightless creature is a symbol of conservation efforts in the region. Exploring the dense forests and remote islets offers the chance to witness these rare birds in their natural habitat, a privilege for those fortunate enough to glimpse their elusive beauty.

Venturing into the mangroves reveals another facet of New Caledonia's wildlife. These coastal ecosystems, teeming with life, are crucial for numerous species. Saltwater crocodiles, though not as commonly encountered as in some neighboring regions, are part of the diverse cast that inhabits these brackish waters. Mangrove crabs scuttle along the muddy banks, while herons and egrets soar overhead, creating a dynamic tableau of life in equilibrium.

The terrestrial wonders of New Caledonia extend to its lush rainforests, where endemic insects, reptiles, and mammals thrive. The phasmids, or stick insects, are masters of camouflage, blending seamlessly with the foliage. As night falls, the forests come alive with the chirps and calls of endemic frogs and insects, creating a symphony of sound unique to this secluded paradise.

For those with a passion for marine mammals, New Caledonia doesn't disappoint. Cetaceans, including humpback whales and dolphins, grace the surrounding waters. From July to September, humpback whales migrate through the region, offering awe-inspiring displays of breaching and tail-slapping. Dolphins, playful and acrobatic, often accompany boats, delighting onlookers with their graceful antics.

On the Isle of Pines, a sanctuary for biodiversity, the rare and endemic Ouvéa Parakeet flits through the trees. With its vibrant green plumage and distinctive red markings, this small parrot is a symbol of the delicate balance that conservationists work tirelessly to maintain. Exploring the island's trails and forests offers a glimpse into the efforts to preserve these unique species and their habitats.

In conclusion, New Caledonia is a sanctuary for wildlife enthusiasts, a place where terrestrial and marine ecosystems harmonize to create a living tapestry of biodiversity. From the vibrant coral reefs to the dense rainforests, every corner of this archipelago tells a story of resilience and adaptation. Through responsible tourism and conservation efforts, New Caledonia strives to ensure that future generations can continue to marvel at the wonders of its wildlife, a testament to the delicate dance between humanity and the natural world.

CHAPTER 4: CUISINE

Traditional Kanak Dishes: A Culinary Journey through New Caledonia's Rich Culture

New Caledonia, nestled in the heart of the Pacific, is not only a tropical paradise of pristine beaches and lush landscapes but also a haven for gastronomes seeking a taste of unique cultural blends. One of the culinary treasures of this archipelago is the traditional Kanak cuisine, a vibrant reflection of the indigenous Kanak people's heritage and connection to the land. In this culinary journey, we explore the flavors, techniques, and stories behind some of the most beloved traditional Kanak dishes.

1. **Bougna:**

At the core of Kanak gastronomy lies the Bougna, a traditional Melanesian feast that embodies the communal spirit of the Kanak people. This dish is a harmonious blend of yams, sweet potatoes, taros, and cassava, accompanied by a choice of meat – often fish, chicken, or pork. The ingredients are carefully layered on banana leaves, seasoned with coconut milk, and then wrapped into a tight package before being slow-cooked in an earth oven. Bougna not only tantalizes the taste buds but also serves as a symbol of unity and togetherness.

2. **Patate Douce Farcie:**

Patate Douce Farcie, or stuffed sweet potatoes, is a delightful dish that showcases the Kanak people's resourcefulness in utilizing local ingredients. Sweet potatoes are hollowed out and filled with a savory mixture of grated coconut, fresh herbs, and sometimes minced meat. The result is a mouthwatering combination of sweetness from the potatoes and a savory burst of flavors from the stuffing. This dish not only satisfies hunger but also pays homage to the bounty of the land.

3. **Boulette de Poisson:**

Boulette de Poisson, or fish balls, is a beloved Kanak appetizer that reflects the archipelago's deep connection to the sea. Freshly caught fish is finely minced, mixed with aromatic herbs, and shaped into small balls. These are then either fried to golden perfection or gently poached. Served with dipping sauces made from local ingredients, Boulette de Poisson is a delectable testament to the Kanak people's mastery of seafood and their appreciation for simple, yet flavorful, culinary creations.

4. **Igname au Coco:**

Igname au Coco, or yams in coconut milk, is a dish that beautifully combines two staples of Kanak cuisine. Yams, a traditional root vegetable, are cooked in a rich coconut milk broth, creating a dish that is both hearty and comforting. The subtle sweetness of yams is complemented by the creamy texture of coconut milk, making Igname au Coco a dish that resonates with the essence of Kanak culinary traditions.

5. **Civet de Rousette:**

For those with adventurous palates, Civet de Rousette, or bat stew, offers a unique and culturally significant experience. While not for everyone, this dish has been passed down through generations and is considered a delicacy by the Kanak people. The bat meat is marinated in a blend of local spices, slow-cooked until tender, and served with root vegetables. This dish not only reflects the resourcefulness of Kanak hunters but also honors the cultural significance of certain fauna in their cuisine.

In every bite of a traditional Kanak dish, one can taste the flavors of centuries-old traditions and the richness of a culture deeply connected to the land and the sea. From the communal gathering around a Bougna to the intricate flavors of Patate Douce Farcie, Kanak cuisine is a celebration of diversity and heritage. As travelers immerse themselves in the culinary delights of New Caledonia, they embark on a sensory journey that goes beyond taste, offering a glimpse into the soul of a people and the spirit of their islands.

Bougna: A Culinary Tapestry Weaving Tradition and Flavor in New Caledonia

Nestled in the heart of the Pacific, the archipelago of New Caledonia is not just a tropical paradise but also a treasure trove of unique cultural experiences. Among the many facets that showcase the indigenous Kanak people's heritage is Bougna – a traditional Melanesian feast that goes beyond being a culinary delight; it is a celebration of community, connection, and the rich bounty of the land.

Bougna, at its core, is a communal dish deeply embedded in the Kanak way of life. Its roots trace back to ancient traditions where the preparation and sharing of food were symbolic acts of unity and shared identity. The word "Bougna" itself carries a resonance of togetherness, and the dish is often prepared during special occasions, ceremonies, or simply as a means of bringing people together.

Central to the Bougna experience are the locally sourced ingredients, a testament to the Kanak people's sustainable and harmonious relationship with their environment. The dish typically includes a medley of root vegetables such as yams, sweet potatoes, taros, and cassava. These are complemented by protein sources like fish, chicken, or pork.

The preparation of Bougna is a meticulous and collaborative process. First, a bed of banana leaves is laid out, creating a natural and aromatic wrapping. The ingredients are then layered on these leaves, each component contributing to the overall flavor profile. Coconut milk, a staple in Kanak cuisine, adds a rich and creamy texture, infusing the dish with a distinctly Pacific taste.

Once the ingredients are arranged, the banana leaves are carefully folded to create a tightly sealed package. This packet is then placed in an earth oven, a traditional method of cooking in New Caledonia. The slow, gentle heat allows the flavors to meld, creating a harmonious union of tastes that is characteristic of Bougna.

Beyond its gastronomic appeal, Bougna carries deep cultural symbolism. The act of preparing and sharing Bougna is a ritual that signifies the interconnectedness of the community. It's a gesture of hospitality and an expression of collective identity. The communal aspect extends to the actual cooking process, often involving multiple generations and community members.

The earth oven, in which Bougna is cooked, represents a direct link to the land. The slow cooking process not only tenderizes the ingredients but also imparts a smoky, earthy flavor that is unique to this traditional method. As the aroma of Bougna wafts through the air, it serves as a call to gather, reinforcing the sense of belonging and shared experience.

While the core elements of Bougna remain consistent, there are regional variations that reflect the diverse landscapes and resources found across the archipelago. Coastal communities might include an abundance of seafood, infusing a briny essence to the dish. Inland regions, on the other hand, may showcase more root vegetables and freshwater fish. These variations highlight the adaptability of Bougna to local resources, making it a truly dynamic and representative dish of New Caledonian cuisine.

In modern New Caledonia, Bougna has not only retained its cultural significance but has also found its way into mainstream culinary experiences. Restaurants and resorts, recognizing the appeal of this traditional dish, often feature Bougna on their menus, offering both locals and visitors a taste of Kanak heritage.

Moreover, the preparation of Bougna has become a popular activity for tourists seeking an authentic cultural immersion. Many tour operators offer experiences where participants can join locals in the entire process – from selecting fresh produce to wrapping the ingredients in banana leaves and savoring the final product. This hands-on approach fosters a deeper understanding of the cultural importance of Bougna and creates lasting memories for those partaking in the experience.

Bougna stands as a culinary masterpiece, a sensory journey through the history, culture, and flavors of the Kanak people. Beyond its delicious taste, Bougna encapsulates the essence of community, tradition, and the sustainable relationship that the Kanak have maintained with their environment for centuries.

In savoring Bougna, one partakes in a ritual that transcends the boundaries of a meal; it is an invitation to connect with the soul of New Caledonia. As the aroma of this communal feast permeates the air, it carries with it the stories of generations, the richness of the land, and the warmth of a people who have embraced their heritage in every bite.

Patate Douce Farcie: A Culinary Odyssey in New Caledonia

In the heart of the South Pacific lies a tropical paradise known for its azure waters, lush landscapes, and a culinary heritage as rich and diverse as the culture itself. New Caledonia, an archipelago teeming with biodiversity, is home to a unique gastronomic experience, with traditional Kanak dishes taking center stage. Among these culinary treasures, Patate Douce Farcie emerges as a delightful exploration of flavors, techniques, and cultural significance.

Patate Douce Farcie, translated as stuffed sweet potatoes, is a testament to the Kanak people's resourcefulness and deep connection to the land. The dish is a harmonious blend of simplicity and sophistication, combining locally sourced sweet potatoes with a savory stuffing that reflects the bounty of the archipelago.

At its core, Patate Douce Farcie is a celebration of ingredients that are not just chosen for their taste but also for their cultural significance. The sweet potatoes, a staple in Kanak cuisine, are not only a source of sustenance but also a symbol of the earth's generosity. The process of preparing Patate Douce Farcie is a culinary ritual that connects the present to the past, embodying the essence of Kanak traditions.

The dish begins with the selection of the sweet potatoes, a meticulous process where the cook considers factors like size, texture, and freshness. The sweet potatoes are then carefully washed, peeled, and hollowed out to create a vessel for the forthcoming medley of flavors. This initial step already sets the stage for what promises to be a gastronomic journey, each potato holding the promise of a unique culinary experience.

The stuffing, a crucial element in Patate Douce Farcie, is where the chef's creativity and regional influences come to the fore. Grated coconut, a staple in Kanak cuisine, adds a delicate sweetness and a satisfying texture to the stuffing. Fresh herbs, often sourced locally, contribute a burst of aromatic complexity, transforming the dish from a simple preparation to a nuanced culinary masterpiece.

The stuffing may also include minced meat, typically poultry or seafood, elevating Patate Douce Farcie to a more substantial and protein-rich offering. The choice of meat reflects the availability of local resources and the Kanak people's dependence on the surrounding seas for sustenance. The meticulous combination of these ingredients results in a stuffing that is not just a complement to the sweet potatoes but a harmonious fusion of flavors.

Once the sweet potatoes are hollowed and the stuffing is prepared, the two components come together in a culinary dance that involves precision and care. The sweet potatoes are generously filled with the stuffing, ensuring that each bite offers a balanced amalgamation of the sweet, savory, and herbal notes.

The cooking process varies, with some opting for traditional methods such as baking in an earth oven, while others embrace modern techniques like roasting or steaming. Regardless of the method, the objective is to achieve a perfect marriage of flavors, where the sweet potatoes absorb the essence of the stuffing, creating a cohesive and mouthwatering dish.

As Patate Douce Farcie cooks, the aroma wafting through the air is an invitation to partake in a cultural experience. The dish is not merely a combination of ingredients but a narrative of Kanak history, a story told through the artistry of food. The communal aspect of preparing and sharing

Patate Douce Farcie is ingrained in Kanak culture, reinforcing the idea that meals are not just a means of sustenance but a binding force that brings communities together.

The presentation of Patate Douce Farcie is an art form in itself. The vibrant colors of the sweet potatoes and the contrasting hues of the stuffing create a visually stunning dish that is as pleasing to the eyes as it is to the palate. The communal aspect of sharing this dish is enhanced by its visual appeal, turning every serving into a moment of shared joy and appreciation.

The first bite into Patate Douce Farcie is a revelation. The sweetness of the potatoes mingles with the savory richness of the stuffing, creating a symphony of flavors that dances on the taste buds. The texture is a play of contrasts, with the softness of the sweet potatoes juxtaposed against the slightly chewy coconut and the succulent bits of meat. It's a dish that engages all the senses, from the enticing aroma to the satisfying crunch and the explosion of flavors in every mouthful.

Beyond its gastronomic appeal, Patate Douce Farcie holds cultural significance in Kanak traditions. It is not just a dish; it is a representation of the symbiotic relationship between the Kanak people and the land that sustains them. The reliance on locally sourced ingredients reflects a commitment to sustainability and a deep understanding of the ecosystems that shape Kanak life.

In conclusion, Patate Douce Farcie is more than a culinary delight; it is a cultural journey that unfolds with every preparation and every shared meal. It encapsulates the essence of Kanak cuisine, where simplicity meets sophistication, and tradition converges with innovation. As travelers explore the vibrant landscapes of New Caledonia, a taste of Patate Douce Farcie offers not just a gastronomic experience but a profound connection to the cultural tapestry of this Pacific paradise.

Boulette de Poisson: A Culinary Symphony of Kanak Delight

In the culinary tapestry of New Caledonia, Boulette de Poisson stands as a testament to the archipelago's profound connection to the sea. This beloved dish, translated as fish balls, is not merely a culinary creation but a cultural ode to the bounties of the Pacific Ocean and the artistry of Kanak cooking.

The preparation of Boulette de Poisson is a delicate dance of flavors, starting with the main protagonist – fresh fish. The Kanak people, with their intimate knowledge of local waters, have

mastered the art of fishing, selecting the finest catches for their culinary creations. The fish, often a white-fleshed variety, is meticulously cleaned and minced, setting the stage for a harmonious blend of textures.

The next act in this culinary symphony involves the incorporation of aromatic herbs. Fresh cilantro, parsley, and sometimes chives join the ensemble, adding layers of fragrance and complexity to the mixture. These herbs not only contribute to the flavor profile but also reflect the lushness of the New Caledonian landscape.

As with many traditional Kanak dishes, coconut plays a pivotal role in Boulette de Poisson. Grated coconut, a staple in Pacific cuisine, is added to the fish and herb medley. The coconut's natural sweetness and creaminess bind the ingredients together, creating a cohesive mixture that will later transform into delectable fish balls.

Local spices, ground to perfection, make a cameo appearance, infusing the Boulette de Poisson with a hint of heat and depth. The precise combination of spices varies among households, each chef imparting a personal touch to the recipe, ensuring a unique and memorable dining experience.

With the ingredients in harmony, the next step is the meticulous shaping of the fish mixture into small, round balls. This step requires skill and finesse, as the chefs strive to achieve uniformity in size to ensure even cooking. The shaping of the boulettes is not just a culinary technique but a cultural practice passed down through generations, a craft that embodies the essence of Kanak gastronomy.

The cooking method for Boulette de Poisson is a matter of preference, with variations found across different regions of New Caledonia. Some opt for the simplicity of pan-frying, creating boulettes with a crisp outer layer that gives way to a moist, flavorful interior. Others prefer the gentle poaching method, allowing the fish balls to absorb the flavors of a broth, transforming them into succulent morsels of delight.

Accompanying sauces add the final crescendo to this culinary masterpiece. Dipping sauces made from locally sourced ingredients, such as lime, chili, and perhaps a touch of soy, elevate the Boulette de Poisson experience. The sauces are not just condiments but complementary notes that enhance the overall symphony of flavors.

In the homes of the Kanak people, Boulette de Poisson often graces the table during festive occasions, family gatherings, and celebrations of cultural significance. Its presence is more than just a dish; it is a symbol of shared moments, of togetherness around a table laden with the culinary treasures of the Pacific.

Beyond the sensory delight, Boulette de Poisson carries with it stories of tradition and cultural pride. It is a dish that speaks of a people intimately connected to the ocean, acknowledging its

role not just as a provider of sustenance but as a source of cultural identity. The act of crafting Boulette de Poisson becomes a ritual, a way of preserving and passing on the culinary heritage of the Kanak people to future generations.

As travelers explore the enchanting landscapes of New Caledonia, a taste of Boulette de Poisson becomes a journey into the heart of Kanak culture. It is an invitation to savor the flavors of the Pacific, to appreciate the skill and love infused into every fish ball, and to connect with a people whose culinary traditions are as rich and diverse as the waters that surround their islands. In Boulette de Poisson, one discovers not just a dish but a story – a story of the sea, of community, and of the enduring spirit of Kanak cuisine.

Igname au Coco: Unveiling the Essence of Kanak Culinary Artistry

Nestled in the heart of the Pacific Ocean, New Caledonia stands as a testament to the amalgamation of diverse cultures and the richness of indigenous traditions. Among the culinary treasures that echo the vibrant history and connection to the land is Igname au Coco, a dish that encapsulates the essence of Kanak gastronomy. In the intricate dance of flavors and textures, one finds a reflection of the Kanak people's deep-rooted relationship with nature and their commitment to preserving culinary heritage.

At its core, Igname au Coco is a celebration of two staples in Kanak cuisine: yams and coconut. These ingredients, sourced locally from the fertile lands of the archipelago, are transformed into a dish that not only satiates hunger but also serves as a sensory journey through the history and culture of the Kanak people.

In the culinary lexicon of New Caledonia, yams hold a revered position. These tuberous roots, with their earthy flavors and starchy textures, have been a dietary mainstay for generations. As the Kanak people worked in harmony with the fertile soils, cultivating yams became more than just sustenance; it became a symbol of resilience and connection to the land. Each yam, dug from the ground with care, carries with it the story of seasons, the cycle of life, and the interdependence between the people and their environment.

The second protagonist In this culinary symphony is coconut, a versatile and abundant resource in the Pacific. The Kanak people, masterful in utilizing the gifts of their tropical surroundings, ingeniously incorporated coconut into their cuisine. The creamy, mildly sweet taste of coconut milk adds a luscious depth to many traditional dishes, and in the case of Igname au Coco, it transforms a simple yam into a culinary masterpiece.

The preparation of Igname au Coco is a meticulous process that reflects the Kanak commitment to culinary excellence. Yams, carefully selected for their freshness and quality, are peeled and sliced into bite-sized pieces. The coconut milk, extracted from freshly grated coconut, is the elixir that binds the dish together. The marriage of yams and coconut milk in a simmering pot creates a fragrant broth that infuses the yams with a rich and creamy essence.

As the pot simmers, the kitchen is filled with the aromatic embrace of yams mingling with coconut. The slow cooking process allows the flavors to intermingle, creating a dish that is not just a convergence of ingredients but a fusion of cultural elements. In this culinary alchemy, the yams absorb the coconut milk, resulting in a texture that is both tender and infused with the essence of the tropics.

Igname au Coco is not merely a dish; it is a sensory experience that transcends taste. The act of preparing and sharing this dish is a ritual, a communal endeavor that brings people together around the hearth. As the aroma wafts through the air, it beckons family and friends to gather, to share stories, and to celebrate the richness of life.

In the heart of Kanak communities, Igname au Coco is often prepared during special occasions and cultural festivities. It becomes a centerpiece, symbolizing abundance, hospitality, and the continuity of traditions. The dish, with its unassuming simplicity, carries the weight of cultural heritage, connecting the present generation to the wisdom of their ancestors.

Beyond its cultural significance, Igname au Coco is a testament to the sustainable and locally sourced nature of Kanak cuisine. In a world increasingly concerned with the environmental impact of food production, the traditional practices of the Kanak people offer a model of harmony with nature. The reliance on locally grown yams and coconut not only reduces the carbon footprint but also fosters a sense of ecological responsibility that is inherent in Kanak culture.

As one savors a spoonful of Igname au Coco, the flavors transport the palate to the sun-kissed shores of New Caledonia. The dish is a passport to the landscapes where yams thrive in the fertile soil and where coconut palms sway in the gentle breeze. It is a journey through time, echoing the chants of Kanak elders and the laughter of children playing in the shadows of towering yam plants.

In conclusion, Igname au Coco is more than a dish on a plate; it is a cultural artifact, a culinary masterpiece, and a living testament to the resilience and creativity of the Kanak people. In each bite, one discovers the soul of New Caledonia – a place where the past and present converge, and where the land speaks through the flavors that dance on the taste buds. Igname au Coco is an invitation to partake in a timeless feast, where tradition, nature, and community come together to create a symphony of flavors that linger in the memory long after the last spoonful is enjoyed.

Civet de Rousette: A Culinary Exploration into New Caledonia's Unique Delicacy

Nestled in the heart of the Pacific, New Caledonia is a haven for culinary adventurers seeking to explore the unique and diverse flavors of its traditional dishes. Among these, one stands out as both a delicacy and a cultural symbol—the Civet de Rousette, or bat stew. As unconventional as it may sound to some, this dish holds a special place in the culinary heritage of the Kanak people, reflecting their resourcefulness, connection to nature, and the preservation of age-old traditions.

The Civet de Rousette Is not merely a dish; it is a culinary experience that unfolds layers of history, tradition, and gastronomic innovation. To understand its significance, one must delve into the cultural tapestry of New Caledonia and the role this unique stew plays in the daily lives and celebrations of the Kanak community.

In the remote villages and tribal communities scattered across New Caledonia, Civet de Rousette is more than just a meal—it's a link to the past, a practice that connects the Kanak people to their ancestors and the natural abundance of the islands. The roots of this dish can be traced back through generations, a testament to the resourcefulness of Kanak hunters who turned to the bounties of the forest for sustenance.

The star ingredient, rousette, refers to the fruit bat that inhabits the lush rainforests of New Caledonia. These bats are not only a source of sustenance but also hold cultural significance, playing a role in traditional ceremonies and rituals. While the consumption of bat meat might raise eyebrows in some cultures, in New Caledonia, it is a practice deeply embedded in the cultural fabric, and Civet de Rousette is a manifestation of this connection.

Preparing Civet de Rousette is a meticulous process that involves a blend of culinary artistry and cultural rituals. The bat meat is first marinated in a concoction of local herbs, spices, and perhaps a hint of the infamous Kanak hot pepper—a staple in their cuisine. This step is crucial not only for flavor enhancement but also for softening the somewhat tough texture of bat meat. The marination process, sometimes passed down through oral traditions, encapsulates the essence of Kanak culinary expertise.

Once marinated to perfection, the bat meat is slow-cooked, often in a communal setting. The communal aspect is intrinsic to the preparation of Civet de Rousette, mirroring the communal nature of other traditional Kanak dishes like Bougna. Families and communities gather around the simmering pot, sharing stories, laughter, and a deep sense of cultural pride as the stew takes form.

The aroma that emanates during the cooking process is a sensory journey in itself, a harmonious blend of earthy tones from the bat meat and the aromatic symphony of local herbs. The slow-cooking technique is not just about tenderizing the meat; it is about allowing the flavors to meld and evolve, creating a dish that is rich, nuanced, and distinctly Kanak.

The final presentation of Civet de Rousette is a moment of celebration. The bat stew is served alongside root vegetables, a staple in Kanak cuisine, and often accompanied by traditional side dishes like yams or sweet potatoes. The stew itself is a visual feast, with the bat meat glistening in a flavorful broth, inviting those at the table to partake in a culinary adventure that transcends the ordinary.

As diners take their first bite of Civet de Rousette, they embark on a journey through New Caledonia's cultural landscape. The taste is a unique amalgamation of flavors—earthy, slightly gamey, and deeply satisfying. The dish pays homage to the Kanak people's close relationship with nature, acknowledging the role of the rousette in their daily lives and emphasizing the sustainable practices that have sustained them for centuries.

Beyond its culinary appeal, Civet de Rousette carries a cultural weight that extends beyond the dinner table. The dish is often associated with traditional ceremonies and rites of passage, underscoring its significance in Kanak rituals. The bat, revered for its adaptability and symbolism in Kanak cosmology, becomes a bridge between the spiritual and the earthly realms when transformed into a hearty stew.

In contemporary times, the consumption of bat meat has sparked debates globally due to concerns about zoonotic diseases. However, in the context of New Caledonia, the practice is deeply rooted in cultural and ecological sustainability. The Kanak people have maintained a delicate balance with nature, respecting the ecosystem and the resources it provides. Civet de Rousette is a manifestation of this harmonious relationship—a dish that reflects not only culinary prowess but also a profound respect for the environment.

As travelers venture into New Caledonia, exploring its landscapes and cultural treasures, Civet de Rousette beckons as a culinary rite of passage. While the dish may challenge preconceived notions, it invites visitors to engage with the Kanak way of life, encouraging an open-minded exploration of the diverse and rich traditions that make this archipelago a culinary destination like no other.

In conclusion, Civet de Rousette is more than a dish; it is a gateway to understanding the Kanak people's deep-rooted connection to nature, their cultural practices, and their commitment to sustainable living. As the bat stew finds its way onto the plates of those willing to embrace this unique culinary adventure, it serves as a reminder that the world's gastronomic tapestry is woven not only with familiar flavors but also with the extraordinary and the unexpected.

French-Influenced Cuisine in New Caledonia: A Gastronomic Delight

New Caledonia, nestled in the heart of the South Pacific, is not just a tropical paradise renowned for its turquoise waters and coral reefs. It is also a culinary haven where French sophistication meets Pacific flavors, creating a unique and delightful fusion of cuisines. In this exploration of French-influenced cuisine in New Caledonia, we dive into the rich tapestry of tastes, textures, and traditions that make the island's food culture a true gastronomic adventure.

1. **Historical Roots:**

To understand the culinary landscape of New Caledonia, we must delve into its history. Colonized by the French in the mid-19th century, the island carries a deep and lasting French influence. This influence extends beyond language and architecture to the very heart of New Caledonian culture—the kitchen. French culinary techniques, ingredients, and a love for fine dining have seamlessly blended with the island's own bounty.

2. The Art of French Cooking:

Wander through the streets of Nouméa, the capital city, and you'll encounter charming bistros and elegant patisseries reminiscent of those found in Paris. French cooking techniques, such as sous-vide and meticulous pastry craftsmanship, are proudly on display. Chefs in New Caledonia often undergo training in France, bringing back not just recipes but a commitment to the artistry of French cuisine.

3. Baguettes and Boulangeries:

The aroma of freshly baked baguettes wafts through the air in New Caledonia, a testament to the enduring French influence. Local boulangeries, or bakeries, offer an array of crusty baguettes, croissants, and pastries. It's a daily ritual for many residents to start their morning with a warm croissant and a cup of coffee, a tradition that mirrors the French café culture.

4. Seafood Extravaganza:

New Caledonia's location in the Pacific provides a bounty of seafood that seamlessly integrates with French culinary finesse. Bouillabaisse, a traditional Provençal fisherman's stew, finds a tropical twist with the inclusion of local seafood like prawns, lobster, and coral trout. The French emphasis on using fresh, quality ingredients aligns perfectly with the abundance of marine treasures surrounding the island.

5. Fusion Flavors:

What makes New Caledonian cuisine truly unique is the fusion of French techniques with local Pacific ingredients. Dishes like "Escargot à la Calédonienne," where snails are prepared with a coconut and lime twist, showcase this harmonious blending of culinary traditions. It's a celebration of diversity on the plate, reflecting the multicultural fabric of New Caledonian society.

6. Wines and Fromages:

No French-inspired meal is complete without the perfect wine and cheese pairing. In New Caledonia, you can savor French wines while overlooking the Pacific sunset. Local markets and specialty stores offer a selection of French cheeses, allowing residents and visitors alike to indulge in the time-honored tradition of ending a meal with a cheese platter and a glass of Bordeaux.

7. Nouvelle Cuisine in the Pacific:

The principles of Nouvelle Cuisine, a movement in French gastronomy that emphasizes lightness and freshness, find a natural home in the tropical setting of New Caledonia. Local fruits, vegetables, and herbs complement French culinary aesthetics, resulting in dishes that are as visually stunning as they are delicious.

8. Festive Feasts:

From Christmas to Bastille Day, New Caledonians celebrate their French connection through festive feasts. Tables are adorned with a mix of classic French holiday dishes and Pacific specialties. It's a time when communities come together to share not only meals but the joy of culinary traditions that bridge continents.

9. Challenges and Innovations:

While French cuisine has left an indelible mark, chefs in New Caledonia are also pushing boundaries, incorporating indigenous ingredients and experimenting with new flavors. This innovative spirit ensures that the culinary scene continues to evolve, offering surprises for both locals and visitors.

10. A Culinary Journey:

In conclusion, the French-influenced cuisine of New Caledonia is not just about food; it's a journey through history, a celebration of cultural diversity, and a testament to the island's ability to adapt and transform. From the bustling markets to the fine-dining establishments, every meal in New Caledonia is a reminder that the fusion of French and Pacific influences has created a culinary paradise unlike any other. Bon appétit!

Exploring Culinary Delights: A Guide to Popular Restaurants in New Caledonia

New Caledonia, with its unique blend of French and Melanesian influences, offers a culinary experience that is as diverse as its stunning landscapes. From charming seaside bistros to upscale restaurants, the archipelago boasts a vibrant food scene that caters to every palate. In this guide, we'll take you on a gastronomic journey through some of the most popular restaurants in New Caledonia.

1. **Le Roof**

Location: Nouméa

Cuisine: French, Seafood

Situated on Anse Vata Bay, Le Roof is a fine-dining restaurant known for its panoramic views of the Pacific Ocean. The menu is a celebration of French cuisine with a focus on fresh seafood. From lobster bisque to seared tuna, each dish is a masterpiece that combines local flavors with French culinary techniques. The elegant ambiance and attentive service make Le Roof a favorite among locals and visitors alike.

2. **Le Bilboquet**

Location: Nouméa

Cuisine: French, Pacific Rim

For those seeking a blend of French sophistication and Pacific influences, Le Bilboquet is a must-visit. This restaurant, tucked away in a colonial-style house, offers a menu that showcases the best of New Caledonian produce. Dishes like coconut crab and vanilla-infused desserts highlight the unique flavors of the region. The intimate setting makes it ideal for a romantic dinner or a special celebration.

3. **La Pirogue**

Location: Île des Pins

Cuisine: Melanesian, French

On the idyllic Isle of Pines, La Pirogue stands out as a culinary gem. The thatched-roof restaurant is known for its fusion of Melanesian and French flavors. Guests can savor dishes made with local ingredients, including the famed Isle of Pines yams. The oceanfront setting adds to the charm, creating a relaxed atmosphere for enjoying a leisurely meal.

4. **Chez Toto**

Location: Lifou

Cuisine: Kanak, Seafood

For an authentic taste of Kanak cuisine, Chez Toto on Lifou is a popular choice. This family-run eatery offers a warm welcome and traditional dishes prepared with love. Grilled fish, coconut crab, and taro-based delicacies dominate the menu. The rustic surroundings and friendly ambiance make Chez Toto a favorite among those looking for a genuine cultural experience.

5. **Le Faré du Palm Beach**

Location: Ouvéa

Cuisine: French, Seafood

Ouvéa's culinary scene is enriched by Le Faré du Palm Beach, a beachfront restaurant renowned for its French and seafood offerings. From escargot to locally sourced lobster, the menu is a

delightful fusion of classic French techniques and Pacific ingredients. The casual setting allows guests to enjoy exquisite meals while feeling the ocean breeze.

6. **L'Hippocampe**

Location: Nouméa

Cuisine: Mediterranean, Fusion

L'Hippocampe, located in the heart of Nouméa, is a Mediterranean-inspired restaurant that brings a touch of the exotic to New Caledonia. The chef's inventive creations, such as prawn ceviche with tropical fruits, showcase a harmonious blend of flavors. The stylish décor and lively atmosphere make it a popular spot for both locals and tourists.

7. **Le Rocher à la Voile**

Location: Bourail

Cuisine: French, Steakhouse

In the scenic town of Bourail, Le Rocher à la Voile is a steakhouse that has earned a reputation for its succulent meats and rustic charm. The menu features locally sourced beef cooked to perfection, accompanied by a selection of fine wines. The outdoor seating area, nestled among lush greenery, adds to the overall dining experience.

8. **Au P'tit Café**

Location: Nouméa

Cuisine: French, Café

For a more casual dining experience, Au P'tit Café in Nouméa offers a cozy setting where guests can enjoy French pastries, sandwiches, and artisanal coffee. The laid-back atmosphere and friendly service make it a favorite spot for breakfast or a leisurely afternoon break.

9. **La Table des Gourmets**

Location: Nouméa

Cuisine: French, Fusion

La Table des Gourmets is a culinary haven in Nouméa, where French gastronomy meets Pacific influences. The chef's tasting menu takes diners on a journey through exquisite flavors, with each course meticulously crafted. The elegant setting and attention to detail make this restaurant a top choice for those seeking a refined dining experience.

10. Kotémer

Location: Nouméa

Cuisine: Fusion, Pacific Rim

Situated on Lemon Bay, Kotémer is known for its fusion cuisine that combines Pacific Rim flavors with local ingredients. Diners can enjoy dishes like coconut and lime-infused fish while taking in the breathtaking views. The restaurant's commitment to sustainability adds an extra layer of appeal for environmentally conscious diners.

In conclusion, New Caledonia's culinary scene is a rich tapestry woven with French sophistication and Melanesian warmth. Whether you're savoring the catch of the day by the ocean or indulging in a gourmet feast in Nouméa, the diverse range of restaurants ensures that every palate is catered to in this tropical paradise.

Le Roof: A Culinary Masterpiece Overlooking the Pacific

New Caledonia, nestled in the heart of the South Pacific, is renowned for its stunning landscapes, rich cultural tapestry, and a culinary scene that seamlessly blends French sophistication with local flavors. Among the myriad dining establishments that grace this archipelago, Le Roof stands tall, both figuratively and literally. Perched on the shores of Anse Vata Bay in Nouméa, Le Roof is not merely a restaurant; it's an experience that transcends the boundaries of gastronomy, offering patrons a sensory journey that extends beyond the palate.

Situated on the edge of Anse Vata Bay, Le Roof boasts a prime location that allows diners to immerse themselves in the natural beauty of New Caledonia. As the name suggests, the restaurant features a spacious terrace with a gently sloping roof, offering uninterrupted views of

the Pacific Ocean. The sight of the sun dipping below the horizon, casting hues of orange and pink across the water, is a spectacle that transforms an evening at Le Roof into a poetic affair.

The architectural design of Le Roof Is a harmonious blend of modern elegance and island charm. The use of natural materials such as wood and stone, coupled with contemporary furnishings, creates an atmosphere that is simultaneously sophisticated and welcoming. Whether one chooses to dine indoors or on the terrace, the ambiance is characterized by a sense of refinement that complements the natural surroundings.

Le Roof is celebrated not only for its panoramic views but also for its exceptional culinary offerings. The menu, curated by a team of skilled chefs, is a testament to the restaurant's commitment to excellence. The cuisine at Le Roof is predominantly French with a focus on fresh seafood, reflecting the bountiful resources of the Pacific.

To commence this culinary journey, diners might indulge in the delicate flavors of a lobster bisque, a signature dish that exemplifies the kitchen's mastery in transforming simple ingredients into a symphony of taste. The selection of seafood is extensive, ranging from locally sourced fish to succulent prawns. Each dish is a work of art, meticulously prepared and presented to elevate the dining experience.

For those with a penchant for land-based fare, the menu at Le Roof features premium cuts of meat cooked to perfection. Whether it's a tender filet mignon or a juicy lamb rack, the chefs at Le Roof showcase their culinary prowess in every dish. The fusion of French culinary techniques with Pacific ingredients results in a menu that is both diverse and harmonious

Complementing the exquisite cuisine is Le Roof's extensive wine list. The restaurant boasts a curated selection of wines from renowned vineyards, both French and international. From crisp Sauvignon Blancs to robust Bordeaux blends, the sommelier at Le Roof ensures that each wine on the list is chosen to enhance the flavors of the dishes.

Diners have the option to seek recommendations from the knowedgeable staff, who are adept at suggesting pairings that elevate the dining experience. The terrace, with its gentle sea breeze and the soothing sound of waves, provides an idyllic setting for a leisurely evening of sipping fine wine and savoring delectable bites.

The staff at Le Roof contributes significantly to the overall experience. The warm and attentive service reflects the Melanesian tradition of hospitality, creating an atmosphere where guests feel not only welcomed but also genuinely cared for. The waitstaff is well-versed in the intricacies of the menu, ready to offer recommendations or cater to specific dietary preferences.

The chefs at Le Roof also embrace the opportunity to interact with diners, occasionally presenting special dishes or explaining the inspiration behind a particular creation. This personal

touch adds an extra layer to the dining experience, transforming it into a dialogue between the culinary artists and their appreciative audience.

Le Roof is not merely a place for everyday dining; it's a venue that lends itself to special occasions and celebrations. The restaurant offers tailored menus for events such as weddings, anniversaries, and corporate functions. The combination of breathtaking views, exquisite cuisine, and impeccable service makes Le Roof a sought-after venue for those looking to create lasting memories against the backdrop of the Pacific sunset.

Le Roof encapsulates the essence of New Caledonian dining—a harmonious blend of French sophistication and Pacific warmth. It's a place where culinary artistry meets natural splendor, and each visit is not just a meal but a celebration of the senses. Whether one is a local resident savoring the familiar flavors of home or a traveler seeking an authentic taste of New Caledonia, Le Roof beckons with its open doors and promises an experience that transcends the ordinary.

In conclusion, Le Roof is more than a restaurant; it's a culinary masterpiece that invites patrons to embark on a sensory journey. With its prime location, exquisite cuisine, extensive wine selection, and exceptional service, Le Roof stands as a testament to the vibrant and diverse gastronomic scene that defines New Caledonia. It's a destination where the beauty of the Pacific meets the artistry of French cuisine, creating an experience that lingers in the memory long after the last dish is savored.

Le Bilboquet: A Culinary Odyssey in Nouméa

Le Bilboquet, nestled in the heart of Nouméa, New Caledonia, stands as a beacon of culinary excellence, inviting patrons on a gastronomic journey that seamlessly blends French sophistication with Pacific influences. In a colonial-style house that exudes charm, Le Bilboquet has established itself as more than just a restaurant; it's an experience, a celebration of flavors that dance between the traditional and the avant-garde.

As one approaches Le Bilboquet, the colonial architecture sets the stage for what lies within. The elegant façade, adorned with lush greenery, hints at the gastronomic delights that await diners. The restaurant's commitment to creating an inviting atmosphere is evident from the moment one steps through the door. The interiors are a harmonious mix of classic and contemporary design, creating a space that is both refined and welcoming.

The ambiance at Le Bilboquet is an integral part of the dining experience. Soft lighting, tasteful décor, and carefully chosen furnishings contribute to an intimate setting that is perfect for a romantic dinner or a special celebration. The restaurant's attention to detail extends to every

aspect of its design, ensuring that patrons feel not just like guests but participants in a culinary event.

The menu at Le Bilboquet is a testament to the culinary expertise of the chefs, who skillfully navigate the realms of French and Pacific Rim cuisines. The dishes are a symphony of flavors, each ingredient chosen with care and each plate presented as a work of art. From the appetizers to the desserts, Le Bilboquet's menu is a carefully curated exploration of taste and texture.

Seafood takes center stage at Le Bilboquet, reflecting the bountiful offerings of the Pacific Ocean. Diners can indulge in creations such as seared tuna with a delicate mango salsa or lobster bisque that captivates the palate with its rich, velvety texture. The menu also pays homage to local produce, with dishes that feature New Caledonia's unique ingredients, adding an authentic touch to the dining experience.

The culinary journey at Le Bilboquet is elevated by a carefully curated wine list that complements the flavors of each dish. Whether it's a crisp white to pair with seafood or a robust red to enhance the richness of a perfectly cooked steak, the sommeliers at Le Bilboquet have thoughtfully selected wines that enhance the overall dining experience.

Service at Le Bilboquet is as impeccable as the cuisine. The staff, trained to anticipate the needs of the guests, contributes to the seamless flow of the dining experience. The waitstaff is not just knowledgeable about the menu; they are passionate about the culinary creations, able to provide recommendations and insights that enhance the dining journey.

Le Bilboquet's commitment to excellence extends beyond the dining room. The restaurant takes pride in sourcing ingredients locally, forging connections with New Caledonia's farmers and producers. This commitment to sustainability is not just a trend but a reflection of Le Bilboquet's ethos — a dedication to preserving the natural beauty and resources of the region.

The dessert offerings at Le Bilboquet are a fitting conclusion to the culinary adventure. From decadent chocolate creations to delicate fruit-infused pastries, the desserts showcase the pastry chef's artistry. The dessert menu is a testament to the philosophy that every meal should end on a sweet note, leaving patrons with a lingering taste of indulgence.

Le Bilboquet is not just a restaurant; it's a culinary institution that has become a focal point of Nouméa's gastronomic landscape. Its reputation extends beyond the shores of New Caledonia, drawing visitors who seek not just a meal but an experience that lingers in memory. Whether one is a connoisseur of fine dining or a casual diner looking for an extraordinary meal, Le Bilboquet welcomes all with open arms and a menu that tells the story of a culinary love affair between France and the Pacific.

La Pirogue

La Pirogue, a culinary gem nestled on the pristine Isle of Pines in New Caledonia, stands as a testament to the fusion of Melanesian and French flavors. This enchanting restaurant, with its thatched-roof charm and oceanfront setting, invites diners on a gastronomic journey that transcends the ordinary.

The moment you step into La Pirogue, you are greeted by an ambiance that exudes warmth and authenticity. The rustic yet elegant surroundings create an inviting space where guests can unwind and immerse themselves in the unique culinary offerings of the region.

The menu at La Pirogue is a masterpiece, carefully crafted to showcase the rich tapestry of flavors that define New Caledonian cuisine. Here, traditional Melanesian ingredients are seamlessly woven into classic French dishes, resulting in a symphony of tastes that captivate the senses.

Seafood takes center stage on the menu, paying homage to the island's abundant coastal resources. Freshly caught fish, succulent lobster, and delicate shellfish are expertly prepared to highlight their natural flavors. One cannot escape the allure of the 'Bougna,' a traditional Kanak dish featuring fish or meat marinated in coconut milk and cooked to perfection in banana leaves.

The culinary journey continues with a celebration of local produce, with the Isle of Pines yams taking a prominent place on the menu. These earthy and flavorful tubers are transformed into delectable dishes that pay homage to the island's agricultural heritage.

The chefs at La Pirogue are not merely cooks; they are storytellers, weaving narratives of culture and tradition through their culinary creations. Each dish tells a tale of the region's history, a story that unfolds with every bite. The infusion of French culinary techniques adds a layer of sophistication to the menu, creating a dining experience that is both authentic and refined.

As you dine at La Pirogue, you can't help but be enchanted by the panoramic views of the Pacific Ocean. The restaurant's oceanfront location allows diners to bask in the natural beauty of the Isle of Pines while indulging in a feast for the senses. The sound of the waves, the gentle rustle of palm leaves, and the aroma of exquisite dishes create a symphony that complements the visual splendor.

The staff at La Pirogue play a crucial role in enhancing the overall dining experience. Their warm hospitality and deep knowledge of the menu guide guests through the culinary adventure,

ensuring that each dish is not just a meal but a revelation. The waitstaff's passion for the cuisine is palpable, adding an extra layer of authenticity to the dining affair.

As the sun sets over the Pacific, La Pirogue takes on a magical quality. The soft glow of lanterns and the play of shadows create an intimate atmosphere that is perfect for romantic dinners or special celebrations. The restaurant becomes a haven where time seems to slow down, allowing diners to savor every moment of their culinary escapade.

La Pirogue is not merely a restaurant; it is a cultural institution that pays homage to the traditions of the Isle of Pines. The décor, the menu, and the overall ambiance are carefully curated to reflect the island's identity, making it a destination within a destination. Visitors to New Caledonia find in La Pirogue not just a place to dine but an opportunity to connect with the soul of the archipelago.

The commitment to sustainability is another aspect that sets La Pirogue apart. The restaurant places a strong emphasis on using locally sourced, seasonal ingredients, minimizing its environmental footprint. This dedication to eco-friendly practices resonates with diners who seek not only exquisite flavors but also a dining experience that aligns with their values.

For those fortunate enough to experience La Pirogue, the memories created at this culinary haven linger long after the last bite. It becomes more than a restaurant; it becomes a touchstone, a reference point for the beauty and richness of New Caledonia's culinary landscape.

In conclusion, La Pirogue is a treasure trove of flavors, a haven where Melanesian and French culinary traditions converge to create a dining experience that is nothing short of extraordinary. As you navigate through the carefully curated menu, you embark on a journey that transcends the ordinary, leaving an indelible mark on your palate and your heart. It is a place where the spirit of New Caledonia comes alive through the artistry of food, where each meal is a celebration of culture, tradition, and the breathtaking beauty of the Isle of Pines.

Chez Toto: A Culinary Journey into Kanak Flavors on Lifou

In the heart of Lifou, an island in the archipelago of New Caledonia, lies a culinary gem known as Chez Toto. This family-run restaurant is more than just a place to eat; it's a cultural experience, a celebration of Kanak traditions, and a testament to the flavors of the Pacific. As you step into Chez Toto, you're not just entering an eatery; you're entering the home of Toto

and his family, where every dish tells a story and every meal is a journey into the heart of Kanak cuisine.

Chez Toto is nestled in the vibrant community of Lifou, surrounded by lush greenery and the rhythmic sounds of the Pacific Ocean. The restaurant's unassuming exterior gives way to a warm and welcoming interior adorned with traditional Kanak artwork and décor. The ambiance is relaxed, reflecting the laid-back lifestyle of the island, and visitors are greeted with the genuine hospitality that characterizes Kanak culture.

The menu at Chez Toto is a culinary adventure that takes diners on a tour of Lifou's bountiful land and sea. Freshness is a cornerstone of Kanak cuisine, and Chez Toto sources its ingredients locally, ensuring that each dish bursts with flavor and authenticity. Seafood, a staple in Pacific diets, features prominently on the menu. From grilled fish to coconut crab, every bite is a taste of the ocean, expertly prepared and served with a touch of familial care.

One of the standout dishes at Chez Toto is the Bougna. Considered a culinary masterpiece in Kanak culture, Bougna is a traditional feast that brings together an array of ingredients, including yams, taro, coconut milk, and a choice of protein. The ingredients are wrapped in banana leaves and slow-cooked to perfection, resulting in a dish that is both aromatic and flavorful. The Bougna at Chez Toto is a symbol of cultural pride and culinary expertise, a must-try for those looking to immerse themselves in the authentic tastes of Lifou.

As you dine at Chez Toto, it becomes evident that the restaurant is not just a place to eat but a stage for the preservation of Kanak culinary heritage. Toto himself often takes the time to interact with diners, sharing stories of the dishes, the island's history, and the significance of each ingredient. This personal touch adds a layer of intimacy to the dining experience, allowing visitors to connect not only with the food but also with the rich cultural tapestry of Lifou.

The restaurant's commitment to sustainability Is another aspect that sets Chez Toto apart. Many of the ingredients are sourced from local farmers and fishermen, supporting the island's economy and promoting environmentally conscious practices. The use of traditional cooking methods, such as earth ovens and open flames, not only imparts a distinct flavor to the dishes but also reflects a commitment to preserving Kanak culinary traditions in an ever-changing world.

Chez Toto is not just a restaurant; it's a cornerstone of the Lifou community. Locals and visitors alike gather here not only for the exceptional food but also for the sense of community that permeates the air. The communal tables encourage shared meals and conversations, creating an atmosphere reminiscent of a family reunion. It's not uncommon for diners to find themselves engaged in lively discussions with Toto and his family, learning not only about the food but also about the island's customs and way of life.

For those seeking an immersive cultural experience, Chez Toto offers more than just a meal. The restaurant often hosts traditional dance performances and musical events, providing a glimpse into the vibrant arts scene of Lifou. The rhythmic beats of traditional drums and the graceful movements of the dancers transport diners to a world where culture is not just preserved but celebrated with every heartbeat and every step.

Chez Toto's popularity extends beyond Lifou, drawing visitors from neighboring islands and around the world. Travelers seeking an authentic taste of the Pacific make their way to this culinary haven, where the essence of Kanak hospitality is served on a plate. The restaurant's reputation has grown through word of mouth, with tales of Chez Toto's culinary delights reaching the far corners of the globe.

As the sun sets over Lifou, casting hues of orange and pink across the sky, Chez Toto comes alive with the glow of lanterns and the laughter of satisfied diners. It's a place where time seems to slow down, allowing guests to savor not just the flavors of the dishes but also the moments that unfold around them. Whether you're enjoying a leisurely meal with loved ones or striking up a conversation with fellow diners, Chez Toto invites you to experience the true essence of Lifou.

In conclusion, Chez Toto stands as a testament to the power of food to transcend cultural boundaries and create connections. It is a place where culinary artistry meets cultural preservation, and where every meal tells a story of tradition, community, and the bountiful gifts of the Pacific. A visit to Chez Toto is more than a dining experience; it's a journey into the heart of Lifou, where the spirit of Kanak hospitality leaves an indelible mark on all who partake in its warmth and flavors.

Le Faré du Palm Beach: A Culinary Journey in Ouvéa

Nestled on the pristine shores of Ouvéa, a jewel in the South Pacific's Loyalty Islands, Le Faré du Palm Beach stands as a testament to the marriage of French culinary finesse and the bountiful offerings of the Pacific Ocean. This beachfront restaurant, with its unassuming charm, beckons travelers to embark on a gastronomic journey that transcends the ordinary.

Ouvéa, often referred to as the "Island of Beauty," boasts powdery white sand beaches and crystal-clear turquoise waters. It is in this idyllic setting that Le Faré du Palm Beach finds its home. The restaurant, with its thatched-roof structure and open-air design, seamlessly blends into the natural beauty that surrounds it. The rhythmic sounds of the ocean waves provide a soothing soundtrack to the dining experience, creating an ambiance that is both tranquil and inviting.

Le Faré du Palm Beach's menu is a canvas that reflects the vibrant colors and flavors of Ouvéa. The chef, with a keen understanding of the island's culinary heritage, crafts dishes that celebrate the freshness and diversity of local ingredients. The cornerstone of the menu is, unsurprisingly, seafood. Ouvéa's rich marine life provides an abundant array of choices, from succulent lobster to delicate fish that practically melt in the mouth.

The fusion of French culinary techniques with Pacific influences Is evident in every dish. The menu is a testament to the chef's commitment to showcasing the unique identity of Ouvéa, making it more than just a dining experience; it becomes a cultural exploration.

Signature Dishes

Escargot Ouvéa Style: Le Faré du Palm Beach introduces diners to a unique twist on the classic French dish. Escargot, sourced locally, is prepared with a delicate blend of island spices, providing a flavorful introduction to Ouvéa's culinary world.

Lobster Medley: The pièce de résistance of the seafood offerings, the Lobster Medley is a celebration of the ocean's bounty. Grilled lobster, infused with a hint of vanilla, takes center stage, accompanied by a medley of fresh, locally sourced vegetables.

Taro Delight: Taro, a staple in Pacific cuisine, takes on a new dimension in Le Faré du Palm Beach. Whether it's crisped to perfection as a side dish or incorporated into the main course, the chef's innovative use of taro adds a local touch to every plate.

Coconut Dream Dessert: The meal crescendos with a dessert that captures the essence of Ouvéa. Coconut, a ubiquitous ingredient in Pacific desserts, is transformed into a velvety, indulgent treat that leaves a lingering sweetness on the palate.

Beyond the delectable dishes, Le Faré du Palm Beach offers an immersive Ouvéan experience. The restaurant's staff, many of whom are locals, warmly welcome guests and share stories that provide insights into the island's traditions and way of life. The laid-back atmosphere encourages diners to take their time, savoring not just the food but also the moment.

The dining tables, arranged to maximize ocean views, create an intimate setting where couples can enjoy a romantic dinner under the stars, and families can relish quality time together. As evening falls, the soft glow of lanterns adds a touch of magic to the surroundings, transforming Le Faré du Palm Beach into a haven of tranquility.

Le Faré du Palm Beach's commitment to sustainability is a key element of its identity. The restaurant actively seeks partnerships with local fishermen and farmers, ensuring that the ingredients used are not only fresh but also sourced responsibly. This dedication to supporting local communities contributes to the preservation of Ouvéa's natural resources, making each meal a small step towards sustainable tourism.

No culinary journey is complete without the perfect accompaniment, and Le Faré du Palm Beach takes this to heart. The restaurant's well-curated wine cellar boasts a selection of French and international wines, carefully chosen to complement the flavors of the Pacific. From crisp whites to robust reds, each wine is a harmonious addition to the culinary symphony that unfolds at the table.

Le Faré du Palm Beach is not just a restaurant; it's a feast for the senses. As the aroma of fresh seafood mingles with the salty sea breeze, and the gentle lapping of waves provides a rhythmic backdrop, diners are transported into a world where culinary artistry and natural beauty converge.

In the heart of Ouvéa, where time seems to slow down and the worries of the world fade away, Le Faré du Palm Beach invites visitors to savor more than just a meal. It's an invitation to partake in the essence of Ouvéan life, where every bite tells a story of tradition, innovation, and the unyielding beauty of the South Pacific.

As the stars twinkle overhead and the ocean whispers its lullaby, diners at Le Faré du Palm Beach are left with memories of a culinary voyage that transcends the boundaries of taste, creating an indelible imprint of Ouvéa's charm on their palates and in their hearts.

L'Hippocampe: A Culinary Odyssey in the Heart of Nouméa

Nestled in the heart of Nouméa, New Caledonia, L'Hippocampe stands as a beacon of culinary excellence, inviting patrons on a gastronomic odyssey that seamlessly blends Mediterranean flavors with the vibrant influences of the Pacific. This restaurant, a cornerstone of Nouméa's dining scene, has earned a stellar reputation for its inventive dishes, stylish ambiance, and warm hospitality.

As one steps into L'Hippocampe, the ambiance immediately captivates. The décor is a harmonious fusion of modern elegance and tropical allure. Soft lighting casts a warm glow, creating an intimate atmosphere that is both inviting and sophisticated. The use of natural materials and a color palette inspired by the surrounding ocean and lush landscapes contribute to a dining space that feels distinctly New Caledonian.

The restaurant is strategically designed to offer a seamless transition between indoor and outdoor dining, taking full advantage of the island's pleasant climate. The outdoor terrace, adorned with lush greenery and overlooking the vibrant cityscape, provides a picturesque backdrop for an unforgettable dining experience.

At the heart of L'Hippocampe's success is the visionary chef, whose culinary prowess is reflected in every dish that graces the tables. The menu is a canvas that showcases the chef's creativity and commitment to using the freshest, locally sourced ingredients. The fusion of Mediterranean and Pacific Rim influences results in a symphony of flavors that tantalize the taste buds and celebrate the rich culinary diversity of New Caledonia.

The culinary journey begins with appetizers that set the tone for the feast to come. Delicate bruschettas with locally grown tomatoes, drizzled with olive oil, offer a burst of freshness. A selection of oysters, sourced from the pristine waters surrounding the island, provides a taste of the sea in every shell.

As Nouméa is surrounded by azure waters teeming with marine life, it comes as no surprise that seafood features prominently on L'Hippocampe's menu. The catch of the day is a highlight, with the chef expertly preparing the freshest fish and shellfish available. Grilled octopus, a signature dish, is tender and flavorful, enhanced by a zesty citrus marinade that transports diners to Mediterranean shores.

Lobster, a delicacy synonymous with indulgence, takes center stage in several dishes. Whether served simply grilled with a garlic butter glaze or incorporated into pasta dishes with handmade saffron-infused linguine, the lobster at L'Hippocampe is a testament to the restaurant's commitment to culinary excellence.

While seafood is a star attraction, L'Hippocampe also pays homage to the lush landscapes that characterize New Caledonia. The menu seamlessly integrates meats and poultry sourced from local producers, creating a symphony of flavors that delight carnivores and seafood enthusiasts alike.

One standout dish is the slow-cooked lamb shoulder, a culinary masterpiece that exemplifies the chef's dedication to precision and depth of flavor. The lamb, sourced from nearby farms, is infused with aromatic herbs and spices, resulting in a dish that is both tender and rich in complexity.

L'Hippocampe's menu is a testament to the art of culinary fusion. The chef skillfully marries ingredients and techniques from the Mediterranean with those indigenous to the Pacific, creating a dining experience that is both globally inspired and locally rooted.

A prime example of this fusion is the prawn ceviche with tropical fruit salsa. The freshness of the prawns is complemented by the sweetness of locally grown mangoes and pineapples, creating a palate-pleasing combination that dances on the taste buds. Each dish tells a story of cultural exchange, where French culinary traditions meet the vibrant spirit of the Pacific.

No culinary journey is complete without a sweet conclusion, and L'Hippocampe delivers in grand style. Desserts are a celebration of sweetness and creativity, with each creation serving as a testament to the chef's mastery of the pastry arts.

The mango and passion fruit tart is a visual and gastronomic delight. The buttery crust cradles a velvety mango and passion fruit filling, creating a symphony of tropical flavors. The dessert menu, like the savory selections, evolves with the seasons, ensuring that patrons can always indulge in the freshest and most delectable sweet offerings.

To complement the culinary delights, L'Hippocampe boasts an extensive wine list that spans the globe. From French vintages that pay homage to the restaurant's roots to New World wines that bring a touch of the exotic, the sommelier-curated selection ensures that every dish is paired with the perfect libation.

The cocktail menu is equally impressive, featuring creative concoctions that showcase local spirits and ingredients. Sipping a cocktail on the terrace as the sun sets over Nouméa is an experience that elevates the dining journey at L'Hippocampe to a moment of pure bliss.

Beyond its culinary prowess, L'Hippocampe is committed to sustainable and ethical practices. The restaurant sources ingredients responsibly, working closely with local farmers and fishermen to minimize its ecological footprint. This commitment to sustainability adds an extra layer of satisfaction for diners who appreciate not only the exquisite flavors on their plates but also the ethical values upheld by the establishment.

In the realm of fine dining in Nouméa, L'Hippocampe stands as a beacon of excellence. The restaurant's commitment to culinary innovation, coupled with its warm ambiance and dedication to sustainability, has solidified its place as a culinary haven in the heart of New Caledonia.

From the first sip of a handcrafted cocktail to the last bite of a decadent dessert, dining at L'Hippocampe is a multisensory experience that lingers in the memory. As patrons depart, sated and satisfied, they carry with them not only the flavors of the Mediterranean and the Pacific but also the essence of a culinary masterpiece that is L'Hippocampe.

Le Rocher à la Voile: A Culinary Odyssey in Bourail

Nestled in the heart of Bourail, a charming town on the western coast of Grande Terre in New Caledonia, Le Rocher à la Voile stands as a testament to the fusion of culinary excellence and rustic charm. This steakhouse, a celebrated establishment in the region, has carved its niche in offering a dining experience that goes beyond the ordinary. As you step into Le Rocher à la Voile, you embark on a gastronomic journey that intertwines local flavors, French culinary traditions, and a commitment to delivering a memorable dining experience.

The restaurant's location itself Is an invitation to indulge in the beauty of Bourail. Surrounded by lush greenery and set against the backdrop of the New Caledonian landscape, Le Rocher à la Voile captures the essence of the Pacific with an air of tranquility and simplicity. It's not just a place to dine; it's an immersion into the soul of the island.

The menu at Le Rocher à la Voile is a testament to the chef's dedication to quality and a celebration of the region's culinary treasures. With a focus on locally sourced ingredients, the restaurant takes pride in presenting dishes that showcase the rich flavors of New Caledonia. However, it's the mastery of meat that truly sets Le Rocher à la Voile apart.

As you peruse the menu, your senses are awakened by the anticipation of savoring some of the finest cuts of meat the island has to offer. From tender filet mignon to flavorful ribeye, each dish is a symphony of taste and texture. The chef's expertise in grilling and preparing meats ensures that every bite is a culinary delight.

One of the signature dishes that patrons rave about is the locally sourced beef, cooked to perfection. The quality of the meat is paramount at Le Rocher à la Voile, and it's evident in every mouthful. The steak, whether ordered rare or well-done, retains its juiciness, a testament to the chef's skill and the premium quality of the ingredients.

Accompanying the succulent steaks are a variety of side dishes that complement and enhance the overall dining experience. From garlic-infused mashed potatoes to sautéed seasonal vegetables, each element on the plate is carefully chosen to create a harmonious balance of flavors. The attention to detail in the presentation reflects the restaurant's commitment to delivering not just a meal, but an artistic culinary experience.

The wine list at Le Rocher à la Voile is a curated selection that complements the richness of the cuisine. Whether you prefer a bold red to pair with your steak or a crisp white to accompany lighter fare, the knowledgeable staff can guide you to the perfect pairing. The sommelier's recommendations add a layer of sophistication to the dining experience, turning each meal into a symphony of flavors and aromas.

The ambiance of Le Rocher à la Voile is a blend of rustic charm and understated elegance. The warm, welcoming décor is inspired by the natural surroundings, with earthy tones and wooden accents creating a cozy and inviting atmosphere. The outdoor seating area allows diners to bask in the gentle breeze and enjoy the sounds of nature, creating an al-fresco dining experience that enhances the overall enjoyment of the meal.

The attentive and friendly staff at Le Rocher à la Voile contributes to the restaurant's reputation for exceptional service. From the moment you step through the door to the final farewell, you are treated with a level of hospitality that reflects the genuine warmth of New Caledonian culture. The staff's knowledge of the menu, coupled with their enthusiasm for sharing recommendations, adds a personal touch to the dining experience.

In addition to its role as a culinary destination, Le Rocher à la Voile plays a significant role in the local community. As a supporter of sustainable practices, the restaurant actively engages in sourcing ingredients from local farmers and producers. This commitment not only contributes to the freshness and quality of the dishes but also fosters a sense of community and collaboration.

The restaurant's dedication to sustainability extends beyond the kitchen. Le Rocher à la Voile has implemented eco-friendly practices, from energy-efficient lighting to waste reduction initiatives. This holistic approach to environmental responsibility aligns with the growing global consciousness about the impact of dining establishments on the planet.

Le Rocher à la Voile has become more than just a place to enjoy a meal; it has become a symbol of culinary excellence in Bourail. Its presence is a testament to the evolving gastronomic landscape in New Caledonia, where local traditions meet global influences. The restaurant's popularity extends beyond locals to become a must-visit destination for tourists seeking an authentic and exceptional dining experience.

As you savor the last bite of your perfectly grilled steak at Le Rocher à la Voile, you can't help but appreciate the seamless blend of flavors, the dedication to quality, and the immersive experience that goes beyond the plate. It's not just a meal; it's a celebration of New Caledonian cuisine, a journey through the senses, and a memory that lingers long after you've left the rustic charm of this culinary haven in Bourail.

Au P'tit Café

Au P'tit Café is a charming establishment nestled in the heart of Nouméa, New Caledonia, where the aroma of freshly brewed coffee mingles with the delightful scent of French pastries.

This café, with its unassuming façade, has carved a niche for itself as a beloved spot for locals and tourists alike, offering a respite from the bustling streets and a cozy haven for those seeking a moment of tranquility.

The café's ambiance is a harmonious blend of French elegance and Pacific warmth. Upon entering, patrons are greeted by the inviting aroma of roasted coffee beans and the soft hum of conversation. The décor is simple yet tasteful, with comfortable seating arrangements that encourage guests to linger and soak in the relaxed atmosphere.

One of the standout features of Au P'tit Café is its commitment to delivering an authentic French café experience. The menu is a testament to this dedication, featuring an array of classic French pastries, artisanal sandwiches, and a selection of carefully curated coffee blends. From flaky croissants that transport you to the streets of Paris to rich éclairs that are a symphony of flavors, each item on the menu reflects the artistry of French pastry-making.

The café's coffee offerings are a highlight for caffeine connoisseurs. The skilled baristas at Au P'tit Café take pride in crafting the perfect cup, using high-quality beans sourced from reputable suppliers. Whether you prefer a robust espresso, a velvety latte, or a creamy cappuccino, the coffee here is a sensory delight that caters to diverse tastes.

In addition to its delectable pastries and expertly brewed coffee, Au P'tit Café also stands out for its commitment to creating a welcoming space for the community. The friendly and attentive staff add a personal touch to the dining experience, making patrons feel like cherished guests rather than mere customers. This warm hospitality, combined with the café's unpretentious charm, contributes to its popularity among both locals and visitors.

Au P'tit Café's location in Nouméa further enhances its allure. Positioned in a vibrant neighborhood, the café becomes a hub of activity throughout the day. Locals stop by for their morning coffee on the way to work, friends gather for leisurely brunches, and tourists stumble upon this hidden gem, drawn in by the irresistible scent of freshly baked pastries.

For those seeking a moment of tranquility, the outdoor seating area offers a delightful escape. Shaded by umbrellas and surrounded by greenery, it provides a serene setting where patrons can sip their coffee, savor their pastries, and watch the world go by. This outdoor oasis transforms Au P'tit Café into more than just a place to grab a quick bite; it becomes a destination for relaxation and contemplation.

Beyond its role as a café, Au P'tit Café has become a cultural touchstone in Nouméa. It is a place where locals gather to share conversations, artists find inspiration, and the rhythms of daily life unfold. The walls often showcase the work of local artists, adding a touch of creativity to the café's ambiance. This integration of art and community creates a dynamic space that transcends the traditional boundaries of a coffee shop.

In the ever-evolving culinary landscape of Nouméa, Au P'tit Café has not only endured but thrived. Its success can be attributed to a combination of factors—the quality of its offerings, the warmth of its hospitality, and its ability to create an environment that feels like a home away from home. As trends come and go, this café has remained a constant, a testament to the timeless appeal of a good cup of coffee and a freshly baked croissant.

In conclusion, Au P'tit Café is more than just a café; it is a cornerstone of the culinary and cultural scene in Nouméa. It embodies the spirit of French café culture while embracing the unique character of New Caledonia. Whether you're a coffee enthusiast, a pastry lover, or someone seeking a tranquil space to unwind, Au P'tit Café invites you to step into its world—a world where the simple pleasures of life are savored and shared.

La Table des Gourmets

La Table des Gourmets, an exquisite culinary haven nestled in the heart of Nouméa, New Caledonia, stands as a testament to the fusion of French gastronomy and Pacific influences. With an unwavering commitment to delivering an unparalleled dining experience, this restaurant has become a jewel in the archipelago's gastronomic crown.

As you step into La Table des Gourmets, you are immediately enveloped in an ambiance of refined elegance. The décor, characterized by a harmonious blend of contemporary sophistication and Pacific-inspired elements, sets the stage for a culinary journey that transcends the ordinary. The muted tones and tasteful furnishings create an atmosphere of understated luxury, allowing the focus to remain on the star of the show—the food.

The culinary team at La Table des Gourmets, led by a masterful chef with a passion for innovation, has crafted a menu that is a symphony of flavors and textures. Each dish is a work of art, meticulously prepared and presented to delight the senses. The menu itself is a carefully curated selection that showcases the best of local and imported ingredients, with an emphasis on freshness and seasonality.

One of the hallmarks of La Table des Gourmets is its commitment to using locally sourced produce. The restaurant's kitchen is a canvas where the chef transforms the bounties of New Caledonia's land and sea into culinary masterpieces. From succulent seafood to vibrant tropical fruits, every ingredient is chosen with precision to create a dining experience that is both authentic and extraordinary.

The tasting menu at La Table des Gourmets is a culinary journey that unfolds in multiple acts. Each course is a revelation, with flavors that dance on the palate and textures that surprise and delight. The chef's artistic flair is evident not only in the taste but also in the presentation, with each plate resembling a canvas where colors and shapes come together in perfect harmony.

The wine list at La Table des Gourmets is a carefully curated selection that complements the flavors of the dishes. From crisp whites to robust reds, each wine is chosen to enhance the dining experience, creating a perfect marriage of food and drink. The sommelier, knowledgeable and attentive, is always ready to guide diners through the extensive wine list, ensuring that the chosen pairing elevates the overall enjoyment of the meal.

Service at La Table des Gourmets is an art in itself. The staff, trained to anticipate every need, provides a seamless and unobtrusive dining experience. From the moment you are seated to the final morsel, the service is characterized by attention to detail and a genuine desire to make every guest feel special. The waitstaff is well-versed in the intricacies of the menu, able to provide recommendations and descriptions that enhance the overall dining experience.

The restaurant's commitment to sustainability is reflected not only in its use of locally sourced ingredients but also in its eco-friendly practices. La Table des Gourmets strives to minimize its environmental impact, from waste reduction to energy efficiency. This dedication to responsible dining adds an extra layer of appeal for those diners who are conscious of the ecological footprint of their culinary choices.

The dessert offerings at La Table des'Gourmets are a sweet conclusion to the gastronomic journey. From delicate pastries to decadent chocolate creations, the desserts are a testament to the chef's skill and creativity. Each sweet bite is designed to leave a lasting impression, ensuring that the finale of the meal is as memorable as the opening act.

The popularity of La Table des Gourmets extends beyond local patrons to attract visitors seeking a transcendent dining experience. The restaurant's reputation has not only elevated it to a top spot in Nouméa's culinary scene but has also garnered attention on a broader scale. Travelers seeking a taste of New Caledonia's gastronomic excellence often find themselves drawn to the doors of this establishment.

In the evenings, as the sun dips below the horizon and Nouméa's lights begin to twinkle, La Table des Gourmets takes on a magical quality. The intimate setting, combined with the skillfully prepared dishes and impeccable service, creates an atmosphere that is both romantic and sophisticated. It's a place where celebrations come to life, where milestones are marked with culinary delights, and where every meal is an occasion.

In conclusion, La Table des Gourmets is more than a restaurant—it's a culinary journey, an exploration of flavors, and a celebration of the art of dining. From the first sip of wine to the last lingering taste of dessert, every moment at this establishment is crafted to leave an indelible impression. For those seeking a gastronomic adventure in the heart of New Caledonia, La Table des Gourmets beckons with open arms, ready to indulge the senses and create memories that linger long after the plates have been cleared.

Kotémer: A Culinary Odyssey in New Caledonia

Nestled along the picturesque Lemon Bay in Nouméa, Kotémer stands as a culinary beacon, beckoning both locals and tourists to embark on a gastronomic journey. This restaurant, with its fusion of Pacific Rim flavors and locally sourced ingredients, has carved a niche for itself in the vibrant culinary landscape of New Caledonia. In this exploration, we delve into the essence of Kotémer, unraveling its history, menu highlights, dining experience, and the unique blend of sustainability and sophistication that defines this culinary gem.

Kotémer's story begins with a vision to create a dining experience that goes beyond the ordinary—a place where the richness of Pacific Rim cuisine meets the freshness of New Caledonian produce. The name "Kotémer" itself is a play on words, combining "côté" meaning "side" in French, and "mer" which translates to "sea." This choice reflects the restaurant's commitment to showcasing the bounty of the sea and the land in every dish.

As you step into Kotémer, you are greeted by an ambiance that seamlessly blends coastal chic with a touch of tropical elegance. The restaurant's design mirrors the natural beauty that surrounds it, with open spaces that allow diners to bask in the gentle sea breeze while enjoying their meals. The décor is a harmonious fusion of contemporary aesthetics and traditional Pacific influences, creating an atmosphere that is both inviting and sophisticated.

The heart and soul of Kotémer lie in its menu, a carefully curated selection that captures the essence of New Caledonian flavors. The culinary team, led by a visionary chef with a passion for innovation, crafts dishes that celebrate the diversity of local ingredients. From succulent fish caught off the shores of Lemon Bay to tropical fruits and exotic herbs, each element is thoughtfully chosen to create a symphony of flavors on the plate.

One of the signature dishes that epitomizes Kotémer's culinary philosophy is the Coconut and Lime-Infused Fish. This delicacy showcases the restaurant's mastery in balancing bold and subtle flavors. The freshness of the fish is complemented by the richness of coconut and the zesty notes of lime, creating a dish that is both comforting and exhilarating. It's a testament to Kotémer's commitment to offering a dining experience that is not just a meal but a sensory adventure.

The menu at Kotémer Is a dynamic canvas that evolves with the seasons, ensuring that diners can always anticipate something new and exciting. Local seafood takes center stage, with dishes like Grilled Lobster with Vanilla Butter and Seared Tuna with Mango Salsa becoming instant favorites among patrons. The chef's ability to harmonize diverse ingredients is a testament to the culinary craftsmanship that defines Kotémer.

Beyond the tantalizing flavors, Kotémer distinguishes itself through its dedication to sustainability. In an era where environmental consciousness is paramount, the restaurant takes meaningful steps to minimize its ecological footprint. Locally sourced ingredients, eco-friendly practices in the kitchen, and a commitment to responsible sourcing contribute to Kotémer's mission of promoting sustainable dining.

The commitment to sustainability is not just a checkbox for Kotémer; it's an integral part of the dining experience. Diners can indulge in a guilt-free culinary journey, knowing that the ingredients on their plates have been sourced with care for the environment. This ethos extends beyond the kitchen to the overall operations of the restaurant, creating a model that other establishments can look to for inspiration.

The beverage selection at Kotémer is as thoughtfully curated as the food menu. A comprehensive wine list featuring both local and international vintages complements the dishes perfectly. The sommeliers at Kotémer take pride in guiding diners through the wine pairing process, enhancing the overall dining experience. For those with a penchant for cocktails, the bar offers a selection of creative concoctions that mirror the restaurant's dedication to innovation.

Service at Kotémer is an extension of the warm Pacific hospitality that defines New Caledonia. The staff, well-versed in the intricacies of the menu, guide diners through their culinary journey with enthusiasm and expertise. Whether you're a seasoned food connoisseur or a first-time visitor, the team at Kotémer ensures that your dining experience is not just a meal but a celebration of flavors.

The success of Kotémer can be attributed not only to its culinary prowess but also to its role as a cultural ambassador. The restaurant serves as a bridge between traditional Melanesian flavors and contemporary global culinary trends. It's a testament to the rich culinary tapestry of New Caledonia, where diverse influences come together to create something truly unique.

In the evenings, as the sun sets over Lemon Bay, Kotémer takes on a magical aura. The soft glow of ambient lighting, the gentle lull of the waves, and the laughter of diners create an atmosphere that is both romantic and convivial. It's a place where special moments are celebrated, whether it's a romantic dinner for two or a gathering of friends toasting to life's joys.

As we conclude our exploration of Kotémer, it's evident that this restaurant is more than just a place to dine; it's an experience that transcends the ordinary. From its roots in the local culinary landscape to its commitment to sustainability, Kotémer stands as a testament to the evolving palate of New Caledonia. It invites us to savor not just the flavors on the plate but the essence

of a culture woven into every dish—a culture that celebrates the union of land and sea, tradition and innovation. In every bite, Kotémer invites us to taste the spirit of New Caledonia.

A Culinary Journey: Exploring the "harm'of Popular Cafés in New Caledonia

Nestled in the heart of the Pacific, New Caledonia is not just a haven for its pristine beaches and vibrant coral reefs but also a delight for those seeking a culinary adventure. One aspect of the local gastronomic scene that captivates both locals and visitors alike is the thriving café culture. From the bustling streets of Nouméa to the tranquil corners of the outer islands, New Caledonia's cafés offer a delightful fusion of French sophistication and Pacific warmth. In this exploration, we delve into the rich tapestry of popular cafés that beckon travelers with their unique ambiance, delectable treats, and a genuine taste of New Caledonian life.

Nouméa's Urban Elegance

Café de la Place: Situated in the heart of Nouméa, this café is a testament to the city's French influence. Enjoy freshly brewed coffee paired with delicate pastries while soaking in the lively atmosphere of Place des Cocotiers.

Le Petit Café: A cozy gem tucked away in a narrow alley, Le Petit Café is a favorite among locals for its artisanal coffee and intimate setting. The menu boasts a blend of French and Pacific flavors, offering a truly unique experience.

Isle of Pines' Tranquil Retreats

Kuto Café: Overlooking the pristine Kuto Bay, this café combines breathtaking views with a menu inspired by local ingredients. From coconut-infused coffees to homemade fruit tarts, Kuto Café is a haven for those seeking a serene escape.

Oro Bay Café: Set against the backdrop of the iconic Oro Bay, this café blends island vibes with French finesse. Indulge in freshly caught seafood and tropical fruit smoothies while basking in the gentle sea breeze.

Lifou's Coastal Charms

Jinek Bay Café: Tucked along the shores of Jinek Bay, this café offers a rustic setting with panoramic views of the Pacific. Local artisans supply the café with fresh produce, creating a menu that reflects Lifou's agricultural bounty.

Easo Beach Café: A casual spot right on Easo Beach, this café is a gathering place for locals and visitors alike. Sip on coconut lattes and savor traditional Kanak snacks while immersing yourself in the laid-back island atmosphere.

Ouvéa's Beachfront Bliss

Mouli Beach Café: With its thatched-roof structure and sandy floors, Mouli Beach Café epitomizes the quintessential beachfront café experience. From tropical fruit smoothie bowls to French-style croissants, every item on the menu is a treat for the senses.

Teouta Village Café: In the heart of Teouta Village, this café is a community hub where locals gather to share stories over strong coffee and hearty meals. The warm hospitality and traditional flavors make it a must-visit on Ouvéa.

New Caledonia's popular cafés are not just places to savor exceptional coffee and cuisine; they are windows into the soul of this diverse archipelago. Each café tells a story of cultural fusion, from the French-inspired pastries of Nouméa to the traditional Kanak flavors of the outer islands. As you embark on a journey through the aromatic landscapes of these cafés, you'll discover that, in New Caledonia, every cup is a celebration of both the past and the present—a perfect blend of Pacific paradise and French sophistication. So, whether you're a coffee connoisseur or a casual traveler, make sure to indulge in the enchanting world of New Caledonia's popular cafés for an experience that lingers long after the last sip.

Nouméa's Urban Elegance

Nouméa, the vibrant capital of New Caledonia, stands as a testament to the unique fusion of Pacific charm and French sophistication. Nestled along the southwestern coast of Grande Terre, the city is not only a hub of economic activity but also a treasure trove of cultural richness and culinary delights. Among the many facets that contribute to Nouméa's allure, its urban elegance is prominently displayed in the city's architecture, lifestyle, and, notably, its café culture.

As you wander through the streets of Nouméa, you'll find yourself immersed in an atmosphere that seamlessly blends the laid-back rhythm of island life with the refined allure of French savoir-faire. The city's architectural landscape is a striking manifestation of this amalgamation, with colonial-era buildings standing alongside modern structures, creating a visual narrative that mirrors the city's complex history.

In the heart of Nouméa, the bustling Place des Cocotiers serves as a central meeting point and a showcase of the city's urban elegance. Flanked by majestic palm trees and adorned with vibrant tropical flowers, the square exudes a lively ambiance that captures the spirit of the Pacific. It is here that Café de la Place, a quintessential establishment, takes its place as a cornerstone of Nouméa's café culture.

Café de la Place is more than just a coffeehouse; it is a microcosm of Nouméa's urban sophistication. The outdoor terrace, shaded by parasols, invites patrons to indulge in the French ritual of sipping espresso while observing the dynamic city life. The aroma of freshly brewed coffee mingles with the scent of blooming hibiscus, creating an olfactory symphony that elevates the café experience.

The menu at Café de la Place reflects the diverse influences that have shaped New Caledonia's culinary landscape. French pastries, meticulously crafted with precision and flair, share the spotlight with Pacific-inspired delicacies. Croissants, pain au chocolat, and éclairs coexist harmoniously with coconut-infused treats and tropical fruit tarts. Each bite is a journey through flavors, a fusion of the familiar and the exotic.

Le Petit Café, tucked away in a narrow alley, presents a contrasting yet equally enchanting facet of Nouméa's café scene. This hidden gem offers an intimate setting, where patrons can escape the urban bustle and retreat into a haven of tranquility. The café's interior is adorned with local artwork and rustic furnishings, creating a cozy ambiance that invites relaxation.

Le Petit Café's menu is a curated selection of culinary delights that pay homage to both French and Pacific culinary traditions. The coffee, sourced from local beans, is a testament to the commitment to quality. From the first sip of a velvety latte to the last bite of a flaky pastry, patrons are treated to a sensory journey that reflects the café's dedication to creating an authentic and memorable experience.

As the sun sets over Nouméa, the city undergoes a transformation, revealing another layer of its urban elegance. The warm hues of the twilight sky cast a soft glow on the city, and the lively energy of the day gives way to a more relaxed and sophisticated evening atmosphere. This transition is beautifully encapsulated at Le Roof, a waterfront establishment that seamlessly combines a restaurant, bar, and lounge.

Perched on the Anse Vata Bay, Le Roof offers panoramic views of the ocean and the city lights. The open-air terrace provides an unparalleled vantage point to witness Nouméa's urban landscape come alive at night. The ambiance is sophisticated yet unpretentious, making it an ideal setting for an evening of fine dining or casual cocktails.

Le Roof's culinary offerings are a celebration of fresh, locally sourced ingredients prepared with a contemporary twist. Seafood takes center stage, reflecting the abundance of marine life surrounding New Caledonia. From grilled lobster to tuna tartare, each dish is a masterpiece that showcases the culinary prowess of the chefs and the richness of the region's natural resources.

The café culture of Nouméa extends beyond traditional coffeehouses and waterfront lounges. Along the city's streets, you'll find charming patisseries, gelaterias, and boutique cafes that contribute to the diverse tapestry of flavors. La Maison Ballande, a historic establishment dating back to the 19th century, is a noteworthy example.

La Maison Ballande, with its elegant façade and inviting storefront, is a living testament to the city's colonial past. The café exudes an old-world charm that transports patrons to a bygone era. As you step through its doors, you're greeted by the aroma of freshly baked baguettes and the sight of decadent pastries displayed in ornate glass cases.

The café's interior, adorned with vintage furnishings and sepia-toned photographs, invites patrons to linger and savor the timeless elegance of French café culture. Locals and visitors alike gather at La Maison Ballande to enjoy a leisurely brunch, indulge in delicate desserts, or simply revel in the nostalgia that permeates the air.

Nouméa's urban elegance is not confined to its coffeehouses and patisseries; it extends to the city's markets, where the vibrant colors of tropical fruits and the fragrant scents of spices create a sensory feast. The Port Moselle Market, a lively marketplace located by the waterfront, is a vibrant reflection of Nouméa's cultural diversity and culinary richness.

Wandering through the market's stalls, you'll encounter a kaleidoscope of produce—from exotic fruits like passion fruit and dragon fruit to locally grown vegetables and herbs. The air is filled with the lively banter of vendors, the sizzle of grills preparing traditional Kanak dishes, and the laughter of locals and tourists alike. The market is a microcosm of Nouméa's urban life, where the convergence of cultures and flavors creates a dynamic and captivating atmosphere.

Cafés within the market, such as Café du Port, offer a respite for those seeking a moment of relaxation amidst the bustling energy. Here, you can sip on a refreshing coconut water or enjoy a freshly brewed coffee while observing the ebb and flow of market life. The café's menu features light bites inspired by the market's offerings, providing a true farm-to-table experience.

Nouméa's urban elegance is not static; it evolves with the city's dynamic spirit. As the city continues to grow and embrace its multicultural identity, new cafés and culinary establishments emerge, adding fresh layers to the tapestry of flavors. The evolving nature of Nouméa's café culture is evident at Le Faubourg, a modern boulangerie and café that seamlessly integrates traditional French baking techniques with Pacific-inspired innovations.

Le Faubourg, with its sleek design and minimalist aesthetic, stands as a symbol of Nouméa's contemporary sophistication. The aroma of freshly baked bread and pastries wafts through the air, inviting passersby to step inside and indulge in a moment of culinary bliss. The café's menu, crafted with precision and creativity, features a selection of artisanal bread, viennoiseries, and desserts that showcase the mastery of the bakers.

In the heart of Nouméa's Latin Quarter, Le Faubourg serves as a meeting point for those who appreciate the artistry of baking and the pleasures of a well-brewed cup of coffee. Whether you're in the mood for a flaky croissant, a hearty baguette, or a decadent éclair, Le Faubourg's offerings are a testament to the café's commitment to quality and innovation.

Nouméa's urban elegance extends to its waterfront, where the Anse Vata promenade offers a picturesque setting for cafés and bistros. Along this iconic stretch, you'll find establishments like L'Instant Présent, where the convergence of land and sea creates a backdrop of unparalleled beauty.

L'Instant Présent, with its open-air terrace and panoramic views of Anse Vata Bay, is a sanctuary for those seeking a moment of tranquility. The café's design reflects a harmonious blend of natural elements, with wooden furnishings and earthy tones complementing the surrounding landscape. Whether you choose to enjoy a leisurely brunch or a sunset cocktail, L'Instant Présent provides an intimate space to savor the simple joys of life.

The café's menu is a celebration of local flavors, with an emphasis on fresh seafood and tropical produce. Dishes like grilled prawns, fish ceviche, and coconut-infused desserts pay homage to New Caledonia's culinary heritage. Each plate is a work of art, a symphony of colors and textures that mirror the vibrancy of the island.

Nouméa's urban elegance is not confined to daylight hours; it flourishes under the starlit sky as well. As night falls, the city's waterfront transforms into a romantic tableau, and establishments like Mondo Bar and Restaurant come to life. Located on the Baie des Citrons, Mondo offers a unique blend of sophistication and island flair.

Mondo's waterfront terrace, adorned with ambient lighting and swaying palm trees, sets the stage for a memorable evening. The gentle sea breeze, the sound of lapping waves, and the distant hum of conversation create an atmosphere that is both refined and relaxed. Whether you're savoring a glass of fine wine or indulging in a gourmet dinner, Mondo provides a sensory experience that lingers in the memory.

The restaurant's culinary offerings are a fusion of French techniques and Pacific ingredients. From seared foie gras to locally caught tuna tartare, each dish is a testament to the chef's dedication to culinary excellence. The wine list, featuring a curated selection of French and New World wines, complements the menu, offering the perfect accompaniment to a night of indulgence.

Nouméa's urban elegance is not solely defined by its physical spaces and culinary offerings; it is also embodied in the city's lifestyle and the warm hospitality of its people. As you navigate the streets, you'll encounter a sense of joie de vivre that permeates the air—a collective spirit that celebrates the pleasures of life and the beauty of human connections.

This spirit is exemplified at La Boîte à Café, a cozy establishment that captures the essence of Nouméa's café culture. Located in the Latin Quarter, the café is a gathering place for locals and visitors alike, fostering a sense of community over cups of freshly brewed coffee. The interior, adorned with eclectic furnishings and local artwork, exudes a homely charm that invites patrons to linger.

La Boîte à Café's menu is a delightful exploration of flavors, featuring a selection of specialty coffees and gourmet treats. From artisanal pastries to savory crepes, each item is crafted with care, reflecting the café's commitment to providing a wholesome and enjoyable experience. The baristas, with their expertise and passion, add a personal touch to every cup, creating a connection between the beverage and the person savoring it.

In conclusion, Nouméa's urban elegance is a multifaceted tapestry woven from the threads of history, culture, and culinary artistry. The city's café culture, with its diverse establishments and dynamic evolution, serves as a microcosm of Nouméa's spirit. From the iconic Place des Cocotiers to the charming alleys hiding hidden gems like Le Petit Café, from the historic charm of La Maison Ballande to the contemporary sophistication of Le Faubourg, each café contributes to the city's narrative.

As you navigate Nouméa's streets, explore its markets, and linger in its cafés, you'll discover that urban elegance is not merely a characteristic of the city—it is a lifestyle, a celebration of the harmonious coexistence of tradition and modernity. Nouméa invites you to savor every moment, to appreciate the artistry of its coffeehouses, and to embrace the allure of its urban elegance—a timeless symphony that resonates with the soul of the Pacific and the heart of France.

The Isle of Pines

The Isle of Pines, a gem in the heart of the South Pacific, beckons travelers with its turquoise waters, lush greenery, and a sense of tranquility that is unmatched. As one explores this idyllic

island, it becomes evident that the Isle of Pines is not just a destination; it's a haven, offering a retreat from the hustle and bustle of everyday life. In this narrative journey, we delve into the soul of the Isle of Pines, uncovering its hidden corners and exploring the essence of its tranquil retreats.

The rhythmic sound of waves breaking against the pristine shores greets visitors as they step onto the Isle of Pines. Kuto Bay, a natural masterpiece, serves as a serene introduction to the island's beauty. Here, amid the swaying palms and soft sand, lies a hidden gem known as Kuto Café.

Kuto Café, perched on the edge of the bay, blends seamlessly with its surroundings. The café, a harmonious marriage of rustic charm and culinary finesse, offers a haven for those seeking a moment of respite. The scent of freshly brewed coffee mingles with the salty tang of the sea breeze, creating an olfactory symphony that lingers in the air.

The menu at Kuto Café reads like a love letter to the island's natural bounty. Freshly caught seafood, plucked straight from the crystal-clear waters, takes center stage. Grilled lobster, a delicacy on the Isle of Pines, arrives at tables adorned with tropical flowers, a visual feast that mirrors the flavors within.

As the sun gently dips below the horizon, casting hues of orange and pink across the sky, patrons at Kuto Café find solace in the simplicity of the moment. Conversations ebb and flow like the tide, and time seems to stand still. It's not just a café; it's a communion with nature and a celebration of the unhurried pace of life on the Isle of Pines.

Further along the coast, Oro Bay Café stands as a testament to the island's ability to marry sophistication with simplicity. Situated against the backdrop of the iconic Oro Bay, the café offers patrons a panoramic view of the tranquil waters. Here, elegance is woven into every detail, from the pristine white tablecloths to the delicate porcelain cups that cradle the café au lait.

Oro Bay Café's menu mirrors the refined ambiance. French-inspired pastries, adorned with fresh tropical fruits, share the spotlight with expertly crafted espressos. The blend of flavors is a dance on the palate, with each bite telling a story of cultural fusion. The café is not merely a place to dine; it's a canvas where local and international influences converge to create a masterpiece of taste.

The journey through the Isle of Pines' retreats wouldn't be complete without a visit to Easo Beach Café. Tucked away on the sandy shores of Easo Beach, this casual spot exudes a laid-back charm that captures the essence of island living. The rhythmic percussion of waves provides the soundtrack to a dining experience that is as immersive as it is delicious.

Easo Beach Café's menu is a celebration of simplicity and local flavors. Coconut-infused coffees, served in intricately carved wooden cups, pay homage to traditional Kanak craftsmanship. The scent of grilled fish wafts through the air as patrons indulge in the freshest catches from the island's waters. It's an unpretentious celebration of the Isle of Pines' culinary heritage.

In the heart of the Isle of Pines, Mouli Beach Café stands as a testament to the island's commitment to preserving its natural beauty. With a thatched-roof structure that blends seamlessly with the landscape, Mouli Beach Café is a beachfront retreat that epitomizes the quintessential island experience.

The café's menu, a symphony of tropical flavors, draws inspiration from the surrounding nature. Exotic fruit smoothie bowls, adorned with edible flowers, offer a burst of freshness. French pastries, expertly crafted by local bakers, showcase the island's ability to seamlessly blend colonial influences with indigenous ingredients.

Mouli Beach Café is not merely a culinary destination; it's a sanctuary for those seeking a connection with the island's soul. As patrons sip on coconut-infused beverages and nibble on delicate pastries, they become part of the rhythmic pulse of the Isle of Pines. The sense of time is fluid, and worries dissipate with the gentle lapping of waves against the shore.

Teouta Village Café, nestled in the heart of Teouta Village, is more than just a café; it's a community hub. Here, locals and visitors converge to share stories, laughter, and a cup of strong coffee. The café's unassuming exterior belies the warmth that emanates from within.

Teouta Village Café's menu reflects the culinary traditions of the Kanak people. Hearty meals, prepared with locally sourced ingredients, offer a taste of authenticity. As the aroma of traditional Kanak dishes wafts through the air, patrons find themselves immersed in a cultural tapestry that transcends language.

In conclusion, the Isle of Pines' tranquil retreats are not just culinary establishments; they are gateways to a deeper understanding of the island's soul. Each café, with its unique ambiance and menu, tells a story of cultural richness and natural abundance. As visitors traverse the shores of Kuto Bay, the vistas of Oro Bay, the sands of Easo Beach, and the tranquility of Mouli

Beach, they discover that the Isle of Pines is not just a destination; it's a sanctuary where time slows down, and the spirit of the island invites you to linger a little longer.

Lifou's Coastal Charms

Lifou, the largest island in the Loyalty Archipelago of New Caledonia, is a haven of natural beauty and cultural richness. Nestled in the heart of the Pacific, Lifou is renowned for its pristine beaches, turquoise waters, and vibrant coral reefs. However, beyond its postcard-perfect landscapes, Lifou hides a treasure trove of coastal charms, and among them, the island's cafes stand out as delightful gems that offer both a taste of the local flavors and a glimpse into the warm hospitality of its people.

As you traverse the coastline of Lifou, you'll encounter a series of charming cafes that invite you to pause, sip, and savor the essence of island life. One such establishment is Jinek Bay Café, a rustic retreat along the shores of Jinek Bay. This café not only provides panoramic views of the Pacific but also serves as a testament to Lifou's commitment to using local ingredients. With its menu crafted from the offerings of nearby farmers and fishermen, Jinek Bay Café seamlessly blends the freshness of the ocean breeze with the flavors of the island's rich soil.

Easo Beach Café, another coastal gem, boasts a more casual setting right on the sandy shores of Easo Beach. This café captures the essence of Lifou's laid-back atmosphere, offering visitors a place to unwind and connect with both locals and fellow travelers. Here, coconut lattes are sipped while overlooking the azure waters, and traditional Kanak snacks provide a taste of the island's indigenous culinary heritage.

As you venture deeper into the heart of Lifou, Mouli Beach Café awaits, nestled amidst the palms with its thatched-roof structure and sandy floors. This beachfront establishment epitomizes the quintessential island café experience. The menu at Mouli Beach Café is a celebration of tropical flavors, featuring fruit smoothie bowls that burst with the sweetness of local produce and French-style pastries that reflect the island's colonial history.

Away from the coastal hubs, in the heart of Teouta Village, lies the Teouta Village Café. This unassuming yet charming spot is a gathering place for the local community. Here, strong coffee is brewed, and hearty meals are shared. The warm hospitality of the locals combined with the traditional Kanak flavors on the menu make Teouta Village Café an authentic and essential stop for those seeking a genuine Lifou experience.

In each of Lifou's coastal cafes, there is a unique story to be told — a story of resilience, cultural diversity, and the intertwining of tradition with modernity. The coastal charms of Lifou are not confined to the breathtaking scenery but are embodied in the very fabric of these cafes, where the pulse of the island can be felt in every cup of coffee, every bite of a pastry, and every conversation shared among locals and visitors alike.

The coastal cafes of Lifou are not just places to satiate hunger or quench thirst; they are living testimonials to the spirit of the island. They are the places where cultures collide, where the past meets the present, and where the beauty of Lifou is not just observed but experienced with every sense. So, as you explore Lifou's coastal charms, take the time to indulge in the hospitality of its cafes, for it is here that the heart of the island beats in harmony with the rhythm of the Pacific waves.

Ouvéa's Beachfront Bliss

Nestled in the heart of the South Pacific, Ouvéa, a pristine atoll in New Caledonia, boasts a unique charm that sets it apart from other tropical destinations. Its powdery white-sand beaches, crystal-clear turquoise waters, and vibrant coral reefs make it a haven for those seeking tranquility and natural beauty. Beyond its breathtaking landscapes, Ouvéa is home to a collection of beachfront cafés that embody the laid-back island lifestyle. In this exploration, we immerse ourselves in the essence of Ouvéa's Beachfront Bliss, discovering the unique flavors, cultural nuances, and the rhythmic pace of life that define these coastal havens.

As the sun rises over Ouvéa, casting a golden glow on the shores, locals and visitors alike begin their day at Mouli Beach Café. This beachfront establishment, with its thatched-roof structure and open-air design, perfectly captures the essence of island living. The sandy floors, a nod to the surrounding beaches, create an immediate connection to nature, and as you take your seat, the gentle sound of lapping waves becomes the soundtrack to your experience.

Mouli Beach Café is not merely a place to enjoy a cup of coffee; it's a destination that encapsulates the spirit of Ouvéa. The menu, a harmonious blend of French and Pacific influences, reflects the island's cultural diversity. Sip on a freshly brewed café au lait while indulging in a warm croissant, a perfect fusion of continental elegance and tropical simplicity. The café sources its ingredients locally, ensuring a farm-to-table experience that showcases Ouvéa's rich agricultural heritage.

Teouta Village Café, situated in the heart of Ouvéa's traditional village, offers a different but equally captivating experience. Here, the rhythm of life is slower, and the café serves as a communal space where locals gather to share stories, laughter, and, of course, good food. As you enter the café, you're enveloped in the aroma of strong coffee and the enticing scents of traditional Kanak dishes.

The warmth of the welcome at Teouta Village Café is as integral to the experience as the culinary delights. The locals, proud of their heritage, are eager to share the flavors of Ouvéa. Try the bougna, a traditional Kanak dish made with yams, taro, and coconut, slow-cooked in banana leaves. It's a hearty and flavorful testament to the island's connection to the land and sea.

Moving from the sandy shores to the heart of the village, the café becomes a social hub. Locals of all ages gather here, creating a vibrant atmosphere where conversations flow as freely as the coffee. The walls of Teouta Village Café seem to echo with the stories of generations, a living testament to the enduring traditions of Ouvéa.

As the day unfolds, the beach beckons again, and a visit to Teouta Village Café is complemented by an afternoon spent at Easo Beach Café. This casual yet inviting spot captures the essence of island time. Situated right on Easo Beach, with its calm azure waters and swaying palm trees, the café invites you to kick off your shoes, feel the sand between your toes, and surrender to the unhurried pace of Ouvéa.

Easo Beach Café's menu is a celebration of local flavors, emphasizing the bounties of the surrounding sea and the fertile land. Freshly caught seafood takes center stage, prepared with simplicity and skill. Grilled fish, marinated in coconut and lime, offers a taste of the Pacific, while tropical fruit smoothies provide a refreshing respite from the warmth of the sun.

The beachside setting transforms the dining experience into a sensory journey. The gentle sea breeze carries with it the scent of saltwater and frangipani, creating an ambiance that heightens the flavors on your plate. It's a reminder that, on Ouvéa, every meal is a celebration of nature's abundance.

As the sun begins its descent, casting hues of orange and pink across the sky, Easo Beach Café transforms into an idyllic spot to witness the magic of Ouvéa's sunsets. Time seems to slow, and the rhythmic sound of the waves becomes a meditative backdrop to the day's end. Savoring a cup of local coffee, you watch as the colors of the sky reflect upon the tranquil waters, and the essence of Ouvéa's Beachfront Bliss becomes an indelible part of your journey.

In conclusion, Ouvéa's beachfront cafés are not just places to satisfy culinary cravings; they are portals to a way of life where simplicity, community, and the beauty of nature converge. Each café, whether nestled in the heart of a village or overlooking a pristine beach, tells a story of

Ouvéa's unique identity—a blend of traditional Kanak heritage and the serene allure of the Pacific. To experience Ouvéa's Beachfront Bliss is to immerse oneself in a tapestry of flavors, cultures, and moments that linger long after the journey has ended.

CHAPTER 5: PRACTICAL INFORMATION

Navigating New Caledonia: A Comprehensive Guide to Transportation in 2024

New Caledonia, nestled in the heart of the South Pacific, is a tropical paradise renowned for its stunning landscapes, diverse culture, and unique blend of French and Melanesian influences. As you plan your journey to this enchanting archipelago in 2024, understanding the transportation options is key to making the most of your visit. This guide provides a detailed exploration of the various modes of transportation available within New Caledonia.

1. Air Travel

1.1 Domestic Flights

New Caledonia is comprised of several islands, and domestic flights play a crucial role in connecting these diverse regions. The main hub is La Tontouta International Airport near Nouméa, offering flights to domestic destinations like Isle of Pines, Lifou, and Ouvéa. Airlines such as Air Calédonie and Aircalin provide frequent services, ensuring convenient access to the archipelago's gems.

1.2 Intercontinental Flights

For international travelers, the primary gateway is La Tontouta International Airport. Major airlines operate flights connecting New Caledonia to destinations worldwide, enhancing the archipelago's accessibility for global explorers.

2. Sea Travel

2.1 Ferries

Inter-island travel by ferry is a picturesque and popular option. Regular services operate between Nouméa and nearby islands like Isle of Pines and Loyalty Islands. The journey offers breathtaking views of the Pacific and a chance to experience the local maritime culture.

2.2 Cruise Ships

New Caledonia is a favored destination for cruise lines exploring the South Pacific. Nouméa serves as a significant port for cruise ships, providing visitors with an immersive experience as they explore the islands' diverse landscapes and cultures.

3. Ground Transportation

3.1 Rental Cars

Exploring the main island of Grande Terre is best done by rental car. Several international and local rental agencies provide a range of vehicles, allowing travelers the flexibility to discover hidden gems and remote areas at their own pace.

3.2 Taxis

Taxis are readily available in urban centers like Nouméa and are a convenient option for short-distance travel. Friendly drivers often double as informal guides, offering insights into local life and attractions.

3.3 Public Buses

An efficient and cost-effective way to navigate Nouméa is by using the public bus system. The buses connect various neighborhoods, making it easy for travelers to explore the city's vibrant culture and attractions.

4. Motorcycles and Scooters

For the adventurous traveler, renting a motorcycle or scooter is a thrilling way to explore the scenic coastal roads and lush landscapes. This mode of transportation provides a unique perspective, allowing visitors to soak in the natural beauty of the archipelago.

5. Bicycles

Nouméa and certain islands offer bike rentals, promoting eco-friendly transportation. Cycling enthusiasts can explore the city or enjoy leisurely rides along the coast, discovering hidden beaches and charming villages.

6. Tips for Efficient Transportation

6.1 Planning Ahead

Given the archipelago's unique geography, it's essential to plan transportation in advance, especially for inter-island travel. Booking domestic flights and ferry tickets ahead of time ensures a seamless journey.

6.2 Language Considerations

While French is the official language, English is widely understood in tourist areas. Familiarizing yourself with basic French phrases can enhance your travel experience and facilitate communication, particularly in rural areas.

6.3 Cultural Sensitivity

Respecting local customs and etiquette, especially when using communal transportation, is paramount. Observing cultural norms enhances the overall travel experience and fosters positive interactions with the welcoming local population.

In conclusion, New Caledonia offers a diverse array of transportation options that cater to various preferences and travel styles. Whether soaring over turquoise waters in a domestic flight, cruising between islands on a ferry, or exploring the mainland in a rental car, each mode of transport contributes to the rich tapestry of experiences awaiting travelers in this Pacific paradise in 2024.

Health and Safety Tips in New Caledonia: A Comprehensive Guide

New Caledonia, with its stunning landscapes and vibrant culture, is an enticing destination for travelers. To ensure a safe and enjoyable journey, it's essential to prioritize health and safety. This guide will explore key considerations, from health precautions to general safety tips, helping you make the most of your visit while staying well-informed.

Health Precautions

Vaccinations and Health Insurance

Routine Vaccinations: Ensure your routine vaccinations are up-to-date before traveling to New Caledonia. These may include measles, mumps, rubella, diphtheria, tetanus, and pertussis.

Hepatitis A and B: Consider getting vaccinated against hepatitis A and B, especially if your travel involves interactions with local communities.

Travel Insurance: Acquire comprehensive travel insurance that covers medical expenses. Confirm that it includes coverage for emergency medical evacuation.

Mosquito-Borne Diseases

Dengue Fever: New Caledonia has reported cases of dengue fever. Use insect repellent, wear long sleeves, and consider staying in accommodations with screened windows to minimize the risk.

Zika Virus: Pregnant women should be cautious due to the risk of Zika virus. Consult with your healthcare provider before planning your trip.

Water and Food Safety

Safe Drinking Water: Stick to bottled or boiled water to avoid waterborne diseases. Ensure that the seal on bottled water is intact.

Food Safety: Enjoy local cuisine, but prioritize well-cooked and hot meals. Avoid street food that might pose a risk of contamination.

Seafood Caution: If you're a seafood enthusiast, ensure it's from reputable establishments to minimize the risk of foodborne illnesses.

Safety While Exploring

Natural Hazards

Cyclone Season Awareness: New Caledonia experiences a cyclone season. Stay informed about weather forecasts, especially if traveling between November and April.

Lagoon Safety: When engaging in water activities, pay attention to local advisories. Some areas may have strong currents or marine life hazards.

Crime Awareness

Petty Crime: While New Caledonia is relatively safe, practice common sense. Keep valuables secure, especially in crowded areas, and be cautious of pickpockets.

Emergency Contacts: Save emergency contact numbers, including local authorities and your country's embassy, in your phone and on paper.

Cultural Sensitivity

Respect Local Customs: Familiarize yourself with local customs and etiquette. This includes appropriate attire when visiting sacred sites and showing respect to the indigenous Kanak people.

Healthcare Facilities

Know the Nearest Medical Facilities: Identify the location of the nearest hospitals or clinics. Carry a basic first aid kit for minor injuries.

Prescription Medications: If you take prescription medications, ensure an ample supply for your trip and carry a copy of your prescriptions.

By incorporating these health and safety tips into your travel preparations, you're not only safeguarding your well-being but also enhancing your overall experience in New Caledonia. Stay informed, be prepared, and savor the beauty and culture that this Pacific gem has to offer. Safe travels!

Communication and Connectivity in New Caledonia: Bridging Islands, Connecting Cultures

New Caledonia, nestled in the heart of the South Pacific, is not just a haven for natural beauty; it's also a place where modern communication and connectivity seamlessly blend with traditional island living. In this exploration of New Caledonia's communication landscape, we delve into the realms of technology, languages, and the unique cultural interplay that defines this archipelago.

1. **Technological Infrastructure**

New Caledonia boasts a modern and well-developed technological infrastructure, particularly in urban centers like Nouméa. High-speed internet is readily available in hotels, cafes, and public spaces, allowing both locals and tourists to stay connected effortlessly. The mobile network coverage is extensive, even reaching some of the more remote islands.

   a. **Internet Connectivity**

The internet infrastructure in New Caledonia is on par with global standards. High-speed broadband and 4G networks are prevalent, ensuring that visitors can easily share their experiences on social media, stay in touch with loved ones, or work remotely if needed.

b. Mobile Networks

The archipelago is well-covered by major mobile network providers. Visitors can purchase SIM cards at the airport or local stores, providing access to cost-effective data plans for the duration of their stay. This connectivity proves invaluable when exploring the more secluded parts of the islands.

2. Language Landscape

New Caledonia's linguistic diversity reflects its rich cultural tapestry. While French is the official language, the Kanak people, the indigenous inhabitants, converse in various Kanak languages. Understanding this linguistic blend is crucial for effective communication.

a. French as the Lingua Franca

French is not only the official language but also the primary medium of instruction in schools and the language of government. Visitors with a basic understanding of French will find it easier to navigate daily interactions.

b. Kanak Languages

The Kanak population communicates in a variety of Kanak languages, each deeply rooted in their respective communities. Learning a few basic phrases in the local languages can foster a deeper connection with the island's culture and its warm and welcoming people.

3. Cultural Communication Etiquette

Communication in New Caledonia extends beyond words. Understanding and respecting the cultural nuances is key to meaningful interactions.

a. Traditional Greetings

The customary greeting in New Caledonia involves a gentle handshake, often accompanied by a slight bow. This simple gesture signifies respect and openness. Visitors are encouraged to reciprocate in the same spirit.

b. Importance of Sharing

In Kanak culture, sharing is a fundamental aspect of communication. Whether it's food, stories, or experiences, the act of sharing fosters a sense of community and belonging. Visitors are encouraged to embrace this communal spirit during their stay.

4. Connectivity on the Islands

While the mainland enjoys robust connectivity, the outer islands offer a more serene escape. This duality allows visitors to choose between staying digitally connected or immersing themselves in the untouched beauty of remote landscapes.

a. Digital Detox on Remote Islands

Some of the outer islands provide a limited digital experience, offering visitors a chance to disconnect from the virtual world and reconnect with nature. This intentional balance caters to both the tech-savvy traveler and those seeking a more traditional island experience.

b. Local Radio and Media

Exploring the islands often involves tuning into local radio stations that play a mix of French and Kanak music. This auditory experience offers a unique glimpse into the local vibe, enhancing the overall travel experience.

5. Challenges and Opportunities

While New Caledonia has made significant strides in communication and connectivity, challenges persist, particularly in the more remote regions. Balancing progress with the preservation of cultural identity is an ongoing effort.

a. Connectivity Disparities

Some remote communities still face challenges in terms of internet access and mobile network coverage. Initiatives are underway to bridge these gaps and ensure that the benefits of connectivity are evenly distributed.

b. Preserving Cultural Integrity

As technology advances, there is a delicate dance between modernization and preserving cultural heritage. Efforts are being made to integrate technology in a way that complements rather than compromises the rich cultural identity of the islands.

In the islands of New Caledonia, communication and connectivity serve as bridges between worlds. The modernity of urban centers harmonizes with the timeless traditions of the Kanak people, creating a unique and enriching experience for visitors. Whether navigating the bustling streets of Nouméa or unwinding on a secluded beach, the communication landscape of New Caledonia is a testament to the delicate balance between progress and heritage.

Printed in Great Britain
by Amazon